Changing Names and Gendering Identity

This book investigates contemporary naming practices on marriage in Britain, drawing on survey data and detailed interview material in which women offer their own accounts of the reasons for which they have changed or retained their names. Exploring the ways in which names are used to create and understand family, to cement commitments and make it clear to the self and to others that subject is in 'true love', *Changing Names and Gendering Identity* considers the manner in which names are used to make sense of the self and narrate life changes and choices in a coherent fashion. A critique of the gender-blindness of sociological theories of individualisation, this volume offers evidence of the continued importance of traditions and the past to the functioning of contemporary society. In dissecting the everyday, taken-for-granted ritual of name changing for women on marriage, it sheds light on the nature of an enduring set of unequal gender relations which are used to organise society, behaviour, and interpersonal relations. Engaging with questions of power, heteronormativity, and gender relations, this analysis of a significant ritual of contemporary heterosexual marriage will interest sociologists and scholars of gender studies with interests in the family, identity, and gender.

Rachel Thwaites is a Lecturer in Sociology at Canterbury Christ Church University.

Routledge Research in Gender and Society

For a full list of titles in this series, please visit www.routledge.com/
Routledge-Research-in-Gender-and-Society/book-series/SE0271

44 **Gendering Globalization on the Ground**
The Limits of Feminized Work for Mexican Women's Empowerment
Gay Young

45 **New Dynamics in Female Migration and Integration**
Edited by Christiane Timmerman, Marco Martiniello, Andrea Rea and Johan Wets

46 **Masculinities and Femininities in Latin America's Uneven Development**
Susan Paulson

47 **Gender, Nutrition, and the Human Right to Adequate Food**
Toward an Inclusive Framework
Edited by Anne C. Bellows, Flavio L.S. Valente, Stefanie Lemke, and María Daniela Núñez Burbano de Lara

48 **Teaching Women's Studies in Conservative Contexts**
Considering Perspectives for an Inclusive Dialogue
Edited by Cantice Greene

49 **Ageing, Gender and Sexuality**
Equality in Later Life
Sue Westwood

50 **Gendering the Memory of Work**
Women Workers' Narratives
Maria Tamboukou

51 **Men's Intrusion, Women's Embodiment**
A Critical Analysis of Street Harassment
Fiona Vera Gray

52 **Neoliberal Bodies and the Gendered Fat Body**
Hannele S. Harjunen

53 **Women's Magazines in Print and New Media**
Edited by Noliwe Rooks, Victoria Pass and Ayana Weekley

54 **Changing Names and Gendering Identity**
Social Organisation in Contemporary Britain
Rachel Thwaites

Changing Names and Gendering Identity

Social organisation in contemporary Britain

Rachel Thwaites

LONDON AND NEW YORK

First published 2017
by Routledge
2 Park Square, Milton Park, Abingdon, Oxon OX14 4RN

and by Routledge
711 Third Avenue, New York, NY 10017

Routledge is an imprint of the Taylor & Francis Group, an informa business

© 2017 Rachel Thwaites

The right of Rachel Thwaites to be identified as author of this work has been asserted by her in accordance with sections 77 and 78 of the Copyright, Designs and Patents Act 1988.

All rights reserved. No part of this book may be reprinted or reproduced or utilised in any form or by any electronic, mechanical, or other means, now known or hereafter invented, including photocopying and recording, or in any information storage or retrieval system, without permission in writing from the publishers.

Trademark notice: Product or corporate names may be trademarks or registered trademarks, and are used only for identification and explanation without intent to infringe.

British Library Cataloguing in Publication Data
A catalogue record for this book is available from the British Library

Library of Congress Cataloging in Publication Data
Names: Thwaites, Rachel, author.
Title: Changing names and gendering identity : social organisation in contemporary Britain / Rachel Thwaites.
Description: 1 Edition. | New York : Routledge, [2017] | Series: Routledge research in gender and society | Includes bibliographical references and index.
Identifiers: LCCN 2016026135 | ISBN 9781472477705 (hardback) | ISBN 9781315571256 (ebook)
Subjects: LCSH: Gender identity—Great Britain. | Sex role—Great Britain. | Personality and situation—Great Britain. | Names, Personal—Great Britain. | Social change—Great Britain.
Classification: LCC HQ75.6.G7 T49 2017 | DDC 303.4—dc23
LC record available at https://lccn.loc.gov/2016026135

ISBN: 978-1-4724-7770-5 (hbk)
ISBN: 978-1-315-57125-6 (ebk)

Typeset in Times New Roman
by Apex CoVantage, LLC

 Printed and bound by CPI Group (UK) Ltd, Croydon, CR0 4YY

Contents

List of figures	vi
List of tables	vii
Preface	viii
Author's declaration	x

1	Introduction: the importance of names to gendered social organisation	1
2	Research design and methodology	22
3	Names and tradition	33
4	Names, 'choice', and gender	50
5	Power, politics, and naming	61
6	Maintaining the status quo? Love, heterosexuality, and emotion work	73
7	'Displaying' and 'doing' family: genetics, social connection, and respectability	94
8	Names, (gendered) self, and society	117
9	Accounting for transgression	136
10	Conclusion	146
	Index	151

Figures

3.1	Whether name-changing participants discussed their decision with their partner beforehand	43
4.1	Who influenced participants' naming decisions	51
7.1	Whether name changers still feel connected to their birth family history	99
7.2	To what extent participants think it is important to share one name within a family	101
7.3	Whether participants changed names on marriage	102
7.4	Childless name retainers considering having children in the future and impact on their naming choice	112
7.5	How name retainers felt about not sharing a name with their children (including count for those who do share and double-barrelled children's names)	113

Tables

2.1	Research questions by method	25
3.1	Crosstabulation of who influenced participants' naming decisions by whether or not they changed their name	41
3.2	Crosstabulation of how participants feel about their naming decision with whether they changed or retained their name	44
7.1	Whether it is important to share names by naming decision	111

Preface

This research sprang in part from an interest in how the everyday and mundane upholds powerful social structures and in part from personal interest in the importance of last names to individual identities, as well as the connections between the two. It is based on my PhD research, and I gratefully acknowledge the ESRC for their funding and the many opportunities they provided throughout (Grant Number: ES/I019154/1).

There are a lot of people I would like to thank across the period of researching and writing up my PhD, as well as those who have been involved in the process of turning it into a book. I would first like to thank the participants who took part in this research, from the pilot studies right through to the PhD research itself. You gave me such rich data to work with and provided the basis for this study. I hope I have done justice to the stories, experiences, and views you shared with me.

Second, to my PhD supervisors: Stevi Jackson and Christine Skinner. Many, many thanks for the help, guidance, and support you gave me throughout. I really appreciate all that you did for me and the advice and encouragement you both gave.

My thanks to everyone at the Centre for Women's Studies, University of York, for their support and generosity, which made my PhD experience a very happy one. Thanks also to Laurie Hanquinet and Emma Uprichard for their input and advice, and to Sandra Seubert and the staff at the IPP, Goethe University, Frankfurt, for their interest and encouragement. I would also like to say thank you to colleagues in Social Policy and Sociology at the University of Birmingham, particularly Shelley Budgeon and Nicola Smith, for encouraging me to hurry up and publish this book!

My thanks to Neil Jordan and the team at Ashgate/Routledge who commissioned this work and have been nothing but helpful and patient in its preparation.

I want also to say thank you to some wonderful friends, whose names tell many interesting stories: Dana Galbraith, Tololy Mahadeen, Hollie Morgan, Amy Pressland, Jennifer Reynolds, Cait Rogan, Patrycja Sosnowska-Buxton, and Paul Tobin.

I would like to dedicate this book to my parents and my sister, with whom I have shared many naming discussions prior to beginning this research and who are part of the inspiration for it; I would also like to dedicate it to my partner, Neil, who has been nothing but supportive throughout both PhD and book writing and ensured I did take the time to finish things up in late 2015 and early 2016. I offer him all my thanks and appreciation.

Rachel Thwaites
Birmingham, March 2016

Author's declaration

This book brings together some of the author's previous work, published in the following journals and edited collections. The author would like to thank the publishers for giving her permission to re-use the publications and datasets in this book.

Thwaites, R. (forthcoming 2017). 'Making a Choice or Taking a Stand? Choice Feminism, Political Engagement, and the Contemporary Feminist Movement'. *Feminist Theory*.

Thwaites, R. (2014). 'Love Stories: Naming Decisions and Narrative in Contemporary Britain' in S. Petrella (ed.) *Doing Gender, Doing Love: Interdisciplinary Voices*. Oxford: Inter-disciplinary Press: 193–217.

Thwaites, R. (2013). 'The Making of Selfhood: Naming Decisions on Marriage'. *Families, Relationships, and Societies*. 2 (3): 425–439.

1 Introduction

The importance of names to gendered social organisation

Names both single us out and link us in. They are a symbol of our individual identity and yet also of our collective identity, with first names usually chosen by others, sometimes in honour of others or for a particular meaning, and last names representative of family, history, and genealogy. Geographical, ethnic, cultural, or other ties may be made clear through names; they have both specific and general resonances. They are an important part of cultures and are not given, taken, or shared randomly; they are understood within cultures and their specific boundaries. Without names, we cannot address one another or make it clear whom we are discussing; without names, we become a mass with no public individuality. Names are a part of delineation, organisation, collectivity, *and* individualism. They act as an identity 'hook' and are therefore a part of the process of calling ourselves selves and thinking of ourselves as individuals with significant and important life stories, tied up by the public (and private) symbol of that life – the name.

The last name, which is the real focus of this book, is also intimately connected with ideas of kinship, genealogy, and history, both personal, familial, and societal. It acts as a means to differentiate one Catherine from another, but also to connect that Catherine in with others and make it clear who she belongs to, who belongs to her, and who she can count as family and kin. Names are a part of personal and wider social identities. Yet in a temporal moment of rapid social change, names are also more complex than ever before, and taking them, changing them, or retaining them displays these social changes and personal preferences, but also makes it clear where society has remained constant or attached to an idea of certain traditions and socially meaningful rituals. This book has one of these naming rituals at its heart – naming decisions on marriage – and will explore why it remains socially meaningful and significant to identity building.

Thus far sociology has left names a little in the background (Finch, 2008). Yet, names are a prime means of social organisation. Last names may seem unproblematic, almost natural, in the way they are passed along, taken, shared, or disposed of at certain points in a life, but this is to ignore the specific patterns involved in that passing, taking, sharing, and disposing. In the case of marriage, ignoring the gendered patterns of naming is to accept and silence the more subtle ways in which gender remains significant to how we live our lives and construct our sense of self.

2   *Introduction*

The name (both first and last together) is a significant symbol of our identities, both in a bureaucratic and a personal sense. The name is an important symbol of who a person is, and a sense of identity can be built up around this symbol; yet women are asked to change their last name at pivotal moments in their lives. Schimmel argues that the name and the person named are one and the same (Schimmel, 1989: ix) – they are interchangeable symbols for one another, so closely related that to think of one is generally to conjure up an image of the other. Even when a person's name is simply written on paper, the name will produce images and have connotations for the reader, who will attempt to classify that person based on what is before them. Without a name, a person cannot legally exist and cannot be properly referred to in conversation between people. The name becomes a symbol of life events, achievements, and the actions of the person named, and therefore represents the person's worth in society. Even after death, the idea of burying a body without a name is seen as tragic and prevents families from properly moving on (Bodenhorn and vom Bruck, 2009: 1).

The name goes beyond the letters grouped together to make a word or a means of distinguishing people from one another. It is invested with emotion and is a part of social organisation, as well as social ideals. Some of those I have spoken to about my project have become irate at the suggestion this needs to be investigated and my emphasis on the need to explore a wider range of possibilities for naming. The very idea that women should consider other options can produce anger, personal questioning, and a desire to have me validate my entire ideological and political standpoint; there has also been excitement, interest, and instant understanding of the project's aims. There is much wrapped up in these reactions and some connect with the experience of my participants, which will be discussed further throughout this book. Significantly though, names – how we use them, and what they mean – are *not* value-free. They are an important part of our social organisation and therefore reflect social and cultural values. Our use of names remains political.

As well as this, names are a part of the everyday, and it is the everyday and mundane which underpins our social world and workings. Though more spectacular events may occupy much sociological thought, the everyday is increasingly recognised as important to interrogate (Smart, 2012). The everyday shows us clearly what is meaningful in a society, what 'oils the wheels' of social relations, what is lauded and what undermined. Without a desire to probe the seemingly innocent parts of our lives, there is little possibility of coming to any greater knowledge of how society works. As Hockey et al. (2010) show in their work on heterosexuality, the things we take for granted, things that we can often hardly articulate our reasons for acting upon and being attracted to, are often the most significant practices and social organisers in any given society.

Major themes

Tradition and choice

This book will explore a number of ways in which names are significant to (gendered) identity building and social organisation, building on the thoughts and experiences of the women who took part in this research (more on the sample in Chapter 2). The substantive chapters will explore tradition, choice, feminism, love and heterosexuality, family, expressions of selfhood, and transgression. Chapters 3 and 4 will examine two major justifications for name changing – tradition and individual choice – which between them suggest the naming decision can be seen as one entirely without agency or one entirely with agency. It is a decision with a long past (though not equally as long in every part of the United Kingdom, as will be seen below) and therefore tradition can be safely appealed to as a reasonable reason for wishing to change a last name.

Shils argues that 'All existing things have a past' (1971: 122). In moments of both change and consistency, the past of an event, process, or person is pertinent and cannot be dismissed (1971: 122). As Adams says, the past continues to influence us all through its 'codes of practice' (2003: 227). These codes of practice are the traditions and norms passed down from one generation to the next. As May argues, 'traditions have not disappeared, but rather remain important features of contemporary societies though their nature and role may have shifted' (Vanessa May, 2011: 365). People use the practices that have become fairly stable over time to help guide their decisions in the present (Young in Vanessa May, 2011: 366). They may well act with little knowledge of what they are doing rather than in a deliberate and careful manner (Vanessa May, 2011: 367), but enacting these social norms within lived relationships gives them continued meaning. Our traditions remain alive, meaningful, and significant to action, but the assumptions they carry will stem from a past historical moment.

This focus on the past and its importance may seem to jar with individualisation theories, which have become so important to recent sociological debate (Giddens, 1996; Bauman, 2003; Beck and Beck-Gernsheim, 2010). The theories of these four major theorists of late modernity will be discussed in more detail in Chapter 3, but the overall sense is of a loosening of tradition. This narrative of choice, increasing freedom for the individual, and the suggestion therein of more happiness and fulfilment in life is powerful – my data are testament to this. However, the continued use of the name change clearly displays the equal significance of tradition and well-understood ritual acts within British society. The tension between the need to reach out to and make use of traditions, while appealing to a narrative of choice and freedom, comes through in the stories of the name changers.

Feminism

This significant narrative of choice is one often linked to feminism and the opening up of new possibilities to women in all aspects of their life (see for example, Snyder-Hall, 2010). In Chapters 4 and 5, I will explore the importance of a feminist narrative to the name retainers as a justification for their actions, but also the tensions between feminism and choice, which have concerning links to a more neoliberal agenda (Craven, 2007), where 'choice' is co-opted to maintain the status quo by not interrogating why certain decisions are made. Saying one is following a norm as an individual 'choice' can

4   *Introduction*

actually be a means of masking the maintenance of gendered, hierarchical social relations.

Scholarship on names has focused on identity building and feminism in the main, and the complex interactions between them, particularly within the American cultural context (Foss and Edson, 1989; Spender, 1998; Mills, 2003; Goldin and Shim, 2004; Suter, 2004; Hoffnung, 2006; Laskowski, 2010; Hamilton et al., 2011). This theoretical background shows clearly the continued importance of tradition in decision-making around names (Suter, 2004) and explores the possibilities for better understanding the more subtle ways in which patriarchy is maintained in contemporary (Western) societies (Hoffnung, 2006; Hamilton et al., 2011). The individual (self) and the collective (family; others) continue to be pitted against one another in discussions of naming, with Hamilton et al. (2011) suggesting a stronger connection with a liberal individualism when non-traditional naming options are supported and a more collective and traditional outlook when they are not. This literature also makes clear the connection of non-traditional naming options – that is not changing one's name – with feminism and the complex and even conflicting identity categories women may feel a need to contend with in forming a coherent sense of self (Mills, 2003). This literature therefore acts as both context and also a means of validating my own data, which is in accord with this, mostly American, research.

Love, emotion work, and heterosexuality

In Chapter 6, I will explore love, emotion work, and heterosexuality. Heterosexuality is 'a largely silent principle of social organisation' (Johnson, 2005: 5). It is something taken-for-granted, presumed to be 'natural' and therefore not worth investigating. This is not to suggest that work critiquing heterosexuality has not occurred, because such work can be traced back to the 1970s (Jackson, 1999: 2), but that too little attention has been paid to it. Both heterosexuality and love are often presented as timeless, 'trans-historical and universal' (Johnson, 2005: 40). They are seen as 'natural' parts of human society and love as a deeply held emotion which can barely be described, never mind subjected to scrutiny (Jackson, 1993: 201). This leaves major structures within our society under-researched and badly understood: love should not be thought of as an unchanging emotion, entirely natural and free from society's influence, yet researchers are loath to tackle it seriously (Johnson, 2005: 45).

Heterosexuality, as Hockey et al. note, can be hard to research as it is barely articulated (2010: 2). Heterosexuals see themselves as the norm, and conversations about heterosexual relationships rarely foreground the fact a *heterosexual* relationship is being discussed: people use 'vague yet important yardsticks' to discuss how 'good' their relationships are (Hockey et al., 2010: 3). People are aware there is a way of being a heterosexual in that they worry over transgressing boundaries – what is not heterosexual can be described, but what *is* is more difficult (Jackson, 2003: 77; Hockey et al., 2010: 10). It pervades our lives yet remains 'absolved from scrutiny, explanation, condemnation or tolerance' (Hockey et al.,

Introduction 5

2010: 5); even if we do not define as heterosexual, we continue to be governed by it as it is such a dominant organising principle (Johnson, 2005: 11). As Rich famously defined it, heterosexuality is 'compulsory' (Rich, 1980) – it is seen as the 'natural' state, around which our society is structured. Thinking about heterosexuality as a specific identity rather than a natural given can cause consternation: the act of labelling – naming – this category is a political act in itself (Kitzinger et al., 1992: 297–298). Heterosexuality is not only natural, however, and to refrain from investigating it leaves this illusion intact, without interrogating the interests that are being served by its present existence (Ingraham, 2008: 16).

In approaching this complex system and attempting to destabilise it scholars have looked empirically at marriage and heterosexual coupledom, revealing power relations, the distribution of labour within the household, gendered emotion work, and the continued power of gendered roles (Leonard, 1980; Askham, 1984; Mansfield and Collard, 1988; Duncombe and Marsden, 1993; Jamieson, 2003; Hockey et al., 2010), some of which will be described in more detail below. Work looking at the convergence of class, gender, and respectability has helped to define the boundaries of heterosexuality and examined the ways in which women's lives are organised by it (Skeggs, 2001).

Theorists have also interrogated heterosexuality on a theoretical level as an organising principle of society which is a normalised part of how the world is perceived and understood (Ingraham, 1996; Wittig, 1996; Beasley et al., 2012). Wittig described this as 'the straight mind' (Wittig, 1996: 146), which takes heterosexuality as a natural and given state upon which knowledges of the world can be built. Ingraham's idea of the 'heterosexual imaginary' (1996: 168) is a similar idea of the way in which the world is perceived through a heterosexual lens, one which structures how the world is viewed. This, she argues, is most worrying when feminist sociologists take heterosexuality for granted and fail to investigate it critically, therefore reinforcing the patriarchal narratives they wish to undermine (1996: 181). Instead, heterosexuality must be problematised and its position of dominance destabilised: recognising its contours, complexities, and contradictions has become a project recognised as vital to feminism (Smart, 1998). Heterosexualities becomes a more salient term than heterosexuality (Smart, 1998: 179).

Feminist scholars have grappled with the tensions of living a heterosexual life, especially when one defines as a feminist (Ramazanoglu, 1992; Jackson, 1999: 11). Domestic living arrangements within heterosexual relationships have been a point of interest for much sociological research but, as Van Every argues, heterosexual domestic life does not have to equate to a hegemonic construction of – and lived experience of – heterosexuality (1998: 53). In attempting to re-imagine heterosexuality away from essentialist ideas of gendered power the argument that heterosexuality is a viable and possibly radical position for feminists to hold has begun to be discussed (Rowland, 1992). The tensions of living as a heterosexual who defines as a feminist will be discussed in Chapter 5, in reference to my participants.

As Jackson argues, everyday heterosexuality is experienced in a number of ways through various rituals, practices, and divisions of behaviour and routine

6   *Introduction*

(1999: 26). The 'natural' heterosexual relationship on which so much of social, political and economic policy is based includes the wedding as a pivotal (and taken-for-granted, 'everyday') moment. The relationships my participants have with their names may well have changed significantly on this day; they will each have had to reflect upon their name around this point in their lives, whatever their decision. Marriage is both an individual and a collective experience – people make choices for themselves and can be creative, but marriage continues to have a social and cultural aspect from which it cannot be severed, and which influences the decisions people make (Mansfield and Collard, 1988: 30–31). Marriage remains 'an important cultural symbol', a sign of growing up and gaining security (Mansfield and Collard, 1988: 52). People attempt to show 'that they belong to a category of normal, respectable, moral people, namely those who are married' (Askham, 1984: 142). Within this setting, women are expected to care and love and not see any of the physical or emotional labour they do as exploitative (Mansfield and Collard, 1988: 35; see Chapter 6). It is, in fact, seen as quite normal, and falling into these patterns and roles confirms one's normality (Mansfield and Collard, 1988: 53). The positive aspirations couples have for their marriage conceal the gendered work that exists within the institution. The 'emotional labour' (Hochschild, 2003a: 7) within relationships is connected to a huge number of gender differentials but is often disguised by the word 'love'.

The proposition I am making is not that love causes heterosexuality but that the social construction of love is bound up with, and legitimises, a range of heterosexual practices. This is the opposite of the biological model where we 'read forward' from love, because I am proposing that we 'read backwards' from sexuality, to see how love is invoked as the basis for a way of being, rather than being a natural basis for that way of being (Johnson, 2005: 3). From this perspective I can consider how love is used to legitimise the practice of name changing, and what social pressures women have to struggle with whatever decision they make (see Chapter 6).

Theories of the 'pure relationship' (Giddens, 2008: 2) and 'confluent love' (Giddens, 2008: 61) suggest that people are only together for as long as they feel satisfaction from the relationship and that the idea of the 'one and only' is receding (Giddens, 2008: 61–62). As Giddens argues, romantic love has always been 'skewed in terms of power', despite people narrating it as egalitarian (2008: 62). Therefore, as women's position in society improves and the gendered power imbalances disappear, Giddens argues that couples will not feel a need to be with each other for life, but only 'until further notice' (Giddens, 2008: 63). Yet empirical research suggests this theory is too simplistic (Langford, 1999; Carter, 2011). Long-term commitment is not something younger people are shying away from and romantic relationships within married coupledom remain something young women strive towards (Carter, 2011). The power of love as a discourse needs to be investigated here to understand why traditional decisions are being taken in its name, as well as taking to task some of the over-simplified ideas around modern relationships.

Wendy Langford's study with 15 women and their experiences of love points out some of the ways in which narratives of love are used by women. These narratives,

Introduction 7

which run along the same lines as romance literature, are compelling and raise the world above the mundane everyday (Langford, 1999: 30). Love acts as a 'secular religion', giving women a sense of transcendence and otherworldliness (Langford, 1999: 35). This study shows love raising women's self-esteem and their sense of self-worth: without love, they feel ordinary, ugly, and often, unable to cope with life's burdens (Langford, 1999: 28). Yet, she points out, women in relationships frequently end up continuing to do all of the work (e.g. in the house; carework) they did previously and do not receive emotional support from their partners (1999: 29): this conclusion is also upheld by other empirical studies (see Mansfield and Collard, 1988; Duncombe and Marsden, 1993). Yet staying in the relationship is considered a better idea than leaving it because 'there is an association between being of value and being in a relationship such that being single is equated with being in some way defective' (Langford, 1999: 28). Love promises to complete these women by providing them with what they lack (Johnson, 2005: 78) and this lack is the power that men possess in all aspects of life – the women in Langford's study doubt their own autonomy and ability to cope with life, so turn to men for this support (Langford, 1999). Elements of these findings are found in my own research (see Chapter 6). Love, heterosexuality, and marriage are bound together, but they are also closely connected to ideas of family, to which I will now turn.

Family

Much sociological enquiry into the family has found that it does not really exist, at least not as one, singular, homogenised unit (Morgan, 2011: 3). There are varieties of families and family life which 'the family' does not encapsulate, including non-married couples, single mothers, and lesbian and gay couples (with children). There can also be 'families' of friends (Chan, 2012: 35–36) or other arrangements which steer away from the heteronormative image of a woman, a man, married and living together with their children. As Morgan argues, to use 'the family' is to oversimplify real lives (Morgan, 2011: 4).

Thinking about how a society conceptualises family is significant. As Luxton and Fox argue, such conceptualisations reveal 'cultural assumptions' which 'inform . . . legislation, policies, and practices', as well as how we live our lives on an individual level (2009: 6). The power of the concept of family is so great that it can limit, but also expand, our imaginations about possible futures (Luxton and Fox, 2009: 6). This last is pertinent: the imagining of gay and lesbian couples as loving units brought about the possibility of arguing for their ability to marry and adopt (Woo, 2007). The very act of imagining can have material and political consequences. Within my study the act of imagining the family – within heterosexuality – impacts on the use of names to create this imagined family in reality (see Chapter 7).

The family has been written about and conceptualised as a place of egalitarianism, care, and love, but also as a place where inequalities are reproduced (Seubert, 2010: 5–6). As Seubert has argued, families are meant to be places in which care is given and received and where we can share our troubles, but this does not always transpire (2010: 6, n6). Inequalities can also be generated through unequal

8   *Introduction*

sharing of resources, work within families, and/or 'immaterial resources' which Seubert defines as 'values, dispositions, abilities, competencies or gender-specific attributions . . . communicated to children by their parent's lifestyle, activities and interests' (2010: 6). Following Bourdieu, Seubert argues that the family unit conceals this inequality (2010: 6). Seubert ultimately wants to create a positive and just conception of family which could impact positively on people's lives (2010: 7) and strives towards this in her arguments. To do this, scholars need first to understand how families work in actuality and move from looking at family as a noun to considering the processes which constitute families of all kinds.

Morgan argues for thinking about family 'practices' and how we 'do' family (Morgan, 2011: 5). It is this 'doing' of family which I focus on in Chapter 7, to understand the use of names in constituting family and kinship connections. Family is actively constructed, daily, through doing certain things. Sharing time, going to designated 'family events', talking with and about one another, perhaps living together, caring for one another, and sharing resources. I would add to this the importance of names and the meanings with which we fill them. As Finch argues, names make connections between people, as well as constituting individual selfhood (2008: 710–711). They are an important, if under-examined, part of sociological research. She puts forward three questions about names and family in particular which need answering: 'How far, in the context of contemporary UK society, are names used publicly to map family connections?'; 'How far do people use the process of naming in constituting their family relationships?'; and 'What do naming practices tell us about the contemporary significance of families and kinship?' (Finch, 2008: 710). My study offers data with which to begin answering these questions (see Chapter 7). Names are alive with meaning and are a part of living, constantly evolving, familial relationships.

In many ways, this 'doing' of family is about who we perceive our family to be: it is about the imagination and construction of family within the mind, which is then cemented by various practices, including naming practices. Ueno has argued that perception is as significant as action to an idea of family (Ueno, 2009: 4). The people who make up a family define its parameters: who is part of it, as well as who is not. Ueno gives an example from Japan, the context in which she works: Japanese war orphans searching for families to sponsor them to live in Japan and declare themselves their kin are looking to be perceived as family despite the lack of biological ties (Ueno, 2009: 4). Ueno points out that the same perception might not exist on both sides of this relationship and could result in one side not seeing the other as 'true' family (2009: 4).

Familial, relational identity is significant to a discussion of names, but so is individual identity. It is the connections between these – the self and other – which I explore in Chapter 8.

Selfhood

There are varied and often conflicting theories of selfhood within long-term relationships. Falling in love and being part of an intimate couple relationship like

Introduction 9

marriage is often described as a merging or fusing of selves, so that individuality is in some way lost (Kern, 1992: 282). Yet there is also a struggle for autonomy within love which Sartre has described as appropriating the freedom of others to make oneself free (Sartre in Johnson, 2005: 79); however, this has a gendered angle which he did not investigate. This angle was theorised by scholars such as Simone de Beauvoir (2010) and Rich, who argues that women's subjectivity is re-orientated to identify with men within heterosexual relationships (Rich, 1980: 646).

Goffman's work on the presentation of self (1990 [1959]) emphasises how important symbols are to interaction in everyday life. Without such symbols, it is hard to make sense of the world around us and fit ourselves into everyday situations. The performance of selfhood requires knowledge and incorporation of 'the officially accredited values of the society' (Goffman, 1990 [1959]: 45). Name changing is one such performance of married selfhood, wifehood, and femininity. As Goffman argues, such performances can be looked upon as ceremonies; ceremonies celebrating the values of the culture (1990 [1959]: 45). Symbols can be many things, both tangible and intangible, but the important element is that they have meaning and order society in a meaningful way. This name changing manages, in a society that finds meaning in gendered hierarchy and inequality, and is a part of the reason name retaining is often seen as threatening and confusing.

Naming practices highlight the tension in self-formation between the 'desire for recognition' by others (Crossley, 2001: 102) and the significance of the individual for women in contemporary Britain, and this tension must be dealt with to create a coherent sense of self. How selves are conceptualised and narrated is significant to the everyday understanding and lived experience of gendered identity, and participants use these narratives in particular ways to make sense of the tension described above and the social norms surrounding names and 'appropriate' heterosexual, gendered behaviour. Here I will outline the main theorists who inform my own conceptualisation of self and whose theories inform this project, first addressing the self of modern reflexivity and my conceptual problems with this particular idea of selfhood before looking at Foucault's idea of 'technologies of the self', Bourdieu's habitus, and Mead's dialectic of the self.

The problem with the modern reflexive self

Recent theorisations on reflexive modernisation have posited that all of life now comes down to choice and individual agency (see above for more detail), and it appears to be an ideology many find appealing. The biography of the self is one built upon these choices: life is open to possibilities, less constrained by tradition, and how the self is defined and played out in individual lives can be creative, shifting and changing with the situation. The amount of reflexive work involved in living in late modernity and the proliferation of choices around all of daily life has created a situation in which reflexivity is unavoidable (Giddens, 1996; Beck and Beck-Gernsheim, 2010). As Budgeon notes, for theorists of reflexive modernisation the fact we must choose is itself not a choice, but it is the only thing we are not free to decide for ourselves in modern society (2003: 106). Through actively

10   *Introduction*

reflecting on the possibilities open to us and the paths we can take in life, we choose the direction of our lives and the make-up of our identities. Our identities are truly there for us to self-create; we are true individuals.

The individual as self and agent became an important figure for political debate in the seventeenth century (Bellah et al., 1988: 143): individual rights and freedoms were significant at a time in which the power of God and His divinely established 'natural' hierarchy of people were being challenged. The concept of the rational, active agent of contemporary Anglo-American philosophy remains central to theorists of reflexive modernisation. This person's

> desires are ranked in a coherent order and [their] aim is to maximize desire satisfaction. This conception of the self isolates the individual from personal relationships and larger social forces. It pays little attention to how the individual's desires are formed, nor does it acknowledge the impact of the individual's emotional life. The self is identified with the instrumental rationality of the marketplace.
>
> (Meyers, 1997: 2)

Meyers' definition of the self in Anglo-American philosophy could equally be applied to the modern reflexive self of sociological theory. The political individual was undeniably less individualistic than the reflexive modern self, but the ideas of freedom and equality, not being under the rule of any other person or group, and the ability to choose contracts to enter into in life (Pateman, 1988: 39–40) are all ideas that remain important to this conception of the post-traditional self (see Giddens, 1996, Bauman, 2003; Beck and Beck-Gernsheim, 2010). Yet this is a set of categories into which it has often been difficult for women to fit, historically in terms of the legal and social position of women, but continuing today in less overt forms. Women remain subordinate in our society and the possibilities open to the reflexive self are curbed by this subordination.

Social positioning makes a difference to how identity can be forged and these positionings are not separate, but intersect and work together to form unique circumstances for each individual within the social framework. The self is always in process and never complete; it is, however, not purely choice that is behind this constant refashioning, but also social positionings, such as gender, class, ethnicity, and sexuality. Regulating these selves is then managed using 'technologies of the self' (Foucault, 1988: 18). It is these '[t]echnologies of the self [which] operate to organize conduct in the context of everyday life and to orient this conduct toward a consideration of the kind of person one should aspire to be and the kind of life one should aim to lead' (Budgeon, 2003: 43).

Foucault and technologies of the self

Any way of speaking of ourselves – including calling ourselves 'a self' – is simply a 'particular style or relation that the human being is enjoined to adopt towards itself' (Rose, 1996: 299). This way of viewing selfhood – for this is what we call

Introduction 11

this site of practices at the present time – reminds us that identity is never fixed, but always changing and in flux and encourages thinking about what authorities there are in society which influence how people think of themselves as 'selves' and what kinds of things produce that experience. Indeed, the word 'self' is historically specific: 'Homeric man [sic] was not the introspective self-conscious being who populates Socrates' dialogues a few hundred years later – The Iliad has no word for 'person' or 'oneself'' (Porter, 2002: 13). Rose argues that changes in social arrangements do not necessarily

> transform the nature and form of 'being human' by virtue of some 'experience' that they produce, but instead the relation a person has to him or herself requires examination i.e. 'the ways in which human beings understand themselves and are understood by others, the kinds of persons they presume themselves to be or are pressured to be in the various practices that govern them.
>
> (1996: 305)

It is these connections between ideas 'by which human beings are rendered thinkable' (Rose, 1996: 305), through which we as individuals process a sense of coherent identity. Rendering oneself thinkable is bound up in names and naming practices and the self in relation to others. Names make the self and its relation to others clear for these others, within a specific societal context of widely followed naming practices.

Foucault's discussion of technologies of the self looks back over Greek, Roman and Christian forms of ethics, looking at whether and how people have been encouraged to 'look after themselves' through meditation, writing, confession, physical exercise or labour, and what authorities were involved in instigating the processes through which particular ideas of how to conduct the self evolved (Foucault, 1988). These 'technologies' are about how human beings regulate themselves and others in relation to particular social ideas or 'truths' such as virtue and self-realisation (Budgeon, 2003: 45). How a person conducts themselves should reflect the kind of person they are or aspire to be and the kind of life they are trying to lead (Budgeon, 2003: 43). In Foucault's own words:

> technologies of the self, which permit individuals to effect by their own means or with the help of others a certain number of operations on their own bodies and souls, thoughts, conduct, and way of being, so as to transform themselves in order to attain a certain state of happiness, purity, wisdom, perfection, or immortality.
>
> (1988: 18)

Any authority on conduct and regulation can be considered a 'technology of the self' and be seen as a part of the creation of (a coherent) identity. Naming practices, bound up with heterosexuality and marriage, are one such authority – they guide our conduct, lead us to act out certain norms and attend to certain symbols, while perpetuating a gendered societal hierarchy.

12   *Introduction*

The institution of marriage, as a technology of the self, regulates a person into a particular social group – the couple or family – and, for many of my participants, does exemplify how they want to be thought of and how they want to live their lives: settled, committed individuals, who love and care for others, who are adults with responsibilities, and a team with common goals. Those who changed their names were often happy to consider this a symbol of their new life stage and hence self-regulation.

In each individual's life there is an amount of being able to decide what kind of life one wants to lead and what one can do to be perceived as a particular kind of self by invoking and making use of technologies of the self, as outlined by Foucault, but this makes little *explicit* reference to the parts of life dictated by habit and a lack of thought and consideration. It is this side of women's decision-making that Bourdieu highlights so clearly; his theory of the self embedded within social fields of habitual action or habitus. This theory is also crucial to explaining the actions of participants as they follow particular, preexisting paths when making their naming decisions.

Bourdieu and habitus

Habitus is derived from social fields – arenas of social activity – and the dispositions and forms of competence that are acquired within these fields; it is 'collective conscious' (Boyne, 2001: 8). Once a person understands how to behave within a particular social context and has obtained or gained the correct kinds and amounts of capital (economic, social, symbolic, and cultural), they can enter and flow through these social fields with ease. They understand the 'rules of the game' (see Crossley, 2001: 100–101). Society, its norms and values, can be looked upon as the fields of habitus and people 'internalise the structure of the external field' (Boyne, 2001: 5). This means that much of what people do comes from an unthinkingness or habit which allows selves to deal with their everyday lives without having to consider each movement or social interaction deeply.

This unthinkingness, which will be an important part of thinking through the way participants discuss tradition in relation to naming decisions, is highlighted by Bourdieu as 'doxa' (see Bourdieu, 1998). Doxa is the part of the public sphere which is unquestioned and full of 'unspoken assumptions upon which the state rests' (Crossley, 2001: 98–99). This idea is useful for thinking through the actions of participants within this study whose decisions come from assumptions about the 'correct' behaviour related to heterosexual weddings: there is a great deal of silence around naming decisions, particularly the traditional decision to change names, which rests on unquestioned assumptions about gender, wifehood, heterosexuality, and intelligible families.

This desire to follow the norms and the accepted patterns of behaviour which make up a part of doxa and habitus comes from what Crossley calls the 'desire for recognition' by others (Crossley, 2001: 102). This is the need for an identity which is intelligible and valued by society and, in terms of this project, meaning to be seen as a committed wife, who may well be a mother as well; an identity forged

Introduction 13

from societal and collective understandings of what these categories ('wife', 'mother') mean. The understanding of social norms and values is therefore critical to any social actor if they wish to be accepted as an understandable part of that society: in other words, others are critical to the perception of oneself as a correctly functioning person. These others – both specific people and a generalised other or society – are critical to this project and their impact will be explored throughout.

Selves, within Bourdieu's theories, are created from within social fields of activity, along with the dispositions and capital that are necessary for acting and speaking with ease within them. This forms habits of action and speech which structures individual lives and allows everyday interactions to be completed with relative ease. Bourdieu did not believe agency to be completely overridden by these structures and held a place for resisting norms and for change within his ideas; however the lack of clarity about agency in his work has given rise to claims of determinism (see Crossley, 2001: 115–118 for a discussion of this). The applicability of Bourdieu's theory to participant claims about their sense of self and the actions they take when naming themselves on marriage is clear, but the need for a more explicit theory of agency in the construction of selfhood is also important. Hence I wish to turn to Mead's conception of self, which deals more clearly with agency within selfhood and is the main theory on which I base my conception of selfhood.

Mead's theory of selfhood

The place of each individual's agency as a human being is vital to selfhood. It would not be fair to construct people as 'slaves to culture' or, equally, as completely free agents; instead we must try and view the ways in which people have choice and constraint in their lives. A person locates themselves within all of this by looking to the boundaries in place as well as the choices available as an active agent.

The whole of the self is social and in constant creation; reflexivity is still important to this self. Here the arguments of Mead, elucidated by Jackson, are useful:

> Mead did not see reflexivity primarily as heightened self-concern, but as the capacity to see ourselves as subject and object, which rests on a dialogic interplay between self and other. . . . While there is no unitary, stable "core self" in Mead's account, our ability to remember (or rather retrospectively reconstruct) selves other than the self of the present enables us to create for ourselves a sense of continuity or wholeness. . . . Reflexive self-hood, then, implies a degree of agency and active meaning-making, but it is always both produced within and bounded by its social context.
>
> (Jackson, 2008: 55)

The self is reflexive and can 'be both subject and object' (Mead, 1964: 201). Mead sees this self as object to itself as 'a social structure, and it arises in social experience' (Mead, 1964: 140). The self may then 'provide for itself its social

14   *Introduction*

experiences, and so we can conceive of an absolutely solitary self. But it is impossible to conceive of a self arising outside of social experience' (Mead, 1964: 204). We all create selves and change responses in relation to others (Mead, 1964: 205).

The 'generalised other', which Mead calls the social community in which people move and act, is a part of building up a sense of self as this needs to be done in relation to these others, their opinions, and thoughts, and whatever social activity is being engaged in (Mead, 1964: 218). It is only by considering the thoughts and feelings of this generalised other that a person can have the necessary discourse with the world about who to be and how to act (Mead, 1964: 220). Fitting ourselves into wider groups, from childhood onwards, is how personality develops (Mead, 1964: 223). Each self is different 'but there has to be such a common structure. . . . in order that we may be members of a community at all' (Mead, 1964: 227). 'Selves can only exist in definite relationships to other selves' (Mead, 1964: 227). Mead argues that the social group must pre-exist for the self to arise: 'there is a social process out of which selves arise and within which further differentiation, further evolution, further organization, take place' (Mead, 1974: 164). This 'social group' can refer to a wide variety of contexts: family, workplace, or a generalised society and suggests that people still need to account to others in a way individualisation theorists often do not allow.

Mead also looks to explain the idea of 'I' and 'me'. He argues that the 'I' of one moment, in the next becomes 'me'; we identify ourselves as 'I', but when we reflect upon our actions we are reflecting upon 'me' (Mead, 1964: 237). The 'I' 'is the response of the organism to the attitudes of the others; the "me" is the organized set of attitudes of others which one assumes' (Mead, 1964: 237). The 'I' may not always react within the social expectations of others, but this response will become a part of the experience of that self and be stored up within their experience of how to react in similar situations; the 'me' knows the social expectations of others as they are stored up as experience (Mead, 1964: 238–239).

My conceptualisation of selfhood then is built on the ideas of the three theorists above and their ideas and concepts will be returned to throughout this book. My participants however use ideas of the self in a variety of ways to make their lives coherent and accountable (see Chapter 8). I would argue, with Gergen, that the unitary, singular self continues to hold imaginative sway in the Western context (Gergen, 1991), but that the idea of a more fluid and even fragmented self is gaining ground and is used, implicitly, by some of my participants as a narrative of selfhood.

Transgression

The final empirical chapter (Chapter 9) takes the overall structure of this book, considering justifications for action, and looks at its opposite: transgression. In this chapter I will use Eli Adams' description of transgression (1993) to explore and understand the name retain as an act of transgression of social and gender norms and the impact this has on the lived lives of name retainers. I will also examine the ways in which our society's bureaucracy actually hinders any attempts at naming

Introduction 15

innovation or transgression of social norms, instead reiterating what is socially acceptable and (re)inscribing it into the everyday ways in which we govern, track, and publicly account for ourselves.

Before turning to the design of the study and how it was carried out (Chapter 2), it is worth a brief reflection on the historical development of naming in the UK, which was not unified. As my participants are from England and Scotland, I have focused on researching the histories of married naming in these two countries.

The historical development of the British naming system on marriage

There is some uncertainty about when surnames came into general use in Britain, but authors place it somewhere between the twelfth and thirteenth centuries (Bardsley, 1969 [1873]: 12; Bennett, 1983: 37). These surnames were not yet hereditary and were certainly not as fixed as now. As Geary states: 'Medieval naming followed complex patterns but never "rules" – decisions about how to designate children involved complicated strategies'(2002: vii). Medieval sources are, of course, very useful for looking at the structure of local society at the time; however, they present a 'surname jungle' (Bennett, 1983: 29) – many people at the time had the same name, or one person used more than one last name. Therefore a researcher may be looking at records which discuss, for example, a John Smith, but he may somewhere else be referred to as John Wood, and the historian would not necessarily be able to recognise these names and historical references refer to the same man – these were often 'aliases' used in different circumstances, although sometimes written together so, 'John Smith, alias Wood' (Pine, 1965: 15).

Surnames were not necessarily able to connect up whole family groups as this was not yet the purpose of the name: it was about social activity rather than kinship (Bennett, 1983: 32). There was also a gender divide: men's surnames came from where they lived, what they did, and so on; women barely had surnames of their own as they were generally identified only by linking them to men in some way: 'the wife of . . .', 'the daughter of . . .'; their husband or father's name, in this way, became a sort of surname (Bennett, 1983: 35). The names that were created during the mid- to high medieval period are still recognisable to us: they were kept and began to be passed on in the hereditary style we now take for granted (Beech, 2002: x).

Within a country, there was not necessarily uniformity as class, gender, and age intersected with naming to create a multitude of different styles of address. In the British royal family, for example, the intersection of names and class can still be seen. Such exalted members of a society often do not need more than a first name and our present royal family only took on a (sort of) surname in 1917 ('Windsor') to rid themselves of their German and, during World War One, politically unacceptable lineage title (Pine, 1965: 15). Those royal households which had last names, such as the 'Tudors' or 'Stewarts', had them because they came, originally, from non-royal stock.

16   *Introduction*

Within the British Isles differences in taking up hereditary surnames can be seen: by the fifteenth century English people had hereditary surnames, but Irish people did not (Hassall, 1967: xv). Attempts by the English King Edward IV to change Irish practices to fit in with English ones failed (Hassall, 1967: 29): names have an important national connection and are important in fostering that national identity. Wales took on surnames later also – somewhere between the thirteenth and fourteenth centuries (Pine, 1965: 12). There was also a religious influence as Christian ideas about paternal authority took shape in one name per family, passed on patrilineally (Beech, 2002: xiii).

In Britain, masculine endings for names are prominent; whatever the sex of the child, it is given a name ending in the masculine '-son'. This is not the case in all European countries of course, but in Britain, only a masculine relationship is represented (Hassall, 1967: 6). There are a minority of names which show a relationship other than father–son: son-in-law, brother-in-law, nephew, and there is the occasional aunt (Hassall, 1967: 6). For example, 'Magh' meant 'brother-in-law' and can be seen in 'Hitchmough', 'Hickmott', and 'Hudsmith' (Hassall, 1967: 6). However, daughter is not to be seen. Masculine endings for names are pervasive and have survived across time in great numbers.

The number of '-sons', '-s' (an abbreviation of '-son'), and the Scottish equivalent 'Mac' in modern Britain is testament to this: Leak and Adnan have created an interactive map of contemporary Great British names (i.e. not including Northern Ireland) which shows the vast spread of these 'son of' names. Though the most common name overall is 'Smith', England is also full of 'Hodgeson', 'Johnson', 'Robinson', and 'Thompson'; Scotland 'MacDonald', 'MacKay', 'MacLeod', and 'Wilson'; and Wales 'Davies', 'Jones', 'Roberts', and 'Williams' (Leak and Adnan, 2013). Names which signify relationships to women are rare in Britain.

However, they are not non-existent. Bardsley has pointed out that there could be several reasons for women's names being used as last names: illegitimacy, adoption of children by lone women, the woman in the couple being more well-known locally than her husband (Bardsley, 1969 [1873]: 80), or perhaps the woman's family were rather better known or of better standing than her husband's so her name was used more than his. Children then became known as 'Elizabeth's/ Libby's' or 'Emma's son', for example, which has led to 'Ibson' and 'Emmott'; other names such as Sissons, Marriot, and Annotson, for example, can all be traced back to women's personal names (Bardsley, 1969 [1873]: 79–80). This shows that surnames were far more flexible at one point than they are now: today, passing on a mother's name is highly unusual, particularly using her personal name as a last name.

The family name is meant to represent who can legitimately say they are part of the family unit: in England, this has meant the woman taking on her husband's name and the children also having that name (Amy Erickson, 2005: 11). This has been a symbolic and real change made by the woman reflecting her place in the hierarchical relationship of 'man and wife' produced by marriage (Leonard, 1980: 241). The children are meant to be related to both the mother and father of that unit – rather than being illegitimate and simply living within it – and be fully related to brothers and sisters. However, in Scotland women only began to

Introduction 17

legally change their name to their husband's after the nineteenth century (Barclay, 2011: 98). It would appear that historically '[t]he distinctions in marital property regimes are reflected in naming practices' (Amy Erickson, 2005: 11), and this can be seen in the different systems of law in Scotland and England.

Scots law

The position of women in Scotland in relation to property and names historically reflects Roman law (though on a much less stringent scale). Roman law upheld patria postestas – the father's right to have extensive power over his children. The difference was that the Roman father, unlike other ancient civilisations, did not lose this power over his children when they grew up and created their own households (Arjava, 1998: 41). In practice, there were ways to free oneself from patria postestas but the idea remained in theory (Arjava, 1998: 41) and was certainly seen as the preferable state for women (Gratwick, 1991: 39–40). To reflect this, the most common form of marriage across the period of the Roman Empire as a whole was marriage sine manu, in which women remained legally separate from husbands and under their father's control, retained their own property and took on the legal status of *suriuris* (meaning 'of one's own right, or able to take care of one's own affairs) after their father's death (Arjava, 1998: 124). Hence, a Roman woman, despite marrying and having children of her own, remained, legally, a part of her father's household (Arjava, 1998: 94).

When freeborn and wealthy, Roman women had a great deal of freedom to deal with their own property, write wills, and sue in court, but they still had a guardian in their father (or a caretaker he had legally appointed) and had to ask certain permissions from him concerning their property (Arjava, 1998: 122). Wives usually legally retained their birth family name on marriage (though could also use their husband's name day-to-day) (Rawson, 1992: 19). There is a suggestion from Roman records that the woman's name could reflect what type of marriage she was in (Rawson, 1992: 20). It seems that the most common form of marriage – remaining under the control of the birth family's head of household – was reflected in the most common form of naming rite, that is retaining one's birth name. As Rawson argues, Roman women 'remained members of their own familia in a very real sense' (1992: 18).

As Gratwick argues, it is possible that marriage sine manus was most popular for the upper classes, where rich heads of household did not want to lose property to another family, while those with less property and wealth would consider marriage cum manus, a more advantageous form of marriage as sons would inherit more if daughters were legally a part of another family and no longer able to inherit (1991: 44). However, most evidence suggests marriage sine manus was the most popular form of marriage in general, certainly from the third century BC onwards (Arjava, 1998: 123).

This brief outline of women, property, marriage, and names in Roman times should make the connections with Scots law clear. Scottish women's naming practices reflected this development from Roman law and the feeling of two families uniting, but ultimately remaining separate, in marriage, and the woman remaining strongly connected with her birth family and its interests.

18   *Introduction*

English law

By the thirteenth-century, English law had 'arrived at the general doctrine that any property which a wife had owned as a *feme sole* became the husband's on marriage' (Baker, 1990: 552). This meant all property, both personal and real. The woman could claim back the real property after the death of her husband, but not her personal property (Baker, 1990: 552). Baker notes that, by the early modern period, equity often intervened in cases of married women's property, and women could be treated as feme sole when it was deemed right (1990: 553). Contracting alone on her own property was unusual though, and this was directly related to women being unable to own property in their own right (Baker, 1990: 555). This is the effect of coverture, when the woman becomes one with the man and is his subordinate in law (see Pateman, 1988 for more on coverture). The naming customs reflect this arrangement of property ownership and married identity, in which a woman moves to a new family, bringing her property and herself to serve the wider interests of this family, whose name she takes on.

However, in both England and Scotland women's property rights could be safeguarded in marriage contracts (only pre-nuptial contracts in England). My research in the National Archives of Scotland shows this option was not always taken up by families on either side of the border and may have been seen to be detrimental to a useful marriage alliance in some cases. One case from the papers of the Fergusson family of Craigdarroch in Dumfriesshire from the 1700s, when their daughter was marrying into an English family, reveals that the family chose to hand over all their daughter's property to her husband to be in accordance with English law and custom (Papers of the Fergusson family of Craigdarroch, Dumfriesshire, National Archives of Scotland, Reference GD77/174). Families had to carefully consider the balance of power and prestige when making marriages, as well as securing their property and their interests in the next generation of the lineage. It was only in the nineteenth century that the English naming practice of women legally changing their names when they married began to be accepted and used across the UK (Barclay, 2011: 98) with the increasing importance of 'Britain' as a cultural and unifying idea.

Naming practices reflected the idea of marriage each nation understood, reflecting law on property as well as gendered hierarchy. Names symbolised these structures and relationships. The empirical work within this book will analyse the significance of names to social organisation and how they express important ideas about marriage and relationships today. Naming systems continue to express (and recreate) what is socially important and valued, they continue to categorise and organise and be connected with power, and they continue to reflect (and reiterate) the history and traditions of the culture within which they work.

References

Adams, M. (2003). 'The Reflexive Self and Culture'. *British Journal of Sociology*. 54 (2): 221–238.

Arjava, A. (1998). *Women and Law in Late Antiquity*. Oxford: Clarendon Press.

Introduction   19

Askham, J. (1984). *Identity and Stability in Marriage*. Cambridge: Cambridge University Press.

Baker, J.H. (1990). *An Introduction to English Legal History*. Boston, MA: Butterworth Ltd.

Barclay, K. (2011). *Love, Intimacy and Power: Marriage and Patriarchy in Scotland, 1650–1850*. Manchester: Manchester University Press.

Bardsley, C.W. (1969 [1873]). *English Surnames*. Newton Abbot: David and Charles Reprint.

Bauman, Z. (2003). *Liquid Love*. Cambridge: Polity Press.

Beasley, C., Brook, H., and Holmes, M. (2012). *Heterosexuality in Theory and Practice.* Abingdon: Routledge.

Beauvoir, S. de (2010). *The Second Sex*. London: Vintage.

Beck, U. and Beck-Gernsheim, E. (2010). *Individualization*. London: Sage.

Beech, G.T. (2002). 'Preface' in G.T. Beech, M. Bourtin, and P. Chareille (eds.) *Personal Name Studies of Medieval Europe: Social Identity and Familial Structures*. Kalaamazoo, MI: Western Michigan University: ix–xvi.

Bellah, R., Madsen, R., Sullivan, W.M., Swidler, A., and Tipton, S.M. (1988). *Habits of the Heart*. London: Hutchinson.

Bennett, J.M. (1983). 'Siblings and Surnames: Reconstructing Families from Medieval Village Court Rolls'. *The Journal of British Studies*. 23 (1): 26–46.

Bodenhorn, B. and vom Bruck, G. (2009). 'Entangled Histories: An Introduction to the Anthropology of Names and Naming' in G. vom Bruck and B. Bodenhorn (eds.) *An Anthropology of Names and Naming*. Cambridge: Cambridge University Press: 1–30.

Bourdieu, P. (1998). *Practical Reason*. Cambridge: Polity Press.

Boyne, R. (2001). *Subject, Society and Culture*. London: Sage.

Budgeon, S. (2003). *Choosing a Self: Young Women and the Individualization of Identity*. Westport, CT: Praeger.

Carter, J. (2011). 'Why Marry? Young Women Talk About Relationships, Marriage, and Love'. Unpublished Thesis, University of York.

Chan, A.K. (2012). 'Doing Family, Contesting Gender and Expanding Affinity: Family Practices of Married Women in Hong Kong'. *Families, Relationships, and Societies*. 1 (1): 25–41.

Craven, C. (2007). 'A "Consumer's Right" to Choose a Midwife: Shifting Meanings for Reproductive Rights under Neoliberalism'. *American Anthropologist*. 109 (4): 701–712.

Crossley, N. (2001). *The Social Body*. London: Sage.

Duncombe, J. and Marsden, D. (1993). 'Love and Intimacy: The Gender Division of Emotion and "Emotion Work"'. *Sociology*. 27 (2): 221–241.

Eli Adams, J. (1993). 'The Banality of Transgression? Recent Works on Masculinity'. *Victorian Studies*. 36 (2): 207–213.

Erickson, A. (2005). 'The Marital Economy in Comparative Perspective' in M. Agren and A. Erickson (eds.) *The Marital Economy in Scandinavia and Britain 1400–1900*. Aldershot: Ashgate: 3–20.

Finch, J. (2008). 'Naming Names: Kinship, Individuality and Personal Names'. *Sociology.* 42 (4): 709–725.

Foss, K.A. and Edson, B.A. (1989). 'What's in a Name? Accounts of Married Women's Name Choices'. *Western Journal of Speech Communication.* 53: 356–373.

Foucault, M. (1988). 'Technologies of the Self' in L.H. Martin, H. Gutman, and P.H. Hutton (eds.) *Technologies of the Self*. London: Tavistock Publications: 16–49.

Geary, P. (2002). 'Forward' in G.T. Beech, M. Bourtin, and P. Chareille (eds.) *Personal Name Studies of Medieval Europe: Social Identity and Familial Structures*. Kalaamazoo, MI: Western Michigan University: vii–viii.

20 *Introduction*

Gergen, J.K. (1991). *The Saturated Self*. New York: Basic Books.

Giddens, A. (1996). *Modernity and Self-Identity*. Cambridge: Polity Press.

Giddens, A. (2008). *The Transformation of Intimacy*. Cambridge: Polity Press.

Goffman, E. (1990 [1959]). *The Presentation of Self in Everyday Life*. London: Penguin Books.

Goldin, C. and Shim, M. (2004). 'Making a Name: Women's Surnames at Marriage and Beyond'. *Journal of Economic Perspectives*. 18: 143–160.

Gratwick, A.S. (1991). 'Free or Not so Free? Wives and Daughters in the Late Roman Republic' in E. Craik (ed.) *Marriage and Property: Women and Marital Customs in History*. Aberdeen: Aberdeen University Press: 30–53.

Hamilton, L., Geist, C., and Powell, B. (2011). 'Marital Name Change as a Window into Gender Attitudes'. *Gender and Society*. 25 (2): 145–175.

Hassall, W.O. (1967). *History through Surnames*. Oxford: Pergamon Press.

Hochschild, A.R. (2003a [1983]). *The Managed Heart*. Berkeley, CA: University of California Press.

Hockey, J., Meah, A., and Robinson, V. (2010). *Mundane Heterosexualities*. Basingstoke: Palgrave Macmillan.

Hoffnung, M. (2006). 'What's in a Name? Marital Name Choice Revisited'. *Sex Roles*. 55: 817–825.

Ingraham, C. (1996). 'The Heterosexual Imaginary: Feminist Sociology and Theories of Gender' in S. Seidman (ed.) *Queer Theory/Sociology*. Oxford: Blackwell: 168–193.

Ingraham, C. (2008). *White Weddings*. London: Routledge.

Jackson, S. (1993). 'Even Sociologists Fall in Love: An Exploration in the Sociology of Emotions'. *Sociology*. 27 (2): 201–220.

Jackson, S. (1999). *Heterosexuality in Question*. London: Sage.

Jackson, S. (2003). 'Heterosexuality, Heteronormativity and Gender Hierarchy: Some Reflections on Recent Debates' in J. Weeks, J. Holland, and M. Waites (eds.) *Sexualities and Society: A Reader*. Cambridge: Polity Press: 69–83.

Jackson, S. (2008). 'Materialist Feminism, the Pragmatist Self and Global Late Modernity: Some Consequences for Intimacy and Sexuality' in L. Gunnarsson (ed.) *GEXcel Work in Progress Report Volume 111*. Orebro University/Linkoping University: 53–67.

Jamieson, L. (2003). 'The Couple: Intimate and Equal?' in J. Weeks, J. Holland, and M. Waites (eds.) *Sexualities and Society: A Reader*. Cambridge: Polity Press: 265–276.

Johnson, P. (2005). *Love, Heterosexuality and Society*. Abingdon: Routledge.

Kern, S. (1992). *The Culture of Love: Victorians to Moderns*. Cambridge, MA: Harvard University Press.

Kitzinger, C., Wilkinson, S., and Perkins, R. (1992). 'Theorizing Heterosexuality'. *Feminism and Psychology*. 2 (3): 293–324.

Langford, W. (1999). *Revolutions of the Heart*. London: Routledge.

Laskowski, K.A. (2010). 'Women's Post-Marital Name Retention and the Communication of Identity'. *Names: A Journal of Onomastics*. 58: 75–89.

Leak, A. and Adnan, M. (2013). 'Most Common Surnames of Great Britain'. Available at: http://www.uncertaintyofidentity.com/GB_Names/Mapping.aspx. [Accessed: 2nd September 2013).

Leonard, D. (1980). *Sex and Generation*. London: Tavistock Publications.

Luxton, M. and Fox, B. (2009). 'Conceptualizing "Family"' in B. Fox (ed.) *Family Patterns, Gender Relations*. Ontario: Oxford University Press: 3–20.

Mansfield, P. and Collard, J. (1988). *The Beginning of the Rest of Your Life? A Portrait of Newly-Wed Marriage*. Basingstoke: Palgrave Macmillan.

May, V. (2011). 'Self, Belonging and Social Change'. *Sociology*. 45 (3): 63–378.

Mead, G.H. (1964). *On Social Psychology*. Chicago: The University of Chicago.

Mead, G.H. (1974 [1934]). *Mind, Self, and Society*. Chicago: The University of Chicago.

Meyers, D.T. (1997). 'Introduction' in D.T. Meyers (ed.) *Feminists Rethink the Self*. Boulder, CO: Westview Press: 1–11.

Mills, S. (2003). 'Caught Between Sexism, Anti-Sexism, and "Political Correctness": Feminist Women's Negotiations with Naming Practices'. *Discourse and Society*. 14 (1): 87–110.

Morgan, D.H.J. (2011). *Rethinking Family Practices*. Basingstoke: Palgrave Macmillan.

Papers of the Fergusson family of Craigdarroch, Dumfriesshire (1620–1840) 'National Archives of Scotland'. Reference GD77/174.

Pateman, C. (1988). *The Sexual Contract*. Stanford, CA: Stanford University Press.

Pine, L.G. (1965). *The Story of Surnames*. London: Country Life Limited.

Porter, R. (2002). *Madness: A Brief History*. Oxford: Oxford University Press.

Ramazanoglu, C. (1992). 'Love and the Politics of Heterosexuality'. *Feminism and Psychology*. 2: 444–447.

Rawson, B. (1992). 'The Roman Family' in B. Rawson (ed.) *The Family in Ancient Rome*. London: Routledge: 1–57.

Rich, A. (1980). 'Compulsory Heterosexuality and Lesbian Existence'. *Signs*. 5 (4): 631–660.

Rose, N. (1996). 'Authority and the Genealogy of Subjectivity' in P. Heelas, S. Lash, and P. Morris (eds.) *Detraditionalization*. Oxford: Blackwell Publishers: 294–327.

Rowland, R. (1992). 'Radical Feminist Heterosexuality: The Personal and the Political'. *Feminism and Psychology*. 2: 459–464.

Schimmel, A. (1989). *Islamic Names*. Edinburgh: Edinburgh University Press.

Seubert, S. (2010). 'Warum die Familie nicht abschaffen? Zum spannungsvollen Verhältnis von Privatheit und politischem Liberalismus'['Why Not Get Rid of the Family? The Tense Relationship between Privacy and Political Liberalism'] in S. Seubert and P. Niesen (eds.) *Die Grenzen des Privaten* [The Boundaries of Privacy]. Baden-Baden: Nomos: 89–106.

Shils, E. (1971). 'Tradition'. *Comparative Studies in Society and History*. 13 (2): 122–159.

Skeggs, B. (2001). *Formations of Class and Gender*. London: Sage.

Smart, C. (1998). 'Collusion, Collaboration and Confession: On Moving Beyond the Heterosexuality Debate' in D. Richardson (ed.) *Theorising Heterosexuality*. Buckingham: Open University Press: 161–177.

Smart, C. (2012). *Personal Life*. Cambridge: Polity Press.

Snyder-Hall, R.C. (2010). 'Third-Wave Feminism and the Defense of "Choice"'. *Perspectives on Politics*. 8 (1): 255–261.

Spender, D. (1998). *Man Made Language*. London: Pandora Press.

Suter, E.A. (2004). 'Tradition Never Goes Out of Style: The Role of Tradition in Women's Naming Practices'. *The Communication Review*. 7 (1): 57–87.

Ueno, C. (2009). *The Modern Family in Japan*. Balwyn North: Trans Pacific Press.

Van Every, J. (1998). 'Heterosexuality and Domestic Life' in D. Richardson (ed.) *Theorising Heterosexuality*. Buckingham: Open University Press: 39–54.

Wittig, M. (1996). 'The Straight Mind' in S. Jackson and S. Scott (eds.) *Feminism and Sexuality: A Reader*. Edinburgh: Edinburgh University Press: 144–149.

Woo, J. (2007). 'Sexual Stories Go to Westminster: Narratives of Sexual Citizens/Outsiders in Britain'. Unpublished PhD Thesis, University of York.

2 Research design and methodology

The focus of this book is on what British women do with their last names when they marry and how this impacts upon their sense of (gendered) self and factors into social organisation. I will focus exclusively on 'name changing' – when women take on the last name of their husband – and 'name retaining' – when women retain their previous last name, be that their birth name, name given to them as a child after a mother's remarriage, adopted name, or name from a previous marriage. The decision to investigate name changing and name retaining exclusively was taken for several reasons. First, that name changing remains the norm in Britain (Valetas, 2001: 2), but despite that there continues to be little empirical evidence about naming practices (Johnson and Scheuble, 1995: 724). It was important therefore to add to the empirical evidence about the naming norm to build up a picture of what women in contemporary Britain are doing with their name and why. Valetas' study (2001) shows that the norm in Britain remains strong and more so than in other European countries, with more people than anywhere else in her study believing women *should* change their name to their husband's on marriage. Taking this into consideration, the decision to completely oppose the normative expectation to change names seems like a daring decision and one which also needed consideration. The two – norm and opposite – are relational and investigating them together was necessary.

In Britain, there are few laws around last names: children's names are legislated for to an extent, but adults have a great deal of freedom. Despite this, the existing evidence (Johnson and Scheuble, 1995; Valetas, 2001) would suggest that innovation with names is limited and British women in particular continue to follow the name-changing norm. This led me to discard considering other naming choices such as hyphenating, combining names, or creating a new name. I asked my participants whether they considered these options and how they felt about them, but did not ask for participants who had chosen these routes. This information would of course be useful and would open up the discussion around those at the forefront of naming innovation and change, but I wanted to focus on the predominant and often unquestioned norm (and its related opposite) to unravel why it remains so powerful and what following it might mean for women in Britain.

Research into naming has occurred previously – looking at patterns of name changing on marriage (Johnson and Scheuble, 1995; Valetas, 2001), the

Research design and methodology   23

connections between naming, migration, and class (Webber and Longley, 2003), the legal ramifications of name changing (Emens, 2007), or feminism and identity (Foss and Edson, 1989; Mills, 2003; Goldin and Shim, 2004; Suter, 2004; Hoffnung, 2006; Laskowski, 2010; Hamilton et al., 2011), though predominantly within the American context – but not with the focus chosen here, on (gendered) identity and social organisation in Britain. I am also taking greater account of the decision not to change names than other studies. I also felt it important to ask women what they actually think of their last names and their naming decisions, and whether and how these impact upon their sense of identity.

When a norm is so clearly gendered – with women being expected to change names on marriage in a way men are not – those affected by the practice should be consulted as to their feelings about it. If names are taken to be important to identity, then to ask a person to change theirs becomes highly significant. It suggests less respect for that person's sense of identity, that their identity may be seen as more adaptable than the person who maintains their name, and it also suggests that the change must be meaningful to society and its organisation on some level or it would be unnecessary. These are points I will investigate further throughout. Questioning the taken for granted and the normalised gender differences in our society opens up to scrutiny the way we organise ourselves, what acts we consider meaningful and why, as well as how gendered inequality is maintained in a society where men and women are formally equal (Jónasdóttir, 1991: 11).

The sample

The focus is on British women, though more specifically on practices in England and Scotland (the two nations of the UK my participants identified as home).

One hundred and two women took part in this project, and they were married between the 1940s and 2011. My sample was made up of 75 women who changed their name (whom I refer to as 'name changers'), and 27 women who retained their name on marriage (the 'name retainers'). They had a rich set of experiences, showing that names are significant to individual identity, as well as a societal or collective identity. It is their experiences, thoughts, and feelings which make up the core basis for this work, and I thank them very much for sharing these with me and for taking part in the project.

Participants were gathered from local advertising in the north of England and the central belt of Scotland, as well as via national websites and personal social networks. There was a small amount of snowballing in collecting the sample, but this was kept to a minimum. Women were expected to be legally British (to hold a British passport); a minority had moved to live in Britain from other countries or were living in other countries although still held British citizenship and defined themselves as British. They came from a variety of ethnic backgrounds although 61 per cent self-defined as 'White British', with another 12 per cent self-defining simply as 'White' and another 9 per cent simply as 'British'. There were further smaller groupings of 'Scottish', 'White Scottish', 'White English', and 'White Anglo-Saxon'. However, there were also small groupings of 'White Irish', 'White

24   Research design and methodology

South African', and 'White American'. There were also women defining their ethnicity as 'European', 'Hispanic', and 'African Caribbean'. Finally, 4 per cent of women self-defined as being from a mixed ethnic background. This means that the sample over-represents mixed race people when compared with 2001 Census data (ONS, 2001), but under-represents black people, for example. The sample was also well educated, with 40 per cent of participants holding an undergraduate degree and another 39 per cent holding a postgraduate degree. Of the participants, 10 per cent held a doctorate. The remaining sample held school qualifications or other vocational or training qualifications. More than half of the sample were aged between 26 and 45, with another 38 women aged between 46 and 65. One woman was aged between 66 and 75, while two women fell into the youngest age bracket (16–25) and two into the oldest (76+). Seventy-six of the women were married, with 11 divorced and in a partnership, 6 divorced and single, 4 divorced and remarried, 3 widowed, and 2 separated.[1]

My sample, as with all samples, is therefore particular in nature, and I am aware has limitations in its scope due to its well-educated, white, and predominantly middle-class make-up. Generalisation in non-representative studies is tricky: making grand claims about the wider population is untenable. Nevertheless, as Williams argues, all studies make some form of generalisation, and instead of ignoring this, researchers should be explicit about how they see their claims applying to others, beyond their sample (Williams, 2000). I follow Mason's outline (2009) of claims to generalisability for qualitative and non-representative research. First, that my analysis is rigorous (Mason, 2009: 196): my methods, their strengths and weaknesses, have been carefully considered, and I have conducted this research accurately and fairly. My use of these methods falls within the acceptable limits of pragmatist mixed methods research, adhering to the stipulations set out by this paradigm (Morgan, 2007). My interpretations are based upon the empirical data and reading of the literature: I have endeavoured to represent my participants accurately, while still being critical, to add to theory around names, gender, and identity. My analysis is presented here for readers to judge, along with my methods, for criticism.

The women in my study are part of their society, and their views are relevant and significant – what they are saying is real to them and therefore real to their understanding and perception of their lives and their society. This means there are material lives being lived out according to the beliefs expressed. To have unrelated respondents from across the country express similar views and give similar explanations suggests something socially and culturally influenced is occurring. As Mason (2009: 195) argues, there is no reason to suspect my sample is atypical of the society of which it is part. Bearing this and the characteristics of my sample in mind, I should be able to cautiously suggest other women of similar backgrounds would express similar sentiments. This is open to relevant, representative testing.

I can only make cautious 'moderatum generalizations' (Williams, 2000). Moderatum generalisations are working hypotheses, open to re-working and change from other research (Payne and Williams, 2005: 297). The claims I make which generalise will be made with this idea in mind, as moderate and cautious, accepting a partial stance:

> To generalize is to claim that what is the case in one place or time, will be so elsewhere or in another time. Everyday social life depends on the success of actors doing just this.
>
> (Payne and Williams, 2005: 296)

Mixed methods

This study is based on a mixed methods design, using an open- and closed-question survey, and in-depth interviews. The strengths of these methods combined offer a way of accessing a larger number of people and the ability to create descriptive statistics about this sample to allow me to see patterns within it, as well as challenging my own viewpoint with a wider range of opinions. The interviews then take this larger, more generalised picture and bring it down to the individual and their life story, explored in-depth. As Arksey and Knight argue, 'although qualitative and quantitative approaches rest on very different ontological and epistemological assumptions, they can be complementary . . . and need not be incompatible' (1999: 14).

I have divided my research questions between the survey and the interviews in Table 2.1 to give an idea of which method addressed what. Some are repeated in both however, as these questions were answered by both methods, but to a different extent. For example, 'how is sense of identity connected to naming?' could be answered, to an extent, by open questions in the survey, but also in a more personal way through discussion of life stories in the interviews.

Table 2.1 Research questions by method

Stage 1 of the Research: Online Survey	Is sense of identity connected to naming? If so, *how* is identity connected? Do British women feel a sense of disjuncture in their identities before and after marriage? What purpose does a change of name serve for them? Have British women's attitudes to their names changed over time? What impact has social change had on the meaning of married names; what does retaining a name mean for those who do? What motivates name retention? What is the reaction of others to naming decisions?
Stage 2 of the Research: Interviews	How is identity connected to naming? Do British women feel a sense of disjuncture in their identities before and after marriage? What purpose does a change of name serve for them? How is name changing reconciled with 'individualism'? What impact has social change had on the meaning of married names; what does retaining a name mean for those who do? What motivates name retention? What is the reaction of others to naming decisions?

26   *Research design and methodology*

There was a final theoretical research question also: 'What are the connections between names, identity, modernity, and gender inequality?' This was in part taken from my empirical data, but was also based on criticism of theoretical discussion of identity, modernity, and gender relations.

The survey

Both survey and interview stages went through a process of planning and piloting, and the project was passed by an ethics committee at the University of York. The survey was planned using literature on how survey questions should be written, the format of the questionnaire, and how informants can be influenced by this, as well as by considering what exactly I wanted to know, whether the survey questions got to the heart of my research questions, and how I would then analyse the answers provided (see Gillham, 2000; Bryman, 2008; Dillman, 2009). The final draft was then piloted on 30 women from Yorkshire and the central belt of Scotland and the results analysed using the Statistical Package for the Social Sciences (SPSS) and thematic coding (see Bryman, 2008). This pilot stage ensured that any problem questions were amended or removed; gaps in information were also identified and questions could be added to fill these. Comments on the pilot survey were incorporated when necessary, in terms of areas of content that should have been included (for example, the aesthetics of the name) and design changes. This resulted in a questionnaire with nine sections, most of which had a mix of both open and closed questions: 'Background Questions'; 'Naming Decisions'; 'Names and Family Connections'; 'Name Changing' (for relevant participants); 'Retaining your Original Family Name' (for relevant participants); 'Names and Working Life' (for relevant participants); 'Divorce and Naming Decisions' (for relevant participants); 'Naming and Identity'; and 'Final Comments'. There was also a space for participants to note whether they would be interested in being interviewed at a later date.

Participants were able to contact me by email or by post (I provided details with my adverts). Once they got in touch, I was able to answer questions about the project and then posted them an introductory letter outlining the aims of the project, a consent form, and a sheet on which they could provide further contact details if they thought they may wish to be interviewed in future; they were provided with the URL for the website, a participant number (which they had to enter into the online survey), and the password to access the questionnaire. Participants were provided with a stamped-addressed envelope to return their forms to me. Not all participants wished to provide their address, and to these I emailed all the details, and they either posted the forms back or signed, scanned, and emailed them back to me.

Coding the survey

Once the survey was closed I coded the numerical data using a simple format: giving values to particular answers, for example, '1' for 'yes' and '2' for 'no', or for age or income bands, for example '1' for '16–25' and '3' for '£26, 000–35, 000'.

String data (i.e. written words) were copied out. I used SPSS to complete this process, as well as to create the descriptive statistics for this project.

I also took detailed notes of what each person had said in the qualitative sections of her survey, including both paraphrasing and direct quotes. I went through this process twice. Following on from this I coded all of the data into themes by hand, rather than using NVivo or a similar package. As Stanley and Dampier argue, CAQDAS packages are not always necessary in managing qualitative projects and may not have the specific capabilities required by the researcher to make their use worthwhile (2010: 30), hence deciding when to use them should depend upon each individual researcher and their project. These data were transferred into an Excel spreadsheet as a means to access and analyse the data more easily after this process was complete – using Excel allowed me to instantly see the connections between one participant's set of comments, as well as between participants.

This process of sorting and coding the data meant I could then move onto a more detailed analysis – though in reality, analysis begins as soon as one begins to sort the data – and begin to see what was most significant to my research questions. The themes I selected as being the most important were used as jumping off points for the topics discussed in the interviews.

The interviews

As with the survey, I piloted the interviews beforehand. Piloting the interview was done with six participants who had taken the pilot survey, but were all known to me via friends and relatives. These six interviews all took place in a Scottish city and lasted between 40 minutes and one and a half hours. They gave me a near equal spread of name changers and name retainers. The pilot was conducted with a semi-structured interview style, and though this worked for some participants, it often felt too interrogatory when asking participants about their relationships, marriages, and emotions. The life history style seemed more suited to the aims of the project, in looking at life turning points and identity, but also gave the participant the initiative back, allowing her to lead the conversation as she saw fit. The interesting and varied conversations I had with these women influenced what topics I saw as important to the project.

In undertaking the life history interviews, I purposively selected a sample of the survey participants. I selected 20 participants from those who had expressed interest in being interviewed, chosen to provide as wide a range of views and naming decisions as possible. As I already had contact details for participants I was able to get in touch with them directly and ask if they were still interested in being interviewed. I emailed them details about the form the interview would take (life history interviewing), how long it might last, and their rights and responsibilities. Attempts at contact resulted in 16 interviews. Participants who agreed to be interviewed were asked to consider the information I had sent them and on the day of the interview were given a consent form to sign confirming they understood their rights and that they gave their consent to be interviewed and have their data treated as I had outlined. Three interviewees had to be recorded over the phone and I asked them to confirm their consent on tape.

28   *Research design and methodology*

The method of interviewing utilised was the life history interview in which participants are encouraged to tell their own life story and bring out the most important points in their own terms. The interviewer acts only as a guide with some open-ended questions and intervenes as little as possible in the narrative. My participants were encouraged to discuss the stages of their life surrounding their childhood, partnership, engagement, wedding, marriage, the naming choices made, and awareness of identity shifts or continuity. My research focus dictated that these areas of life must be discussed, but participants were able to bring up whatever they felt useful or interesting to expand their story. The life history interview encourages participants to go through their life in a chronological order and produce a coherent narrative, in this case explaining their decisions around names and emphasising what they felt to be the most important aspects of significant life moments. There were, however, several pointed questions asked at the end of interviews to gauge feeling and challenge assumptions if these ideas were not touched on by participants in the main part of the interview.

The act of telling a life history is an act of storytelling, which Atkinson argues is a 'fundamental form of human communication' (Atkinson, 1998: 1). We use stories to make our lives understandable to ourselves and others; we learn more about ourselves 'through the process of reflecting and putting the events, experiences, and feelings that we have lived into oral expression' (Atkinson, 1998: 1). A person describing their life and its events is reminded through the very act of storytelling about obstacles, conflict, and resolution: the narrative form brings out detail and depth.

The document created from transcribing the story of the interviewee is entirely in their own words and in the first person. It is an account created through the collaboration of the interviewer and interviewee, though minimal interference from the interviewer during the storytelling is required. As with all interviewing the interviewer has to accept that they may not be getting an exact retelling of an event, but are getting one perspective, and that perspective which the interviewee wants to be heard – it may be how they remember it or it may be that they wish to recount the events in a way which brings certain ideas to the fore. This does not invalidate the account as it remains truthful to that person and is useful to the researcher as one person's viewpoint. In my research, I am looking for accounts of selfhood and identity creation, therefore the idiosyncratic details of a person's account are necessary data in understanding how they build up a picture of themselves in the world. Atkinson sums up the process thus:

> Whatever form it takes, a life story always brings order and meaning to the life being told, for both the teller and the listener. It is a way to better understand the past, the present and a way to leave a personal legacy for the future. . . . A life story gives us the vantage point of seeing how one person experiences and understands life, his or her own especially, over time.
>
> (Atkinson, 1998: 8)

The interviews took place between December 2011 and May 2012; they lasted between 45 minutes and two and a half hours. Interview participants were given details of the life history interview before it took place, so that they would know

Research design and methodology 29

what to expect and not be surprised by the amount of initiative they were expected to take. I believe this prior explanation is ethical as participants should know what they are signing up for, but it also means participants are more likely to talk without prompting. This did not always work: sometimes I had to go over the structure of the interview – or indeed, lack of – when participants seemed confused, and occasionally a participant was simply unable or unwilling to carry out this kind of interview, despite having initially agreed to it. Some people were constrained by time and could only offer me an hour at lunchtime or a maximum of two hours while their husband looked after the children; the interviewee who took part in the shortest interview did not elaborate without a significant degree of prompting and was, even then, often uncomfortable about giving me details of her life. In this situation the life history format seemed unhelpful and a much more question and answer interview had to take place.

Transcription and write-up

I coded the interviews for themes, as I had done with the qualitative sections of the survey. This meant I could now move between data from the survey and the interviews, comparing commonalities and disjuncture to see whether and how the two methods agreed or disagreed with one another in terms of the data produced. I went back and forth between survey data (both numerical and written) and the interview data throughout the transcription, analysis, and write-up phases.

I offered all interview participants the chance to see the transcription of their interview and comment on it. Only two participants took me up on this offer: one did not comment further on her transcript, but the other discussed it with me and added certain comments and clarifications. I wanted to offer the chance for participants to see and comment upon their transcripts because I see trying to keep the power balance between researcher and researched at an equilibrium as part of being a feminist researcher. It was an attempt to ensure my voice, biases, and assumptions were not getting in the way of the participant's narrative (Bloom, 1998: 10).

As a feminist researcher, I subscribe to the idea that a researcher should offer information about herself in the interview situation. This makes the sharing of information balanced and reduces the feeling of exploitation in the interview (Dickson-Swift et al., 2007: 333–334). This meant offering up information about my partnership, influential women in my life, my feminist political standpoint, and, when requested, my thoughts on names, naming, and marriage. I was generally happy to offer this information, although I sometimes worried about the impact of revealing my views to the interviewee. I was fortunate in that these kinds of questions usually came at the end of the session. However, throughout I was prepared to validate participant stories with my own.

The interviews touched on many emotional and sensitive issues: when asking someone about something as intimate as their marriage a whole range of deeply personal events can emerge. I heard stories of physical, financial, and emotional abuse, alcohol and substance abuse, depression and other mental health problems, the breakdown of marriages, the death of children, and a description of

30 *Research design and methodology*

the final moments of a husband's life. These were sometimes difficult to hear and produced emotional reactions in both myself and, of course, the woman telling me. In the consent form and before the interview, I told participants not to feel they need tell me anything they did not want to and that they had the right to refuse to answer questions; afterwards, and especially after these emotional encounters, I reminded my participants that they could ask me to remove certain sections from the transcript if they decided they did not want their words to be included in the project.

I always engaged with these stories and shared my emotional response with my participants; I wanted to ensure participants felt listened to and that I understood the emotional and physical toll these life events had taken. It felt like the only course of action available; acting in some 'objective' manner would have been appalling, both as an ethical researcher and just as a person. As it was, there was no way I could stop my reactions and I did not think to act in any way other than I did. This is a part of my ethical obligation to these women, and I do not take it lightly (Dickson-Swift et al., 2007: 340). I am privileged to have heard all of my participants speak about their lives, but these stories especially – some of which had never been described in such detail to another person – were deeply moving and I am grateful to my participants for sharing them with me. This book does not give me the scope to fully represent all of these complex life events, for which I am sorry. I am pleased and relieved that none of my participants asked for their stories to be removed from the transcript – I hope this indicates that they felt safe enough to leave them in my keeping.

A note on referring to participants

Before I turn to the empirical data and the main body of this book, I want to note two things about how I refer to participants. They are represented by a number, for example 'participant 12' or P12 throughout. As this project reflects on the importance of names and the thought processes around identity when asked to change a name, assigning a pseudonym seemed incongruous. Instead, using numbers throughout emphasises the importance of the name by its absence. Therefore, all participants will only be referred to by number: when data have come from an interview rather than the survey, this will be indicated.

All details which may identify participants have been removed from the written up data. I also use the acronym 'OFN' at points throughout: this stands for 'original family name'. I do not use the term 'maiden name' because its connotations of what forms of sex and sexuality are appropriate are unacceptable to me; furthermore, my participants may have had a previous name which was not the name they were given at birth, because of adoption, marriage, divorce, and so on, hence I use 'OFN' or 'previous name'.

Note

1 This information has been presented in a very similar way in Thwaites (2013).

References

Arksey, H. and Knight, P. (1999). *Interviewing for Social Scientists*. London: Sage.

Atkinson, R. (1998). *The Life Story Interview*. London: Sage.

Bloom, R. (1998). *Under the Sign of Hope: Feminist Methodology and Narrative Interpretation*. New York: State University of New York Press.

Bryman, A. (2008). *Social Research Methods*. Oxford: Oxford University Press.

Dickson-Swift, V., James, E.L., Kippen, S., and Liamputtong, P. (2007). 'Doing Sensitive Research: What Challenges Do Qualitative Researchers Face?' *Qualitative Research.* 7 (3): 327–353.

Dillman, D.A. (2009). *Internet, Mail, and Mixed-Mode Surveys: The Tailored Design Method*. Hoboken, NJ: Wiley and Sons.

Emens, E.F. (2007). 'Changing Name Changing: Framing Rules and the Future of Marital Names'. *The University of Chicago Law Review.* 74 (3): 761–863.

Foss, K.A. and Edson, B.A. (1989). 'What's in a Name? Accounts of Married Women's Name Choices'. *Western Journal of Speech Communication.* 53: 356–373.

Gillham, B. (2000). *Developing a Questionnaire*. London: Continuum.

Goldin, C. and Shim, M. (2004). 'Making a Name: Women's Surnames at Marriage and Beyond'. *Journal of Economic Perspectives.* 18: 143–160.

Hamilton, L., Geist, C., and Powell, B. (2011). 'Marital Name Change as a Window into Gender Attitudes'. *Gender and Society.* 25 (2): 145–175.

Hoffnung, M. (2006). 'What's in a Name? Marital Name Choice Revisited'. *Sex Roles.* 55: 817–825.

Johnson, D.R. and Scheuble, L.K. (1995). 'Women's Marital Naming in Two Generations: A National Study'. *Journal of Marriage and Family.* 57 (3): 724–732.

Jónasdóttir, A. (1991). *Love Power and Political Interests*. Örebro: University of Örebro.

Laskowski, K.A. (2010). 'Women's Post-Marital Name Retention and the Communication of Identity'. *Names: A Journal of Onomastics.* 58: 75–89.

Mason, J. (2009). *Qualitative Research*. London: Sage.

Mills, S. (2003). 'Caught Between Sexism, Anti-Sexism, and "Political Correctness": Feminist Women's Negotiations with Naming Practices'. *Discourse and Society.* 14 (1): 87–110.

Morgan, D.L. (2007). 'Paradigms Lost and Pragmatism Regained: Methodological Implications of Combining Qualitative and Quantitative Methods'. *Journal of Mixed Methods Research.* 1 (1): 48–76.

Office for National Statistics (2001). Census: Standard Area Statistics (England and Wales). ESRC/JISC Census Programme, Census Dissemination Unit, Mimas (University of Manchester).

Payne, G. and Williams, M. (2005). 'Generalization in Qualitative Research'. *Sociology.* 39 (2): 295–314.

Stanley, E. and Dampier, H. (2010). 'Towards the Epistolarium: Issues in Researching and Publishing the Oliver Schreiner Letters'. *African Research and Documentation.* 113: 27–32.

Suter, E.A. (2004). 'Tradition Never Goes Out of Style: The Role of Tradition in Women's Naming Practices'. *The Communication Review.* 7 (1): 57–87.

Thwaites, R. (2013). 'The Making of Selfhood: Naming Decisions on Marriage'. *Families, Relationships, and Societies.* 2 (3): 425–439.

Valetas, M.-F. (2001). 'The Surname of Married Women in the European Union'. *Population and Sociétés.* 367: 1–4.

32 *Research design and methodology*

Webber, R and Longley, S. (2003). 'Geodemographic Analysis of Similarity and Proximity: Their Roles in the Understanding of the Geography of Need' in P. Longley and M. Batty (eds.) *Advanced Spatial Analysis: The CASA book of GIS*. Redlands, CA: ESRI Press: 233–266.

Williams, M. (2000). 'Interpretivist and Generalisation'. *Sociology*. 34 (2): 209–224.

3 Names and tradition

Thomas Dumm suggests that the modern world is suffused with loneliness: it is a powerful and political emotion which pervades the most important aspects of our lives (Dumm, 2008). In outlining this loneliness Dumm notes that in modern relationships people are estranged from one another and their attachments are weak – our 'lives in common' are far less significant to us now (2008: ix); hence feeling lonely is the most common state for modern people. Dumm's thesis on loneliness is part of a wider-ranging discussion on the state of the modern world in which theorists of individualisation have come to the fore. The names of Giddens, Beck, Beck-Gernsheim, and Bauman are significant within these debates for their ideas on the individualising modern world moving away from, and in some theories escaping, the bonds of the past. The separation from others and the loss of a 'life in common' in late modernity are important to all of these theorists, to differing degrees.

Bauman's description of late modernity is the most pessimistic. He describes the late modern world as 'liquid' 'because like all liquids, it cannot stand still and keep its shape for long' (Bauman, 2010: 1). Things change quickly and people have a short attention span, which moves from one fad and excitement to the next (2010: 1). We have little control over the fast pace of our lives and therefore, to survive, we must be 'flexible' (2010: 2). The internet allows us more information than we could ever have previously imagined in our pockets and at our fingertips – this is a mixed blessing for Bauman, as we can never escape the onslaught and have to wade through information attempting to sort the 'grains of truth . . . from the chaff of lies, illusion, rubbish and waste' (2010: 2). The people moving within this fast-paced society are increasingly individualised and look to their own goals for satisfaction, rather than pulling towards a life in common directed by authorities and institutional structure (Bauman, 2011: 49). Though Bauman argues that the 'job with which humans are charged today remains much the same as it has been since the beginning of modern times' (2011: 48), the sheer amount of information and choice available to humans makes this task somewhat different. People are now expected to make coherent identities, 'solid enough to be acknowledged', but flexible enough to be able to move as necessary in an insecure world (Bauman, 2011: 50).

He argues that this insecurity and transience is not just confined to the world of work, but also spreads to relationships with other humans in which a '[d]isbelief

34 *Names and tradition*

in unity . . . goads people away from each other and prompts an urge to escape' (Bauman, 2003: 33). Relationships are short, lasting only as long as the intense emotions do and the individuals feel some sense of personal satisfaction (Bauman, 2003: 34) – this means that working at a relationship or tying oneself into a lifetime commitment such as marriage is seen as 'oppression' (Bauman, 2003: 47). In a society of consumers looking for the new and casting off the old, Bauman argues that long-lasting relationships are not justifiable (2003: 47). He asserts that '[l]iquid modern rationality recommends light cloaks and condemns steel casings' (2003: 47): why commit to one person when some other, better, situation may present itself?

Giddens is on the opposite end of the scale to Bauman, portraying the late modern condition as one of positivity and progress, opening up opportunity to all and breaking down the constraints of tradition and social positioning. He describes self-identity in late modernity as being a 'reflexive project of the self' (1996: 5) in which people must constantly evaluate and revise their biography, making a coherent story out of a huge number of possibilities (1996: 5). Constraint on choices due to social positioning, as with the other theorists of individualisation and late modernity, is little mentioned by Giddens (1996), and when it is, he appears to suggest that many choices remain available to the underprivileged, despite what may look like impossibly restricted situations. For example, Giddens discusses the position of a black woman, living in poverty with several children to care for and the fact her life may seem entirely bounded by her problems and her social positioning (Giddens, 1996: 86). However, he argues that the awareness of possibilities will make the experience of lack of privilege a different experience than that of the past – poverty may even make tradition seem so irrelevant that 'the creative construction of lifestyle may become a particularly characteristic feature of such situations' (1996: 86). This argument seems weak and overly optimistic about the reality of such a life as the one he offers as an example. His arguments, though attempting to provide a positive interpretation of the social changes that he argues are happening, do not fully address the reality of lived lives, particularly for those who do not have many resources.

In terms of intimate relationships, Giddens argues that the 'pure relationship' grows from this high modern self-reflexivity (1996: 6), and couples are together simply for the benefits of being in that particular relationship. He states that commitment in pure relationships is 'presupposed' and that this is part of the dimension of trust key to these relationships, built through 'mutual disclosure' (Giddens, 1996: 6). This trust and commitment is part of an 'internally referential system' which needs no outward 'criteria of social kinship, social duty or traditional obligation' (Giddens, 1996: 6). This important point on commitment and outward criteria will be problematised below and throughout this book.

In-between these two poles are Beck and Beck-Gernsheim, offering up a more neutral description of the late modern condition. Smart (2012: 20) has argued that Beck and Beck-Gernsheim's work allows the reader to 'superimpose one's own meaning' onto their writing and this may account for the fact I see them as taking up more middle ground. Their theories suggest that people are indeed becoming less traditional and less attached to one another through the oppressive structures of institutions, but that this lack of security actually makes people more desperate to find love and partnerships (Beck and Beck-Gernsheim, 2004: 190). Couples have to create their own rules and standards in love; love is 'dogmatism for two' (Beck and Beck-Gernsheim, 2004: 191).

It is the changing place of women in society that these authors give as the major reason for the pace of change within human relationships, suggesting that men have changed very little (Beck and Beck-Gernsheim, 2004: 150). The combination of change and stagnation that Beck and Beck-Gernsheim (2004, 2010) discuss is sometimes puzzling, as is making sense of their mixing of essentialist notions of gender and sociological attempts to break down the categories of gender. Smart has argued that the writing style of Beck and Beck-Gernsheim can make 'the meaning opaque' (2012: 20). However, their writings show the complex and contradictory nature of late modernity, and the problems with attempting to make sense of a time period that is present rather than past. Importantly they argue that tradition and the past are not completely devoid of interest and importance and that people *are* constrained by institutions, but that this constraint and influence usually occurs in a more subtle way, as 'individuals must, in part . . . import [regulations and guidelines] into their biographies through their own actions' (Beck and Beck-Gernsheim, 2010: 2).

The idea of changing one's name is linked to patriarchal power structures within heterosexual relations: it is a guideline for marriage which people continue to import into their biographies, in line with Beck and Beck-Gernsheim's theories. Such traditions hold a powerful sway, and the actions of women and men are governed by them: the decisions we make are influenced by cultural and social tradition (Adams, 2003: 224; Gross, 2005; Jackson et al., 2013). As Gross argues, the difference between regulative traditions and meaning-making traditions needs to be more fully respected by theorists of individualisation (2005: 294). Regulative traditions are those which stems from communities within our society which regulate out behaviour – religious communities, firms and companies in which one works, local community groups – and tell us which sorts of behaviour are acceptable and which are not; meaning-making traditions shape social action and what is even thinkable in a given situation (Gross, 2005: 294–295). Certain regulative traditions may be declining in significance as individualisation theorists suggest, but not all and not for everyone, while meaning-making traditions are *not* declining and continue to shape what action is meaningful to the self and understandable to others (Gross, 2005: 295). Western societies are 'characterized by the co-existence of traditional and modern elements' (Jackson et al., 2013: 669).

It seems there is a tension for women living in modernity, a period of rapid social change. It cannot be denied that women's lives *are* freer than they have been in the past – women can work outside the home, make their own money, and live independently, as Beck and Beck-Gernsheim discuss (2010), yet living freely is not as easy for women as it might seem at first due to gendered inequalities within the working world and the social pressure to conform to the path of marriage and family. Carter's work (2011) has shown that younger women – who

36   *Names and tradition*

might be expected to be wholeheartedly enjoying their modern, individualistic freedoms – are conforming to traditional ideas of marriage. The meaning-making traditions surrounding marriage, love, wifehood, and name changing are as significant as ever (Gross, 2005).

In individualisation debates the past often seems to be held up as a homogenous and almost mythical time when people did exactly as they were told and followed rigid structures with no individual thought. Phillips argues that it is modernity that is usually of analytical interest and it is therefore easy to discard the past (or tradition) in favour of analysing the apparently more important concept (Phillips, 2004: 17). However, pulling apart the taken-for-granted is highly significant to this study and to the understanding of why the name-changing ritual continues to exist and have meaning. It is imperative then to examine ideas of the past and what 'tradition' might actually mean, as well as where our ideas of tradition come from, to contextualize the narratives of the participants in this study.

The past and tradition

Individualisation theorists pit the past against the present. The past is presented as stable and unchanging, whereas the present is in constant flux. This reductionist view of the past is in part, Vanessa May argues, because we look at the past through its structures, whereas we look at the present via the personal (2011: 365): structures then easily appear unchanging, while our own personal lives appear to be moving fluidly. However, it is pointless to separate the two as this presents an unrealistic view of the world: the personal and structural – self and society – are 'interdependent and permeable, each affected by the other' (Vanessa May, 2011: 365–366). Simmel used the term 'sociation' instead of society because he saw society as something people *do*, not something that is (Vanessa May, 2011: 366). Structures are themselves the 'sedimented practices' of individuals over time and in a particular place – consequences of the sedimentation of these practices can be material and also intangible, as with social norms and particular ways of thinking (Vanessa May, 2011: 366). 'Sedimentation' should not imply fixing immovably, but practices being open to development, variation, and (to an extent) change (Phillips, 2004: 12). Traditions do not remain perfectly the same: their very power to remain relevant comes through adaptation and development.

Tradition is, then, the 'recurrence in approximately identical form of structures of conduct and patterns of belief over several generations of membership or over a long time within single societies' (Shils, 1971: 123). It is rarely expanded upon (Shils, 1971: 123): tradition is a cause and an explanation for action. This means that the past is ever important to present-day members of a particular culture. Shils argues that anyone newly entering an ongoing situation has to conform to its traditions and codes of practice, and that this is as true for a child being born into a family (and wider society) as it is for someone entering a new workplace (1971: 125). To find a place within whichever institution a person must make their actions acceptable and intelligible to those already within it; to secure a place for themselves they must become a part of the prevailing culture (Shils, 1971: 125).

Names and tradition 37

In this way, individuals must always interact with those around them and the wider society, including its ever-present past. Traditions therefore need to have been accepted practice through time. It is time itself which becomes a legitimation for tradition: 'it has been accepted practice for a long period so why change now?' or 'it has worked well for those before us so why should we change?' (Shils, 1971: 126). Importantly, it need only be *believed* to have existed previously (Shils, 1971: 126), and this is an important point in name changing to which I will return below.

The final point to make about the nature of tradition is how little people may think about it. Shils makes several important points about this 'unthinkingness' which I will work through when looking at my participants' words in more depth:

> The unthinkingness of the acceptance might be tantamount to the acceptance of the model of the already existent as a whole. Alternatively the model might be accepted after scrutiny to determine whether it conforms with certain criteria which are themselves unthinkingly accepted. Or again it might entail the discovery of a new pattern of belief by the application of criteria which are unthinkingly accepted.
>
> (Shils, 1971: 128)

The most fully traditional of beliefs though 'is one which is accepted without being assessed by any criterion other than its having been believed before' (Shils, 1971: 128). This links with Bourdieu's idea of 'doxa' in which much of social interaction is based on unquestioned assumptions and is not discussed (Bourdieu, 1998: 56–57). The link with these concepts of tradition and name changing is strong for many of my participants, particularly those over the age of 40.

Temporal tradition: powerful stories

Hobsbawm and Ranger's *The Invention of Tradition* (1987), draws together various examples of British traditions created and cemented throughout the nineteenth century. They argue that many British traditions stem from this period in history and that it is the thoughts, ambitions, and desires of nineteenth-century British people which continue to influence today's Britain most directly (Hobsbawm, 1987: 1). Such venerable traditions become things of pride, to be upheld and cherished. These traditions are nevertheless nineteenth-century inventions, based on the social and political priorities of this period; they uphold the questionable idea that the British monarchy is an 'unbroken' line of 1,000 years and cement the country's image as a world-power. This is a story about power: the power of Britain to colonise others, the power of Britain to command the respect of other countries, and the power of the British monarchy to rule over its own citizens and those it was subjugating in other parts of the world. 'Tradition' can be utilised to uphold the position of those in power.[1]

The idea of 'traditions' as the stories of the powerful looking to maintain their power can be applied to the context of name changing. First, as has been discussed in the introduction, the naming traditions of England and Scotland are different:

38   *Names and tradition*

English women have changed names for centuries (Amy Erickson, 2005: 11), while Scottish women predominantly retained names until the nineteenth century (Barclay, 2011: 98). During the nineteenth century Scottish women increasingly changed their last name to their husband's after marriage, in line with the English practice. This change in 'tradition' is in step with the politics of the day: the making of a unified British state, in which Scotland was playing its part, with a number of English bureaucratic processes being imported (Pittock, 2008). The significance of the British state and its homogenised practices became vital to the project of Britishness and creating a wider British empire; this in practice meant a cultural change towards English practices.

There is a paucity of research into this particular naming practice in Scotland and most people I have communicated with during this research have mentioned the fact that name retaining for women was simply 'how it was in Scotland' (personal correspondence with the staff at the *National Archives*, 2011), though I have raised my own thesis about this tradition in the introduction. Before the nineteenth century, and even early twentieth century, women in Scotland were able to legally retain their birth name and be referred to by this name in contracts and so on, though they could be referred to by both their original and their husband's name socially. The *National Archives of Scotland* holds papers relating to binding marriage contracts – both pre and post marriage – in which women's original family names are used. For example,

> Mutual agreement between John Glas, merchant burgess of Perth, and his spouse, Janet Halyburtone, superseding their marriage contract, which was 'cancelled and destroyed as not being answerable to these ends and purposes intended of it'.
>
> (April 1672; Catalogue Reference: B59/37/5/16)

> Interim act and decree appointing Franc Gibb Dougall to be judicial factor on the trust estate created by the contract of marriage entered into between the deceased George Knox and Mrs Eliza Ferguson or Knox dated 4 Jun 1849 and recorded in the sheriff court books of Lanarkshire 5 May 1875 and granting warrant to complete title.
>
> (April 1883; Catalogue Reference: CS46/1883/4/71)

Changing names had not been a legal and 'normal' part of Scottish culture until the nineteenth and early twentieth centuries. Yet this past has been lost under the homogenising narrative of 'Britain'; what is 'normal' now has been a tradition for less than 100 years for sections of Scottish society, yet the participants in my study set their own decisions within this story of 'tradition' wherever in Britain they lived.

This chimes with Hobsbawm's (1987) argument that most of our present traditions were born in the nineteenth century, and Shils' argument that people need merely to *believe* that what they do is a long-standing tradition to give it credence.

It also shows that the stories of the powerful come to take on the credibility and venerability of 'tradition'. Therefore, to suggest we are free from the past is to ignore the reality, which can be seen in the narratives of my participants. I will therefore turn initially to look at the Scottish participants separately to illustrate these claims, before turning to look at the wider sample.

Scottish participants' narratives of 'tradition'

Within my larger survey study of 102 women, 6 defined themselves as being from Scotland specifically. All six of these women changed their name on marriage and were *situated agents* – they were involved in their own decision-making, but all recognised the importance of other people and wider society. Participant 11 commented that sharing one name in a family was important to her, but she was aware that this was 'culturally bound'; P62 wrote that name changing is 'expected culturally and I never thought about not conforming', though, on her second marriage, had begun a process of reclaiming her original family name as she was unhappy with her change. These two participants show just how quickly name changing has become accepted as a part of Scottish culture and marriage practice. Until recently in historical time these women would not have been able to make this appeal to culture and would instead have had a different narrative to claim as their own. Both what action would have been normative and expected, and the importance of that action, would have been viewed, interpreted and written about differently.

Participant 15 spoke directly of the name change as being 'the norm at the time'. She is of course correct in saying the name change is historically specific, but she was referring to the fact that things may have changed *since she married*; an understanding of the recentness with which her own action has become the norm was not present in her discussion. Participant 15's narrative fits within that of linear progression and present and future progresses being pitted against the past. She believes modern society has moved on from when she made her decision in the 1980s (marrying when she was under 25) and does not require women to make this gesture; the modern choice narrative of theorists such as Giddens (1996) is pervasive. The structures which regulated the lives of women in Scotland before the twentieth century, when it came to marriage and names, have been forgotten entirely.

This appropriation has been quickly made and become totalising in its normalcy. Participant 112, who is delighted with her decision to change names even after divorce, spoke of her family's total acceptance of name changing – it was the expected course of action for her. Despite the fact her name may die out and that she feels her family history will be lost without more effort to understand the history of this name, no one questioned her action. Participant 2 noted that all her female relatives had changed names so it was 'traditional' – she had a set example of how a woman behaves in this situation which legitimised the practice as 'normal' and 'correct'. Indeed, for P2, if she had not changed, she would have felt she

40 *Names and tradition*

was 'holding back from the marriage'. The much older Scottish tradition is not to be seen, and there is no narrative there for this participant to use.

The appropriation of the inequality of the name change and the power it entails can be seen by the reactions from husbands-to-be and their families in these participants' accounts. Participant 15 wrote that her husband's family would have been 'shocked' by retaining, while P2 noted that her husband would have 'taken offence' had she not changed. The idea of participants asserting a separate name and connection to birth family through retaining names is seen as offensive and upsetting by others. It is more than unusual: it is a deliberate attempt to be rude and snub the partner and his family. Both P62 and 95 had changed names because their partners wanted them to. Participant 95 wanted herself and her partner to change to a new name but her partner was 'very against this', while P62's second husband was 'very disappointed' when she said she did not want to change names again. The powerful stories – traditions – told about name changing are gendered, as well as geographical, social, and political; this story maintains a sense of masculinity for some men separate from the feminine behaviour (of name changing) they expect in their partners. Name changing symbolically separates men from women in heterosexual relationships, maintaining a (symbolic) hierarchy and set of gendered social relations. Giddens' ideas of partnerships which run without reference to outside authorities and yardsticks is not upheld.

These data show how naming practices, power, 'tradition', and narrative combine; what is *believed* to be tradition gains credence. As name changing now *is* the norm within British society, it is best to turn and examine how 'tradition' is discussed by participants more widely and what influence it has had on their naming decisions.

Name changing and 'tradition'

When coding this particular theme in my qualitative data, I coded words and phrases such as 'tradition', 'what was expected', and 'the done thing': all stemming from the same idea of a long-standing and accepted norm, seen as the normal course of action by the individual as well as significant 'others'. These significant others may include a husband, family, friends, institutional structures and reactions from workers within institutions, as well as the generalised other of society. Thirty of the 75 name changers (40%) mentioned tradition as a reason for changing their names in the qualitative sections of the survey, with many participants indicating the influence of societal expectations, as can be seen from Table 3.1.

'Tradition' as a reason for name changing was more frequently given by members of my survey who married in the 1980s or earlier, but was not exclusive to them. For example, a participant who married in 2002 stated that:

> It was 'the thing to do' when you marry. I thought nothing of it – I assumed it would be the only time I changed names.
>
> (P26)

Table 3.1 Crosstabulation of who influenced participants' naming decisions by whether or not they changed their name (Count)[2]

		Did you change your name on marriage?		Total
		Yes	No	
Who influenced your decision?	Myself only	23	15	38
	Myself and societal expectations	11	2	13
	Myself and my partner	3	2	5
	Myself, my partner, societal expectations	7	0	7
	Societal expectations only	5	0	5
	My partner only	4	0	4
	Other variations including the self	15	7	22
	Other variations not including the self	7	1	8
Total		75	27	102

When participants had grown up with a shared family name there was little example of being able to act differently and the shared name was taken without question as the norm:

> I just completely accepted [one family name] as normal . . . didn't really think about it at all.
>
> (P15; interview data)

This same participant went on to note that many things about getting married were barely thought about, including having a church wedding though the church was not a significant part of her life: 'you know, it was, "of course we'll get married in a church"'. When discussing her own name change, she said 'I didn't even consider keeping my own name': most women around her changed their name on marriage, the only exception being a cousin who was an actress and used a variety of names throughout her acting career. Participant 15 noted that she found it hard to trace this cousin now after the number of name changes she had gone through. This point, though usually with fewer changes, applies to the tradition of name changing: women are far harder to trace than men in historical records because of the patrilineal nature of the name-changing system in Britain.

When asked about her feelings about her married name, P15 said, 'I don't like the name [married name] but that didn't occur to me that . . . you know it just didn't seem like an option, it was just what was going to happen.' The idea of choice in women's naming decisions had not been a part of P15's framework for

42 *Names and tradition*

thinking about herself and naming choices. In a conversation concerning feelings about first names, she said, 'yes, well, I mean that's a choice isn't it whereas your last name . . . well . . . well I didn't think I had a choice.'

Though P15 realises part way through this sentence that she could indeed have chosen what to do with her last name, the norm was so prevalent and normalised that it did not feel as if choices were open to her. However, she goes on to say that 'I probably knew I didn't *have* to, but it just wasn't an issue . . . for me.' Participant 15 presents a complex picture: she says several times that she did not know she had a choice, and then finishes the discussion by saying that she might have known but it was not an issue for her. She may mean, had she thought about it, she would have known there was no legal requirement to change, but that she would have done so anyway. However, the number of times she states that she thought she had no choice would suggest that there was very little thinking done at the time about changing her name, and that instead she simply followed the tradition. The lack of thinking surrounding this tradition once more becomes apparent.

In accordance with Shils' description of tradition (1971), participants often felt no need to expand on 'tradition' as an explanation for their action, writing 'Part of the ceremony of marriage and lifelong partnership' (P61); 'Just something one did' (P87)' or even just 'Expected' (P89). As with P26 quoted above, there was a level of 'unthinkingness' (Shils, 1971) around the tradition, thus making it a fully traditional idea – these women have changed names simply because it is what is done, has been done and is expected to be done. They do not consider the norm in any deeper sense and perhaps find it difficult to articulate any deeper meaning in their action.

Silence and order

The power of silence around norms is as significant as the justification narratives used – what is said, as well as what is left unsaid, form the contours of a norm and what entails crossing a boundary. Much of society is based on such unquestioned assumptions which are little, if ever, discussed (Bourdieu, 1998: 54–55). Sheriff (2000) argues that silence cannot be seen as straightforward acceptance of powerful ideologies. Silence is complex and scholarly attention needs to be paid to it – it is as important to the 'powerful stories' as speech. The norm of name changing and the discourse around it as a part of marriage, a sign of love and commitment, and a bind between family members, has layers of silence connected to it. This silence has changed in kind in recent decades as name changing has begun to be discussed in Britain in terms of patriarchal relations. Yet, despite this emerging discussion, silence remains significant and continues to play a powerful part in the maintenance of this particular tradition, as the name changing issue is dismissed as trivial and women are encouraged not to take time to reflect upon it. This kind of silence corresponds to Shils' description of the 'unthinkingness' of full traditions and the kind of silence which suggests 'acceptance of dominant narratives and the naturalization of power' (Sheriff, 2000: 127).

Names and tradition 43

Figure 3.1 shows how many participants who changed names discussed their decision with their partner before acting. It shows that total silence around the norm was the second most common response by my survey participants, while even an initial discussion could quickly lead to acceptance and silence, and this was the most common response of all. Furthermore, some participants wrote in the survey that they had rarely spoken about this topic or had not thought or spoken about it in a very long time. Though discussion is more common than in previous centuries, as Figure 3.1 shows, silence and lack of thinking around this norm remain.

However, Sheriff's (2000) point that silence is more complicated is important here, as some participants who changed names considered their decision beforehand, discussed it with their partner, and a number continued to feel ambivalence after the act. A very few went onto 'reclaim' their birth name. Though these responses will be discussed further below, here it is worth noting that these responses show that complete silence is not always what occurs. The silence may emerge after discussion with other people who influence decisions, particularly partners. At this point the women are silenc*ed* by the powerful stories told about this norm. Continued ambivalence will usually be ignored or worked through

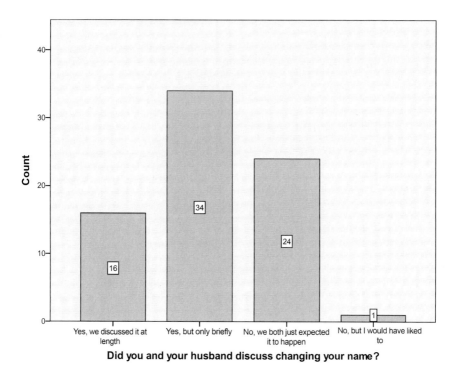

Figure 3.1 Whether name-changing participants discussed their decision with their partner beforehand (Count)

44 *Names and tradition*

until participants feel happy. For example, in the time between P80 taking the survey – when she said she felt 'quite negative' about her decision – and the interview taking place, she said she had come to feel better about her choice overall saying 'you go through phases I guess', yet later in the interview saying again that she did still feel ambivalent: 'Yeah, I do feel very ambivalent about it.' I asked her to explain her general feelings towards the name-changing norm, and she said:

> Em . . . I suppose it's, for *me* anyway, I had more of a feeling for my name than I realised. I thought it kind of *was* just a name, you still are who you, I mean I could change my name by deed poll to something mad and I'd still be me, but actually I had more of a strong reaction to [changing my name], I *did* have more of an identity in my name so . . .

> (interview data)

Ultimately, whatever their decision, the majority of participants said they felt (to a greater or lesser extent) positive about their decision (see Table 3.2), but P80 shows the complex nature of this positivity and the shifts in feeling over time. Working on feelings to fit what is expected seemed especially important for name changers, which will be returned to in Chapter 6.

The number of women who chose 'neither positive nor negative' in response to the question of 'How do you feel about your [naming] decision?' is worth investigating further. Table 3.2 shows a relatively large number of women within my sample choosing this option and having changed names. There is a problem of categorisation here as several emotions could plausibly come under feeling 'neither positive nor negative': being ambivalent, being unsure of feelings, or feeling indifferent (though it could be argued that feeling unsure and being ambivalent are akin to one another). Feeling ambivalent is rarely discussed in the public domain; the norm is generally *publicly* upheld. Participant 80 appears to

Table 3.2 Crosstabulation of how participants feel about their naming decision with whether they changed or retained their name (Count)

| | | *Did you change your name on marriage?* | | *Total* |
		Yes	*No*	
How do you feel about your decision?	Positive	34	23	57
	Quite Positive	15	3	18
	Neither positive nor negative	19	1	20
	Quite negative	6	0	6
	Negative	1	0	1
Total		75	27	102

hold ambivalent views over her name, veering from negativity to positivity when asked to define herself using a tick-box, and showing her continued ambivalence through speaking in interview. Participant 86, stated clearly that she remains 'very ambivalent' about her decision, while P30, faced with the fact she felt sharing one name was important on having her first child, did not know what to do for the best for herself and for her family: these two were not entirely juxtaposed (herself and her family), but she could feel tensions between them. This ambivalence shows that some women in my sample are aware of the possible problems of identity loss that a name change may entail or that they feel some sense of reservation that they *must* conform to this practice, yet continue, predominantly, to change their last name.

The silencing of dissent from the norm is key to its dominance. As Hockey et al. (2010) argue, heterosexuality is a largely silent term of social organisation, and this is part of its power – it is accepted and goes largely unnoticed; it is normalised. The sub-institutions of heterosexuality, such as marriage and name changing, are also organised through a great deal of silence.

There is a general cultural silence around the name-changing norm in Britain. Mead's generalised other may provide standards of behaviour and acceptability by which people judge themselves (1964: 218); this other can make these standards clear as much by its silences. The name-changing norm is little explicated or discussed because it is deemed unimportant and frivolous to do so, and thereby its nature and connection to the gendered organisation of society often goes undisturbed. Sheriff discusses this kind of 'cultural censorship' of certain discourses (2000: 114), saying it is 'social and customary' but also that it

> demands collaboration and the tacit communal understandings that such collaboration presupposes. Although it is contractual in nature, a critical feature of this type of silence is that it is both a consequence and an index of an unequal distribution of power, if not of actual knowledge. Through it, various forms of power may be partly, although often incompletely, concealed, denied, or naturalized. Although the type of silence I refer to may be a more or less stable and widely shared cultural convention, it is constituted through, and circumscribed by, the political interests of dominant groups.
>
> (Sheriff, 2000: 114)

The significance of names and name changing as a norm is discredited through the act of saying as little as possible. As Scott and Lyman argue, the 'deviant' forms of action are the ones which need accounting for: if one acts in accordance with norms accounting for action is deemed unnecessary (Scott and Lyman, 1968: 62). Language is key to deciding who is inside a community and who is outside, by providing the means to articulate and defend culturally appropriate forms of action (Phillips, 2004: 21). Tradition and reason are not separate (Phillips, 2004: 19): action through tradition comes from a place of understanding what is and is not acceptable in one's community or culture. Though there is increased discussion of name changing and there are other possibilities for what one does

46 Names and tradition

with one's name after marriage, these remain minority or unusual decisions which require justification.

Eight name *retainers* reflected very explicitly on the norm, away from their own personal experience of it. Their discussions focused on the inequality of name changing, as something women are expected to do but not men, as well as on the lack of good reasons to change names. Two of these eight mentioned that 'tradition' was not a good enough reason to change, in their opinion, but all eight women questioned the way in which the norm is taken for granted[3]:

> It should not be an automatic assumption that a woman has to give up her heritage because it's tradition or 'the done thing'. It should be made easier for a man to change – as simple as it is for a woman. 'Maiden' name is a ridiculous idea and it should always be 'previous' name.

> (P16)

> I feel it is odd that men keep one name for their whole life and that you can't tell if they're married or not from their name, whereas women are split into married and unmarried.

> (P8)

The name-retaining participants could not use tradition as a justificatory narrative and instead 12 name-retaining participants (just over 44%) looked to feminist narratives to justify their actions, which I will explore in Chapter 5, as well as to ideas of strong individual selfhood, which will be discussed in Chapter 8.

As with any institution, speaking up against its norms is seen as somewhat dangerous and could result in negative responses – be that from family, local community, or generalised 'society' – and is therefore discouraged through practices of silence (Wolfe Morrison and Milliken, 2000). Silence is complex and works on various levels and at various points for women coming into contact with the name-changing norm in their lives. If silence is a part of dominant discourses this means that power is working at various levels also: through the generalised other and 'cultural censorship' (Sheriff, 2000: 114), through individual people who influence the woman making the decision, through institutional, bureaucratic organisation, and through the self-censorship and silencing that individuals perform on themselves, in connection with all of these other influences. Patriarchal, gendered relations – or the 'gender order' – are a product of this power, and name changing is a part of the maintenance of this power.

The gender order is a concept initially developed by Jill Julius Matthews (Pilcher and Whelehan, 2005: 61). Matthews argues that all societies 'distinguish between women and men, but the particular forms of this distinction vary' (1984: 12). The gender order intersects with other positions such as class or race and is not an unchanging, monolithic system, but one which takes on a different shape depending on the context (Matthews, 1984: 12–14). However, she goes on to argue that 'the gender order of any particular society creates an ideology of femininity, which establishes both the imperative and the meaning of being a good or true woman' (Matthews, 1984: 15). There are then, she argues, societal imperatives for women to attempt to achieve this kind of womanhood through various sorts of acceptable behaviours and actions (Matthews, 1984: 15). This gender order guides and shapes how we perceive the world and how our sense of self is developed.

The naming norm is a part of this gender order: it encourages women to act in a particular way in relation to men, and for women and men to be separated from one another through gendered acts. It is a part of the gendered organisational principle of heterosexuality, which organises men and women in certain ways, encouraging certain forms of behaviour, work, and sacrifice. In considering acceptable behaviours as expressed through the modern British gender order, the women note the expectation to act in a certain way and the worry over not living up to these expectations. Furthermore, they note the previous actions of other women adhering to the gender order as examples and encouragement. Others note the lack of thought or discussion of the naming norm meant they had no idea there were other options – the naming norm has become an imperative despite the lack of laws making it obligatory. The naming norm is, in fact, so normalised and 'unthought' that it feels 'natural' and 'proper'. The 'traditions' of the past act as exemplars and encouragement for others to act in a particular way; the gender order of modern Britain continues to encourage this kind of organisation of women. Individuals understand themselves through gender and fit themselves into a particular gender order, attempting to follow its rules and regulations of acceptable behaviour with the purpose of becoming (being perceived as) a successful and credible (gendered) human being.

Another major justificatory narrative is that of choice, and it is this which will be explored in the next chapter: this narrative was, once again, most significant for name changers.

Notes

1 I do not accept Hobsbawm, Ranger, and their colleagues' arguments uncritically, but I would argue that their thesis of 'invented tradition' remains useful for me in conceptualising the relations between power, tradition, and geography.
2 It can also be seen from this table that two name-retaining participants felt societal expectations were the only other influence on their decision than themselves. These two – P40 and P51 – give little information on this, but it may be suggested that societal expectations influenced them to act contrary to the norm as they did not agree with them.
3 Other name-retaining participants also did this, but in relation to themselves and their own experiences which felt different in quality to the generalised reflections of these eight participants.

References

Adams, M. (2003). 'The Reflexive Self and Culture'. *British Journal of Sociology*. 54 (2): 221–238.

48 *Names and tradition*

Barclay, K. (2011). *Love, Intimacy and Power: Marriage and Patriarchy in Scotland, 1650–1850*. Manchester: Manchester University Press.

Bauman, Z. (2003). *Liquid Love*. Cambridge: Polity Press.

Bauman, Z. (2010). *44 Letters from the Liquid Modern World*. Cambridge: Polity Press.

Bauman, Z. (2011). *Liquid Modernity*. Cambridge: Polity Press.

Beck, U. and Beck-Gernsheim, E. (2004). *The Normal Chaos of Love*. Cambridge: Polity Press.

Beck, U. and Beck-Gernsheim, E. (2010). *Individualization*. London: Sage.

Bourdieu, P. (1998). *Practical Reason*. Cambridge: Polity Press.

Carter, J. (2011). 'Why Marry? Young Women Talk about Relationships, Marriage, and Love'. Unpublished Thesis, University of York.

Dumm, T. (2008). *Loneliness as a Way of Life*. Cambridge, MA: Harvard University Press.

Erickson, A. (2005). 'The Marital Economy in Comparative Perspective' in M. Agren and A. Erickson (eds.) *The Marital Economy in Scandinavia and Britain 1400–1900*. Aldershot: Ashgate: 3–20.

Giddens, A. (1996). *Modernity and Self-Identity*. Cambridge: Polity Press.

Gross, N. (2005). 'Detraditionalization Reconsidered'. *Sociological Theory*. 23 (3): 286–311.

Hobsbawm, E. (1987). 'Mass-Producing Traditions: Europe, 1870–1914' in E. Hobsbawm and T. Ranger (eds.) *The Invention of Tradition*. Cambridge: Cambridge University Press: 263–307.

Hockey, J, Meah, A., and Robinson, V. (2010). *Mundane Heterosexualities*. Basingstoke: Palgrave Macmillan.

Jackson, S., Ho, P.S.Y., and Na, J.N. (2013). 'Reshaping Tradition? Women Negotiating the Boundaries of Tradition and Modernity in Hong Kong and British Families'. *The Sociological Review*. 61: 667–687.

Matthews, J.J. (1984). *Good and Mad Women in Twentieth-Century Australia*. Sydney: Allen and Unwin Australia.

May, V. (2011). 'Self, Belonging and Social Change'. *Sociology*. 45 (3): 363–378.

Mead, G.H. (1964). *On Social Psychology*. Chicago: The University of Chicago.

National Archives of Scotland Holdings. (April 1672). 'Mutual agreement between John Glas, merchant burgess of Perth, and his spouse, Janet Halyburtone, superseding their marriage contract, which was "cancelled and destroyed as not being answerable to these ends and purposes intended of it"'. Catalogue Reference: B59/37/5/16.

National Archives of Scotland Holdings. (April 1883). 'Interim act and decree appointing Franc Gibb Dougall to be judicial factor on the trust estate created by the contract of marriage entered into between the deceased George Knox and Mrs Eliza Ferguson or Knox dated 4 Jun 1849 and recorded in the sheriff court books of Lanarkshire 5 May 1875 and granting warrant to complete title'. Catalogue Reference: CS46/1883/4/71.

Phillips, M.S. (2004). 'What Is Tradition When It Is Not "Invented"? A Historiographical Introduction' in M.S. Phillips and G. Schochet (eds.) *Questions of Tradition*. Toronto: University of Toronto Press: 3–29.

Pilcher, J. and Whelehan, I. (2005). *50 Key Concepts in Gender Studies*. London: Sage.

Pittock, M. (2008). *The Road to Independence? Scotland since the Sixties*. London: Reaktion Books.

Scott, M.B. and Lyman, S.M. (1968). 'Accounts'. *American Sociological Review*. 33 (1): 46–62.

Sheriff, R.E. (2000). 'Exposing Silence as Cultural Censorship: A Brazilian Case'. *American Anthropologist*. 102 (1): 114–132.

Shils, E. (1971). 'Tradition'. *Comparative Studies in Society and History*. 13 (2): 122–159.

Smart, C. (2012). *Personal Life*. Cambridge: Polity Press.

Wolfe Morrison, E. and Milliken, F.J. (2000). 'Organizational Silence: A Barrier to Change and Development in a Pluralistic World'. *The Academy of Management Review*. 25 (4): 706–725.

4 Names, 'choice', and gender

Choice is an important idea in discussions of late modernity and individualisation. Giddens' idea of the 'reflexive project of the self' (Giddens, 1996: 5) suggests that there are now more choices and options available to people than ever before. Life trajectories are not bounded as they once were by traditions and rigid rule structures. However, the previous discussion should make it clear that this argument ignores the continuing fact that some people have more choice than others due to their social positioning. The choice narrative also ignores the very important place of 'unthinkingness' (Shils, 1971) within 'traditions' and that some seemingly freely made decisions are so influenced by societal practice and opinion that they cannot be considered truly free, in Giddens' sense. As Lukes argues, some powerful social norms may be so ingrained that conceiving of other possibilities for action is practically impossible (2005: 113). Choices remain limited by the past, by resources, by the society in which a person lives, including the influence of the gender order and the ethical and moral standards of the day. Yet the narrative of freely made and informed choice is powerful: Figure 4.1 shows the importance of thinking one has made a free and individual choice, whatever the influence of culture, 'tradition', and close personal examples.

The idea that women should be able to do whatever they want that makes them happy is a part of this narrative of reflexive choice; it is also a part of the pervasive neoliberal rhetoric which is so significant to modern capitalist societies. Though neoliberalism, globalisation, and the impacts these systems have on the world are presented as inevitable forces – unstoppable in their linear progression – they are in reality the consequence of human decisions and policies (Heron, 2008: 95). These decisions have created vast inequalities and, as Heron argues, the 'role of international and political economic structures and interests as co-determinants to poverty and continuing inequality is not recognized' (Heron, 2008: 95). Instead of investing in social equality and welfare, states look to solve problems through the market – and inequalities widen.

The idea that we can improve our lives through consuming is an important force within neoliberal capitalism. The consumer makes choices based on the idea of the consumer's *right* to choose (Craven, 2007): the consumer should be given a full range of choices and decide which is best for them. Yet, our choices are bounded, as I have argued. Silence prevents certain thoughts from even arising, as

Names, 'choice', and gender 51

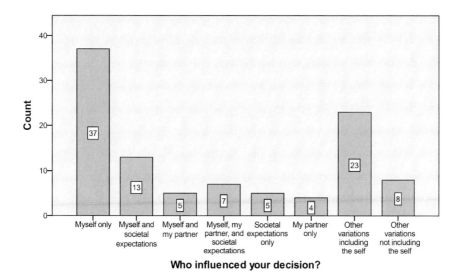

Figure 4.1 Who influenced participants' naming decisions (Count)

name-changing participants discussing 'tradition' have shown. An agent may look as if they have made a totally free choice when in fact the powerful cultural norms at work can prevent 'an agent or agents' desires, purposes, or interests . . . [from being fulfilled] or even from being formulated' (Lukes, 2005: 113). Choices which have such heavy cultural influences and powerful stories of their 'traditional' status are incredibly forceful in shaping action: the woman giving up a part of her selfhood for her partner/marriage is rarely questioned. The unequal nature of this naming practice could be seen as no longer significant or meaningful, a hangover from the past, with connotations of gender inequity which this 'modern' society no longer subscribes to; yet it continues to be deeply embedded in gendered conceptions of the self and the maintenance of unequal gendered relations. As has been argued through the schools of pragmatism and symbolic interactionism, we maintain those ways of interacting which are meaningful and *useful* to us; we do not simply maintain signs, symbols, and rituals which lose all sense of importance.

Upholding all women's decisions may seem like a feminist action in not belittling or talking down to other women, but it remains that feminists should be critical of the taken for granted norms which are unequally gendered. 'Choices' are not entirely free, but the rhetoric is clearly highly important. Feminism has been involved with using the rhetoric of choice to attempt to improve the position of women. Craven points out that feminists called women making decisions about their reproductive rights 'consumers' to attempt to get away from the generally paternalistic relationship with male doctors that women were entered into on becoming pregnant: female patient versus male doctor (2007: 701–702). However liberating this narrative was intended to be, the use of 'choice' by feminists within a neoliberal capitalist society needs more careful examination by feminists

52 *Names, 'choice', and gender*

themselves. The neoliberal rhetoric of choice is often invested in maintaining the status quo, by removing the agency of the less powerful and enhancing that of the established powerful elite (Heron, 2008: 95): norms are maintained and name changing is one such norm. Instead a re-imagining of what choice means and indeed whether neoliberalism is really 'inevitable' is needed.

The power of the imagination is significant to being critical and opening up other possibilities: what courses of action we follow are in part influenced by whether or not we can even imagine them (Lukes, 2005: 113). De Certeau argues that 'the *thinkable . . .* is identified with what one can *do*' (1988: 190. Emphases in original). In other words, if we can think it we believe we can do it. Contrary to this, if we cannot think it we cannot do it – it takes being able to imagine an action first before it can become a reality. Name changing is the prevalent norm. Name retaining is not so well articulated: there are fewer examples and bureaucracy often actively discourages it. The horizons of our imagination limit the possibilities for action: discussion is vital to allowing women to see the variety of naming options available and that following tradition is not necessary. Naming decisions could then be taken with a more genuine freeness, with selfhood and equality in mind. The fact name retaining is now even an imagined possibility is a step towards making it more normalised.

'Choosing' a name?

The narrative of 'choice' in which the modern 'self made self' (Giddens, 1996) is held entirely responsible for their own actions and decisions, posits that people have a wide variety of choices and courses of action available and there is little to prevent them from choosing what they truly want. The 'normal biography' is 'the "elective biography", the "reflexive biography", the "do-it-yourself biography"' (Beck and Beck-Gernsheim, 2010: 3). Beck and Beck-Gernsheim point out that this does not always succeed and that we are constantly in a state of risk due to these choices we, ironically, *must* make. In terms of naming, if truly making a DIY biography, women are simply *choosing* to take on their partner's name, as opposed to following social rules and indeed most participants state that their decision was indeed a 'choice' they made: the modal figure for influence on the decision to change or retain names was '1' or 'Myself' (see Figure 4.1). Participant 32 said that 'it was *my* choice, and for me, it has been a happy one', while P59 noted that 'changing names is an individual choice.' However, the fit with wider patterns and trends on name changing/retaining is so close that it seems unlikely that pure choice is creating these figures.

As has been mentioned previously, Beck and Beck-Gernsheim argue (2010: 2) that we must look to understand carefully what new forms of life are coming into being, and that, in their theorisation, individualisation does not mean the total destruction of 'regulations, conditions, provisos', but that 'far more than earlier, individuals must, in part . . . import [regulations and guidelines] into their biographies through their own actions' (2010: 2). Our present moment holds both change and consistency, but individuals are left with the burden of making sense of this in their own lives (2010: 4–5). This stressful state of choice and risk for modern individuals leads them to seek 'expert' help and guidance, to take away some of the responsibility for actions and decisions (2010: 7). Traditional choices may well be made to deliberately stand against the growing number of possibilities (Beck and Beck-Gernsheim, 2010: 5).

Moving away from the traditional is also difficult in a society which continues to have important socio-structural dimensions and influential traditions and historical examples. Marriage may be increasingly a matter of choice (Beck and Beck-Gernsheim, 2010: 8), but it remains an institution with institutional structures and goals. However, in a time of individualisation, people must *look as if* they are taking responsibility for their own actions: actively *choosing*. It is therefore unsurprising that 37 per cent of my participants stated that they were the sole influence on their decision (see Figure 4.1).

However, closer examination of the qualitative evidence shows the important influence of others, including a general 'other' or 'society'. This influence could be so significant that participants put their own feelings absolutely on the back-burner to the point where they changed their name purely to please someone else, usually their partner. In this way they follow the gendered social rules of love power and love work, which will be discussed in more detail below. However, by playing down or completely disguising the influence of tradition, past example, and wider social rules and practices, the gendered inequality of love and naming decisions is masked by the story of 'free choice', unfettered by anything outwith the person themselves.

This kind of choice, perhaps best displayed in Giddens' theorisation on the 'self made self', is in fact impossible – no one can escape the importance of past example and other people in making decisions, as well as the limits of social and historical positioning. There is a dialectical relationship between self and society (Beck and Beck-Gernsheim, 2010). Participants display the efficacy and reality of this dialectic when making decisions as an individual who lives within a particular society. However, they also display the significance of the idea of totally free choice: it is important to *look as if* one has taken a fully informed and responsible decision *on one's own*.

Marriage, Beck and Beck-Gernsheim argue (2010: 11), has increasingly become about this story of free choice and responsible decision-making, as opposed to familial or societal interests. The ideology of marriage and the increasingly 'free' nature of it, chosen and entered into for nothing but love and care for one another, is shown developing in Beck and Beck-Gernsheim's analysis of German society. It is also shown, Beck and Beck-Gernsheim argue (2010: 11), in the official German marriage manual of the 1970s, in which the possibility of dissolving the marriage if it becomes impossible to live with one another is discussed – the idea of marriage has shifted entirely to one of individualised contentment. Being 'in love' is the officially accepted reason for marriage *par excellence*: an individualised emotion which leads to a free decision to marry one's partner. Marriage and its rituals, including naming decisions, are seen as a matter of free choice in contemporary society, however this simplifies and even ignores the complexity of the choice narrative and what invoking it achieves.

The choice narrative in naming accounts: its significance and what it achieves

Throughout the study, individual choice was threaded through discussions of naming decisions in relation to all of the significant themes: selfhood, family, love and commitment, and tradition. The narration of individual choice seemed highly significant and was maintained even in the face of quite explicit stories of partner and family pressure to act in a particular way. As Figure 4.1 shows, the majority of participants chose 'Myself' as an influence on their naming decision, with the largest number of both name changers and name retainers saying they alone had influenced their choice.

These numbers read as positive affirmation that women are choosing what to do with their names at the point of marriage, thinking about what they would like and prefer, and making a decision which is related to their sense of self at this pivotal life moment. A number of participant quotes can be used to illustrate the use of the choice narrative; the stories I utilise below are illustrative of the wider sample. Participants used words and phrases like 'my choice', 'decided to', 'I wanted to' when discussing their name change and their reasoning for doing so.

> It was *my* choice, and for me a very happy one.
>
> (P32; survey data; her emphasis)

> Changing names is an individual choice.
>
> (P59; survey data)

> I decided to take on my spouse's name because I felt it would be more of a commitment to our marriage on my part.
>
> (P34; survey data)

> I wanted to show my love and commitment by changing my name.
>
> (P54; survey data)

> Ultimately it was my choice . . .
>
> (P77; interview data)

These strong words and phrases frame their narratives in the context of freely made, active choice and set their wider life story in this context of choice. Being able to choose is a valued status to have; being unable to choose suggests a lesser social position and/or less trust placed in you by others. People who cannot choose for themselves must either be in need of protection and care, like children, for example, or in the unpleasant position of not being allowed to follow their own desires: this person may be oppressed by those in power around them. It is understandable that few adults would wish to see themselves as being in one of these positions. To show that one is actively choosing how one lives and is the lead in one's own life suggests agency and freedom (Brannen and Nilsen, 2005: 412).

Furthermore, describing oneself as an individual, who is the active agent in one's own life story, is a very positive and significant narrative in western cultures, including the UK in the contemporary moment (Brannen and Nilsen, 2005). Using this narrative to make sense of life decisions will be understood by others, making your life intelligible to others, and therefore making you an acceptable – non-troublesome – member of society. Forming a coherent narrative of self is therefore pressing: the overarching narrative of our lives needs to make sense, both to ourselves and to others (Atkinson, 1998: 1). This need to account for decisions around marriage and selfhood suggests Giddens' theory that relationships are becoming increasingly inwardly referential (1996: 6) is not correct. Participants must justify themselves to others and consider the thoughts and wishes of these others as they do so, as will be described in more detail below.

Attaching oneself to positive social narratives allows one to see oneself as valuable and successful in that society, as well as portraying oneself in this light to others. Participant 61 wrote that 'When I changed my name I took on a new identity as a married woman which I still feel very positive about. I feel my name gives me status in society and also confirms me as both my husband's partner and the mother of my children.' The name change has provided social approval and intelligibility of family relationships: it is constructed as a positive choice, taken by an individual woman, and confirms one's place in society.

Yet, despite the significance of this narrative, it was often undermined by the in-depth interviews, when participants had the time to go into detail about their life story. Mixing the survey and interviews therefore produced some interesting and conflicting results. These in-depth stories revealed a gendered set of work going on around decision-making, involved with emotional labour and the social construction of gendered commitment, love, and roles; the men in these heterosexual partnerships were much more free to make the choices they wished to and to impose their thoughts and feelings about which choices are 'correct' upon their partners.

Gendering narratives of choice

By comparing and contrasting the data from both the survey and in-depth interviews, it became clear choice in marital naming decisions is gendered. As women described the process of coming to a decision about their name the thoughts and feelings of others were paramount: they did not want to offend their partner or in-laws by not changing names, they wanted to show love and commitment to their partner by changing names, and they wanted to ensure others were happy and felt included in the family – husbands, in-laws, but also children; even imagined, future children – by all sharing one name. Then, describing their male partner's approach to naming decisions: he was described in the main as making a decision based on his own feelings (influenced of course by social context) and which feelings were considered more important than his wife's and allowed to override hers when they were not in agreement. Marital naming choices were therefore not freely made and were gendered in the range of responses available

56 *Names, 'choice', and gender*

as to how to make that choice. Those women that retained their birth name were much more likely to consult their own feelings, *despite* social norms, and were a smaller group working against the more common gendered norm within heterosexual relationships.

Participant 77, mentioned above as providing a choice narrative, went on to change her name, despite mentioning in her interview that she had some reservations: 'I did hum and haw because a few people at work were going, you know, "just leave it as it is"', as she had told them of her concerns about changing her name again, after being divorced previously and feeling connected to her original name on returning to it. However, she had seen a work colleague who had retained her name have a bad reaction from their husband on doing so: 'actually one of the other girls who got married not long before me, she'd left her name as it was and her husband really wasn't happy about it.' She had therefore tested this option with her fiancée to see what his reaction might be: 'I'd sort of jokingly said to [him] a couple of times "I don't know if I'm going to change my name" and he said "well I don't know if I'm going to marry you then" (laughs).' Participant 77 laughs at this statement, feeling it to be jokey and not completely serious. However, her husband's feelings won out over her own and she changed her name. Her 'choice' was less than free, influenced by her partner's lack of ease with the idea of her not changing and the example of her work colleague. Participant 77 had had a very difficult previous marriage and had found the change back from her first married name to her original name highly empowering; the fact she changed name again on her second marriage shows the strength of the norm and the strong influence of her partner.

The comments of P34 and P54 above also reveal the influence of others and the particularly gendered need to display love and commitment (see Chapter 6 for more). The fact that women need to display their commitment so conspicuously – or, as I have called it, 'conspicuous commitment' – while men are exempt from this requirement, suggests a highly gendered decision-making process around names. Arlie Hochschild has argued (2003a, 2003b) that women putting the feelings of others before their own is a framing rule – it frames thoughts and actions – and, I would argue, therefore makes these thoughts and actions intelligible to self and others. This rule was certainly applied by participants within my study, who spoke in strong terms of choice and individual action, but underlying their comments were forceful gendered ideas of appropriate action and behaviour. In deciding to change their name to show their love and commitment, these women were acting upon taken-for-granted norms and behaviours that guide decisions in contemporary Britain. In this case, a gendered rule for love, commitment, and display which turns a narrative of 'individual choice' into a much more complex and messy story of gendered decision-making, in which the feelings of male partners are paramount.

The above examples show that choice narratives are in fact much more complex than they might initially seem, and that 'free choice', connected with late modernity, is not a neutral category, but one with highly gendered overtones. It could be argued that partners always try to do what will make the other happy, and this is merely an example of this selflessness; however, the pervasiveness of women following this norm suggests something rather more social is occurring. Certainly acting in a sacrificial manner has been shown to be a highly gendered phenomenon (Woodhouse, 1988: 380), with women seeing it as their duty to give things up in a way men do not. The name changers act, more generally, for the collective, in gendered ways. These findings also confirm the previous literature on the importance of names to identity and feminist politics: more traditional naming decisions were frequently based on an idea of acting for the collective, which was seen as a good (Suter, 2004). The gendered nature of this 'choice' becomes increasingly clear when the reactions of partners and families to the suggestion that the wife-to-be may keep her name or that the male partner could consider changing his name are taken into account.

Almost 20 per cent of my sample described their husbands becoming agitated and upset when the idea of her not changing her name was raised. This emotional response, and the resulting pressure on the woman to follow the norm to please her partner, ensured some women who may not otherwise have followed the norm did end up 'choosing' a traditional naming route. This suggests a further framing rule (Hochschild, 2003a) in decision-making around names in heterosexual partnerships: men are allowed to respond in a highly emotional way to naming decisions which may upset the gendered social order, and this response is to be taken seriously by those around him, due to his privileged gendered social position in relation to the naming norm.

Men could also use this privileged position to refuse to do anything with their own name, even when it would give the impression to the outside world that he and his partner had followed the naming norm: 'He refused to change his' (P11; survey data). Men's gendered sense of self around names, their feelings, and privileged social position give a credibility to the idea that men should not be asked to change their name and that they might be seen as less masculine by family and friends, and probably by themselves as well, though their action to change their name to their partner's would give strangers the same impression of togetherness and intelligibility as following the norm. It would appear from these data that men have more agency and power within intimate heterosexual decision-making. They are able to refuse to make a decision as much as to make it. The gendered power surrounding decision-making remains significant and clear within my data and confirms the data of Lockwood et al. (2011), who also found that upsetting family dynamics was one reason women chose to follow a traditional naming path. Choice, in any sense approaching that of Giddens, remains a privileged action – or even thought process – and one which is highly gendered.

The gendered nature of the 'choice' to change a name was further emphasised when women decided to go against the norm and were subject to hostility by partners and families. When making this decision, women have already overcome powerful social norms around gender and action and made what comes the closest, in my sample, to a genuine 'free choice'. Such individual decision-making and agency, despite the earlier positivity attributed to it by participants and its overarching positivity within Western cultures (Brannen and Nilsen, 2005) was

58 *Names, 'choice', and gender*

not upheld when these choices were made. Gendered rules around how women and men should make 'choices' came to bear on these participants and they experienced negative reactions. For example, P8 was accused of 'making a point' by her husband's family, and he was criticised for 'settling' for a bad situation which his own brother said 'he would never settle for': in so doing the family criticised the participant's femininity and her husband's masculinity and control of her. Participant 48 described being manipulated by her husband as he informed her that her decision not to change her name would impact negatively on the lives of any future children they had and that she was being disrespectful to him and to her own mother's decision to change her name on marriage.

The emotional responses and the gendered accusations thrown at both participants and their husbands show how difficult it is to make genuine choices which go against the grain of a social norm. As P71 said starkly about the decision to change her name in the survey: 'It requires less explanation', and P35 reflected this feeling when she said she changed her name because 'I just didn't want to be asked why [I had kept my own name] all the time.' The sheer effort of making a decision which is unusual and likely to make you to some extent socially unintelligible was too much for these women. Making 'free choices' around names within heterosexual partnerships is therefore a fallacy: gendered ideas of tradition and gendered framing rules for emotions and expected action make themselves strongly felt. The possibilities open to women around names are therefore curtailed and decisions must be made carefully bearing these rules and traditions in mind, not freely and openly. These results are of course in reference to the specific sample I worked with, but considering the fairly privileged nature of this sample it may suggest a similar picture would appear for those with even less social power.

Choice, names, and heterosexual partnerships

The choice narratives of active agency used by participants are suffused with past traditions, gendered emotional labour, and gendered notions of acceptable behaviour. When viewed in this light, the decision-making around names becomes far less a benign and frivolous process and one much more significant to understanding contemporary social relationships and the impact of gender upon them. The gendered nature of choice in heterosexual relationships goes beyond this particular choice. Studies from the 1970s and 1980s showed that, despite apparent changes in the socio-economic position of women, the inequality between husbands and wives persisted (Bell and Newby, 1976: 166) and that women continued to have their ideas and desires around timing of children and work overruled by their husbands (Leonard, 1980: 242–243). Though we are now more than 30 years on from these studies their comments continue to ring true: more recent research has found that women's earning capacity does not necessarily relate to their power within the marriage as spouses look to preserve gendered expectations and minimise possible anxieties or arguments when a woman earns more than her husband (Tichenor, 2005). Along with my data, these examples suggest a gendered

Names, 'choice', and gender 59

approach to decision-making within heterosexual couples that continues to exist over time.

Therefore, describing decisions around names as free choices becomes distinctly problematic and is a narrative which should be challenged. The choice narrative is significant and achieves a number of things important to creating a sense of self in the contemporary 'West'. As outlined above this includes showing agency, independence, and freedom; it also suggests a creativity and lack of restraint from past traditions which are no longer needed in a fast-changing modern world. However, it manages to do a number of other things, which are more concerning. It conceals the emotion and love work women undertake in these relationships and therefore accepts, and even masks, gendered inequality in relationships, including the expectation that women will be happy to give up their name for their new relationship and married role. The act is normalised behind 'choice', while the suggestion that change is needed is trivialised: women are happy, so what is the problem? In fact, this trivialisation of women's lack of choice and the continued significant impact of social positioning on the paths we can take ensures gendered inequality in decision-making within heterosexual relationships goes unchallenged. The status quo is maintained.

This raises questions about how we think of choice. 'Choice' should not be referred to or used without relating it to gender and other social positionings; the realities of and restrictions on choices and who can make them need to be interrogated by sociologists. Gender is an especially significant factor to take into account as, within heterosexual relationships, the most intimate decisions are being made based on power and gendered inequality. It actually begs the question of whether 'choice' is really a useful term in itself. *Decisions* are made based on the intersections of social positionings and power, and the conscious and semi-conscious knowledge gained from living within a society of how to act and be accepted; *choices* on the other hand, made freely from several equal options, are a much rarer occurrence and a socially privileged one.

This discussion of choice leads into Chapter 5, which investigates the impact of feminism on naming choices within my sample, particularly the decisions of the name retainers. Second-wave feminism, names, and choice are frequently closely connected in the popular imagination, and yet I have here argued that 'choice' is a much more complex and troubling concept, which may actually work with a neoliberal agenda. I will unpack these arguments in much more detail, while exploring the place of feminism in contemporary British naming decisions.

References

Atkinson, R. (1998). *The Life Story Interview*. London: Sage.

Beck, U. and Beck-Gernsheim, E. (2010). *Individualization*. London: Sage.

Bell, C. and Newby, H. (1976). 'Husbands and Wives – The Dynamic of the Deferential Dialectic' in D. Leonard Barker and S. Allen (eds.) *Dependence and Exploitation in Work and Marriage*. London: Longman: 152–168.

60   *Names, 'choice', and gender*

Brannen, J. and Nilsen, A. (2005). 'Individualisation, Choice, and Structure: A Discussion of Current Trends in Sociological Analysis'. *The Sociological Review*. 53 (3): 412–428.

Craven, C. (2007). 'A "Consumer's Right" to Choose a Midwife: Shifting Meanings for Reproductive Rights under Neoliberalism'. *American Anthropologist*. 109 (4): 701–712.

De Certeau, M. (1988). *The Practice of Everyday Life*. Berkeley, CA: California University Press.

Giddens, A. (1996). *Modernity and Self-Identity*. Cambridge: Polity Press.

Heron, T. (2008). 'Globalization, Neoliberalism and the Exercise of Human Agency'. *International Journal of Politics, Culture, and Society*. 20 (1/4): 85–101.

Hochschild, A.R. (2003a [1983]). *The Managed Heart*. Berkeley, CA: University of California Press.

Hochschild, A.R. (2003b). *The Commercialization of Intimate Life*. Berkeley, CA: University of California.

Leonard, D. (1980). *Sex and Generation*. London: Tavistock Publications.

Lockwood, P., Burton, C., and Boersma, K. (2011). 'Tampering with Tradition: Rationales Concerning Women's Married Names and Children's Surnames'. *Sex Roles*. 65: 827–839.

Lukes, S. (2005). *Power: A Radical View*. Basingstoke: Palgrave Macmillan.

Shils, E. (1971). 'Tradition'. *Comparative Studies in Society and History*. 13 (2): 122–159.

Suter, E.A. (2004). 'Tradition Never Goes Out of Style: The Role of Tradition in Women's Naming Practices'. *The Communication Review*. 7 (1): 57–87.

Tichenor, V.J. (2005). 'Maintaining Men's Dominance: Negotiating Identity and Power When She Earns More'. *Sex Roles*. 54 (3/4): 191–205.

Woodhouse, L. (1988). 'The New Dependencies of Women'. *Family Relations*. 37 (4): 379–384.

5   Power, politics, and naming[1]

Naming is a meaningful and political act. There is a long history of using names to symbolise political viewpoints, and to actualise them. In this chapter I wish to explore some of these political uses – and abuses – of names to explore the power and politics invested in names and naming practices. This is most explicitly a part of black American history; in the case of American slavery the point of renaming was to change a person's status, erase their history, and force a change of identity. However, there are many acts of naming that can be used to illustrate the ways in which names are not meaningless combinations of letters passed, changed, and taken in arbitrary ways. Names in the context of Britain and gender are closely tied up with feminism and women taking control of their own lives: this may at first seem an odd connection, but as this chapter will argue, not when names are understood politically as representing who has power, authority, and control over others. Therefore, I will begin by looking at names in a variety of political examples before turning to feminism in particular and the narratives my participants used to connect their naming decisions with feminism and feminist principles.

Naming as political

People taken from Africa to become slaves in the United States underwent a *renaming* by their slave masters – their own names connected them to their African heritage and traditions, as well as to their freedom, and as such were, in the eyes of their white slave masters, dangerous symbols of another life which needed to be erased. As the African names of slaves were no longer used every day as legally and socially enshrining their identity, they stopped having any power and their meaning to the wider social body was complicated. As Benson argues, names are not only a personal symbol, but equally a social one: they have to be used by others to have any real meaning and as such, 'they are constituted within and are ratified by the symbolic order, the order of power and its inscriptions' (Benson, 2009: 179).

Renaming acted as erasure of identity and displaced slaves' sense of grounding in history, which ensured greater submission. Slaves were re-named to constantly

62   *Power, politics, and naming*

remind them of their inferior status: English diminutives which were childlike such as 'Doll or Bess' were used, names that were insults such as 'Villain, Trash, Whore', or overly grand names to make the slave feel worthless in comparison such as 'Dido, Venus, Nero' (Benson, 2009: 190–191). The slave was given the last name of his or her master as a public sign of ownership – slaves belonged, bodily, to their slave-master. The power of the name was clearly felt by slave-owners, and no doubt by slaves themselves.

The loss of identity through renaming, which slaves experienced throughout their lives, can be seen in the reaction after emancipation in which freed slaves began to rename themselves. Frederick Douglass is a well-known example of a former slave who renamed himself several times, before settling on 'Douglass' with the help of another emancipated slave (Benston, 1982: 3).[2] Malcolm X is another famous example of a man who refused a last name given by a slave-master in his family's past, using 'X' to show up the dislocation of his ances-tral history by slavery (Benston, 1982: 3). In the example of American slavery, the person is re-named so that they can be placed into the new category of 'slave' rather than 'free person'. Names categorise people, and categorisation is always bound up with power – those with the power to define and sort, and those without.

This can be seen in other examples of naming throughout history. Claiming power over lands and cultures and building empires in the 'New World' was in part achieved through the creation of maps and the naming involved in these representations of the lands newly discovered by Europeans (Livingstone, 2003: 155). By drawing lines across long established settlements and communities, and naming locations and geographical features with the names of Spanish, French, or British royalty and cities, Europeans staked their claim to the land, its resources, and its people (Livingstone, 2003: 155–156). They obliterated the history of the indigenous people as they re-drew and re-named their landscape, suggesting to patrons at home that the land was empty and ready to be exploited (Livingstone, 2003: 155). The new names erased the old and silenced the history of the local people, making the spaces intelligible to Europeans:

> When James Cook named well over one hundred Australian capes, bays, and isles, frequently using the names of European naturalists, he at once effaced local designations and brought those spaces into European circulation for the first time.
>
> (Livingstone, 2003: 156)

These acts of renaming are bound up with race, ethnicity, nationalism, and power and are crucial and clear examples of the political nature of naming.

The power to name is also gendered, and feminists in particular have pointed this out, binding feminist politics more closely with acts of naming and taking control over one's identity. A prominent feminist theologian, Mary Daly, argues that the Christian story was a 'prototypic case of false naming' (1985: 47), in which the world has been named (ordered, organised) according to the wishes

Power, politics, and naming 63

and interests of the dominant group; these are acts of naming intended to oppress women and bolster the claims of men to their power and status (Daly, 1985: 46; Spender, 1998: 167–168). The Bible's story of Adam and Eve gives a clear message about the Christian belief in *man's* ability to name and therefore to control; Christian stories have had – and continue to have – a powerful influence on British culture. God creates all of the animals and birds of the natural world and allows Adam to name them: 'So God formed out of the ground all the wild animals and all the birds of heaven. He brought them to the man to see what he would call them, and whatever the man called each living creature, that was its name' (Genesis 2: 19). Adam also has the power to name 'Woman' when she is created from his rib, and later he gives her the specific personal name 'Eve': 'The man called his wife Eve' (Genesis: 3:20). Schimmel argues that the reason God allowed Adam to name is so that he may rule over all he names (Schimmel, 1989: ix) – naming and classifying gives the namer a power and implies a certain obedience from the one named. As 'woman', and specifically 'Eve', is named by Adam, along with the rest of the natural world, the Christian creation story gives Adam as Man a power over Woman, and Adam as Husband a power over his Wife. The power imbalance within these relationships is made obvious through this act of naming. As Leonard states, there is '[n]o doubt Adam's naming of Eve is a sign of his authority over her' (Leonard, 1990: 39).

Other feminist sociological discussions of naming and gender have focused on the important elements of power and control which reside in naming processes, most prominently Dale Spender (1998). Through naming the world is ordered and without names things are hard to perceive and to discern. This is made clear in Spender's discussion of naming when she says 'By naming the world we impose a pattern and a meaning which allows us to manipulate the world' (1998: 163). As part of the feminist discussion of gender, inequality, and names Spender discusses this manipulation of society by those in dominant positions to fit the world to their interests, noting that women's experiences are often unaccounted for by a lack of fitting names and that feminists must work to create names for these experiences (1998: 183). In doing so women's experiences become normalised and move into the centre rather than being seen as peripheral and 'Other' to the norm of men's experiences.

Spender argues that if women had more power to name their own world these words would be different and more positive towards women. Positive words, particularly in terms of heterosexual relations, are more often reserved for men, while normal, healthy sexuality in women is nameless (1998: 175), and has therefore even been seen as a sign of ill-health (1998: 175). Spender makes clear that the power of naming is a male one and that this power has informed how the world is viewed, (re)created, and *experienced* by both men and women. Spender's analysis has been widely critiqued (see for example Black and Coward, 1998) as needing more context as to how language is created and constructed, and that it is embedded within, as well as a part of, creating society. However, Spender's argument about the power of naming to influence how the world is perceived and understood is significant; the person with the authority to name is a person

64   *Power, politics, and naming*

with a wider social power and status. The name-giver, then, has authority over the named.

Within this wider context of naming, and the patriarchal history of women's name changing on marriage (see Pateman, 1988), the name changing ritual and its connected social meaningfulness continues to be an important issue for feminists. It connects to deep and vital debates about social values and gender hierarchy, as well as to why the trivialised acts of the everyday are ignored. Attempts at closing down conversations about names as 'silly' and 'trivial' point to deeper concerns around this ritual and the social need to keep it alive that should worry feminists. The everyday may seem mundane but is in fact the very fabric of our society and holds within it the values which social actors aspire to hold dear and use to become intelligible actors (Hockey et al., 2010; Smart, 2012). Naming is a political act, closely connected with power and identity in many different contexts, and feminism's connection with the gendered naming rituals of British society is not therefore random or strange but something to be explored and maintained.

Feminism and the last name in contemporary Britain

Giddens has linked the rise of 'the reflexive project of the self' (1996: 5) with feminism and the move away from identities for women 'defined so closely in terms of the home, and . . . domesticity' (Giddens, 1996: 216). Women, the feminist movement argued, should be given more choices in life and control over these decisions. Choice is now a powerful rhetoric in society generally, including for feminists. 'Choice' appears to open up decision-making and a sense of freedom to women; the ability to have agency in one's own life. Of course, to an extent this is absolutely true and a powerful message about women taking control. However this narrative has pitfalls and is now bound up with neoliberalism (Craven, 2007) which is opposed to the egalitarian message of the feminist movement, as has been explored in the last chapter.

With naming decisions tightly bound up with a narrative of choice and it being a woman's 'own decision' this discussion is an important one to raise, and in particular in the light of its apparent feminist background. Second wave feminism is particularly important here. The debate over names is often connected to this period in time and the concerns of this moment in the feminist campaign (Mills, 2003). Feminism has often been lambasted as a force which breaks down tradition in a negative and destructive way, yet the tradition of name changing, as explored in Chapter 3, continues. The complicated connection between feminism and names will be explored here.

The anger and vitriol against feminism emerged early in the movement's history as can be seen from the number and variety of anti-suffrage cartoons from the early nineteenth century (see for example, the collection on Ben Vincent's blog, www.genderben.com[3]). However, the anger against feminism and the actions of women to improve their own and others' lives continues to provoke backlash. Recent debates in the United States over reproductive rights have produced particularly vicious attacks in cartoon form (see 'Sandra Fluke Cartoon Creates Controversy of Its Own', *The Huffington Post*, 2012).

These cartoons depict women as emotional (in a negative and irrational way), loud, and stupid, as they make confused or contradictory statements. The women are shown as 'unfeminine' and are often depicted as in some way immoral for acting in unconventionally feminine ways, that is, seeking more rights for themselves. The aim of the cartoonists is to undermine the feminist convictions, thoughts, and actions of these women through ridicule and attempt at defamation of character, be it through an unspecified group 'type' or a particular woman. Over 100 years lies between the anti-suffrage cartoons and the Sandra Fluke cartoon, and these years have seen a great deal of social change, but the methods used to make particular points remain remarkably similar. The ultimate message is that feminists should not be listened to or taken seriously, and this because they are acting against traditional ideas of 'proper' behaviour for women by attempting to change power structures in their countries to improve women's position.

Feminism is, then, often used as a scapegoat by those in positions of power for problems in society. This phenomenon has occurred over the last few years in discussions over parenting, the family, and feminism. Diane Abbott, speaking to *The Guardian* newspaper in January 2013 about the rise in obesity being related to poor parenting and family breakdown, argued that feminists needed to re-think their discussions of the family and not 'abandon that terrain to the right' (Wintour, 'Diane Abbot Outlines Plan to Curb Fast Food Shops', 3rd January 2013). Although Abbott made the point that 'the family' need not refer to the heteronormative nuclear family model, she made comments about feminist discussions of the family unit as oppressive to women which could be interpreted as dismissive of feminist politics and this resulted in several right-wing newspapers using these comments to fuel articles on the feminist movement's place in 'destroying the family' (see for example in *The Daily Mail*, Shipman, 'How Feminism is to Blame for the Breakdown of the Family, by Left-Winger Diane Abbott', 3rd January 2013). The questions about health and emotional well-being are lost and instead the focus is on blaming the changed position of women in our society for perceived social ills. The traditional story is revived and attempts to question it repressed; instead attempts are made to undermine feminism and to maintain the status quo.

Name changing is one of these traditional stories of the powerful; those working against it can be ridiculed and their lives made difficult. The process and the norm have come under attack from the feminist movement more widely, but it is a topic associated with second wave feminism in the general imagination. It is difficult to find definite connections with British second wave feminists: the United States has a much more defined and organised approach to the discussion of naming norms through the Lucy Stone League (www.lucystoneleague. org). This organisation connects its origins to nineteenth-century suffragist and abolitionist Lucy Stone, the first American woman known to retain her birth name after marriage ('Who is Lucy Stone?', n.d., Lucy Stone League website).

66 *Power, politics, and naming*

However strong the empirical evidence for second-wave interest in names may or may not be, the popular imagination connects the decision to retain the last name with a feminist stance. This can be seen from participant experience: 'I'm a feminist' (P37, when asked to explain her decision to retain her name), while P51 described receiving several sarcastic comments from family members about being a feminist once she explained that she would not be changing her name. As I said at the end of the previous chapter, name retainers used feminism as a major justification narrative for their decisions. However, for name changers their relationship to feminism was complicated by the connection of name retaining and being a committed feminist. This left some of them questioning their decision and their feminist ideals, but provoked others to defend their decision *as well as* their feminist identity.

Feminism and naming decisions

Name retainers who identify themselves and their actions as feminist wrote that they have particular principles which make name changing impossible, and/or they see no need to change their name in favour of another person's. They are aware of the gender imbalance in the name-changing norm, and this is a source of irritation and anger. There was a hope for some that they could influence others or open up further feminist debate through the discussions provoked by their naming decision. Not all of these participants were free of ambivalence about marriage or naming, as the examples below will show, but had ultimately come to accept marriage, with name retention, as a sign of their feminism, their break from tradition, and their independence.

Participant 3 spoke of her involvement with the feminist movement in the 1970s which made her 'more aware of being proactive and proud about my female identity and questioning the patriarchal status quo'. She wrote of not understanding why women change their names as there is no need: 'I do feel women sell themselves short by thinking that they must adopt their husband's name.' Though she changed her mind about the married state itself she said 'I think that women can become more invisible by changing their name on marriage, it seems an indicator that women are prepared to play second fiddle to men by changing their names. This is the wrong signal to send out!' She spoke of her belief in the power of women to change gendered social norms and that it was up to women to do so.

Participant 5 spoke of her and her partner's dislike of the 'perceived dominance of the partner who keeps and bestows their name over the one that adopts the new name.' They went to great lengths to try to remove the 'patriarchal baggage' from their wedding, including researching the possibility of removing the words 'husband' and 'wife' from their ceremony, researching going abroad for a heterosexual civil ceremony, and having their ceremony in Scotland rather than the south of England where they live to be able to put their mothers' occupations, as well as their fathers', on their marriage certificate. Participant 5 noted her initial embarrassment at having married, and doing so in a 'big white wedding dress', as

Power, politics, and naming   67

she did not feel this reflected her feminism. The name retain became a sign of her feminist principles.

Participant 46 wrote that changing her name seemed 'too enormous' a move, considering the history of the surname change as being an indicator of the woman as property. Men do not have to present themselves to the world as married and she felt it was important not to present herself as such. She wrote of the ambivalence she feels knowing her last name is still just her father's name, but that '[i]t's important to remember the centuries of struggle women have had to progress from being treated as second class citizens' and that naming decisions are a part of that history.

These comments suggest the idea of a standard of feminism and a 'proper' feminist, which participants are measuring themselves against. Certain actions and beliefs are associated with (Western) feminism and being critical of marriage, aware of the historical subjugation of women, and retaining one's name seem to be a part of this standard, for my participants at least. This reflects the findings of other studies into feminists and naming decisions (see Mills, 2003). When name-retaining participants felt they might have acted contrary to this standard, or not quite matched up with it, as with P5, they felt the need to justify their actions almost apologetically. The retaining of their birth name was one action that displayed their feminist beliefs to the world. Participant 48 (name retainer) wrote that she knew someone who took on 'a beautiful Spanish name' when she married and that 'everyone is envious of that', 'even the most hardened feminists!' It does not matter how much one may like a name or want a name to be one's own, one should not follow the norm as a 'true' feminist, this quote suggests, albeit in a playful manner. When articulating these standards self-identified feminists are creating a vocabulary around what it means to be a feminist in Britain today: name retaining is one such standard course of action and forms a sort of 'social control' within feminist circles of what is expected and what needs to be justified (Mills, 1940: 907–908).

Participant 76 described herself as a feminist and told a story in her interview which suggested a standard of (Western) feminism: not being as interested in marriage as other women may be. She said:

> I was very much a feminist. I did a lot of work in the 70s and 80s, I took a degree in Women's Studies . . . and I was very much a part of this and thought that "this is my life" and . . . (laughs) just today I was in [a university department] and a girl came out and was talking to one of my staff and she said "ooh, I got engaged!" and the other girl said "I got engaged too! When did you get engaged?" and I was thinking "I don't care!" (laughter) I really don't, didn't have that concept and none of my friends did either.

It appears that this standard of feminism is what name changers are also measuring themselves against, and this measurement produces a complex picture. Out of the thirteen name changers who mention feminism in some way, three explicitly state that there is no link between name changing and a lack of respect for feminism

68 *Power, politics, and naming*

or women's rights. Participant 39 said that she has considered politics, principles and theories behind name changing, but has concluded that feeling right about one's name within oneself is what should be aimed for; P52 thought she would not marry or change names and have church and state approval of her relationship, but she did all of these things. She does not accept that taking someone's name means accepting other inequalities. Finally, P44 said that name changing has nothing to do with rights, oppression or a denial of feminism. It annoys her when people believe women who change names are subservient or less intelligent than women who do not or who hyphenate.

Participant 120 was in a slightly more ambivalent position, writing that she had thought she would never change her name or marry, but that at the time it ended up not being a big decision. She is a feminist and 'perhaps it is strange that I changed my identity for a male name', but she feels more concern over the use of titles and the declaration of marital status these entail. She feels unease over having changed her name and gone along 'with a tradition that is born out of inequality', but she wanted a family name for her children and felt happy to take his name. The feminist 'standard' of a person who would not change her name and is therefore independently minded and unaccepting of inequality is a figure these women feel they need to address. They do not feel they should be discounted as independent, thinking women because they have changed their name, but feel that this is suggested by a (feminist) generalised other.

The remaining nine of those name changers who mentioned feminism spoke of their unhappiness with the norm, as it means that women are declaring their marital status in a way men are not. The problem of titles was brought up time and again by this group, who felt unhappy with the double declaration of marriage they were asked to make. Participant 86 had 'strong reservations about the practice on feminist and equality grounds' and 'about what changing your name says as a statement about women's role in society'. She worries she has set a bad example to her daughter, but sharing a name was more important to her husband than these reservations were to her, hence she decided to change names. Participant 93 wrote that her viewpoint has changed over time and that she has 'come round to a much more feminist viewpoint' and wishes she 'had made a stand against this kind of unthinking tradition'. She would rather not use titles or last names at all. Participant 62 is in the process of reclaiming her OFN as she feels it is a way of feeling and showing (to others) that her relationship is an equal one.

There was only one participant who mentioned feminist expectations of behaviour but did not feel any need to match herself up to them. Participant 74 said she might have retained her name because it was 'trendy' in her 'feminist-leaning social circle', but she did not see 'any compelling reason' to do this. It seems there is a general assumption that feminists will look kindly on name retaining and will scorn name changing. The history of the movement as breaking with tradition, the association of second wave feminism in particular with name-retaining debates, and the idea of a 'standard feminist' who does not change her name, hold imaginative sway.

Name retainers can see and articulate a clear relationship between feminism and name retaining, if they wish. The popular connection of second wave,

Western feminism and name retaining remains powerful and the name retain is seen by many as a feminist act. In this way the name retainers juxtapose tradition and feminism – feminism offers a new route around names and thinking about one's identity and the importance of that identity. Feminism is the opposite of tradition, but in a positive manner. It may be breaking down old 'traditions', but not without reason – the narrative of feminist action is in opposition to the narrative of 'tradition' for these participants. For name changers it is more complex. For those who define as feminist the 'standard feminist' becomes a problem for them, as explaining why they have taken part in this symbol of female subordination (name changing) while maintaining a feminist identity is difficult. Problematic categories arise: can an individual be a heterosexual, married, name changing, *feminist?*

The feminist bride?

A brief look at feminist bride websites will in itself show how powerful the pull of heterosexual marriage remains (see for example, www.feministbride.com; www.offbeatbride.com; www.feministwedding.com). The authors of these sites attempt to question the norms of marriage and the amount of money involved in the wedding industry, but there are conflicting and conflicted discussions of whether or not a feminist can change her name. *APracticalWedding.com* offers up the viewpoint that feminists can and do change names, but they do so after a period of thought and only when making the decision that is right for them (Keene, 'What Should We Call Me? Changing My Name as a Feminist Choice', 12th September 2012).

TheFeministBride.com however, advocates not changing names as the feminist decision: the owner of this website provides a video link to her own university presentation on this matter (Majkut, 'Why do Bride's [sic] Take Their Husband's Name?', 18th May 2012). There is no obvious answer to what a feminist should do in this situation: the 'standard feminist' would suggest not changing names but the individualised narrative of choice is also significant. On *www.feministwedding.com*, site visitors are asked to fill in a short quiz about name changing. The results show that most women who answered felt there was considerable pressure on women to change names, that they were irritated that it is seen as only a woman's problem, that they were in the main going to keep their own name, but that they expected backlash for this decision.

These answers may seem to be 'standard feminist' thoughts, but the final question on whether women who change names are making an anti-feminist choice proves difficult to answer, despite clear thoughts from quiz takers on all the previous questions: 30 per cent think it is an anti-feminist choice, 47 per cent think it is not, and the remainder are unsure (results examined on the 28/1/13). This is one short poll, but the comments on the other feminist bride sites reveal an equally mixed viewpoint on this question. *TheFeministBride.com* author has some support for her viewpoint from site users, but the idea of choice as more important to feminism begins to creep in; *ThePracticalWedding.com* article has a long comments section following it in which feminists argue this point, but most appear to

70 *Power, politics, and naming*

agree that feminism is about offering women *choice* and that all decisions should be supported not belittled.

As I have already argued, 'choice' is not a value-free concept and its increasing use within feminist politics is a concerning one. Though supporting all women's decisions seems tolerant and inclusive, it also encourages a lack of criticality around taken-for-granted norms and gendered practices. There needs to be an alertness to the wider patriarchal context in which decisions are being made. 'Choice feminism' and its close connections with a neoliberal discourse should be something the feminist movement confronts to ensure its political and emancipatory role is maintained (see Thwaites, forthcoming, online early view 2016).

The feminist bride websites show up something interesting about justifying one's actions with one's name and one's identity and the right to call oneself part of a group within a particular context: the name-retaining feminist need not justify herself, but the name-changing feminist must do so; within this circle the 'deviant' action is name changing and therefore needs an explanation and justification that name retaining does not (Scott and Lyman, 1968: 62). This was the only time in my research that it appeared that the name-changing participants had to justify themselves more than the name-retaining participants. The different groups one is involved in present different 'cultural' standards and contexts: whether one needs to justify oneself for an action depends on this context.

Conclusions

Naming and its connection with feminism is therefore a complex issue. It is clear from my participants and the feminist bridal websites that *retaining* one's name is connected with feminism and seen as a 'standard' feminist act. Nevertheless, the rhetoric of choice is very powerful and appeals to feminist sensibilities about opening up possibilities to women and giving everyone an equal chance in life to fulfil their potential and find happiness. However, these 'choices' can become uncritical and actually help to maintain the status quo. Feminist participants within my study – those that actively spoke of their feminist identity – were much more likely to retain their original name than those who did not mention feminism, and were able to account for their actions by mentioning a history of women's oppression, with which they associated name changing. However, not all of my feminist participants retained their name and their relationship to the 'standard feminist' ideal of name retaining was complicated; they were often angered and frustrated by it.

Naming is certainly political and, as my discussion at the beginning of this chapter and throughout will have shown, connected with various acts of repression, domination, power, and control throughout history. In the British context this connection between name changing and power is no longer explicit and no longer accepted by everyone. It, however, lives on in how the majority of my feminist participants understand the name change and hence their decision not to follow this norm. Its connection with gender, heteronormativity, particular ideals of the family, and social organisation of people into certain groups ensures the name change is still a live and contested issue within the current feminist movement.

Power, politics, and naming   71

The emotional nature of naming decisions has already begun to be highlighted in this chapter, by mentioning the idea that women are meant to do what is best for them to be 'happy'. In the next chapter, I will look in more depth at love, commitment, and the search for a sense of happiness in connection with naming decisions.

Notes

1 With thanks to Sage and *Feminist Theory* for use of some of the material printed originally with them, citation: Thwaites, R. (forthcoming April 2017, issue 18.1, with Early View 2016). 'Making a Choice or Taking a Stand? Choice Feminism, Political Engagement, and the Contemporary Feminist Movement'. *Feminist Theory*.
2 In his own narrative of his time as a slave, Douglass specifically used names to highlight the character of the person he was discussing. For example, Mr Sevier became Mr Severe. One does pronounce both the former and the latter in the same way, but Douglass wanted to show up his former master publicly and explicitly. Names labelled a person for Douglass, hence why his own was so important to him and why he changed it repeatedly until he felt comfortable (see Stepto, 2009).
3 Many thanks to Ben Vincent for permission to mention their blog in this book.

All Bible quotes taken from *The New English Bible*. (1970). Oxford University Press/ Cambridge University Press.

References

Benson, S. (2009). 'Injurious Names: Naming, Disavowal, and Recuperation in Contexts of Slavery and Emancipation' in G. vom Bruck and B. Bodenhorn (eds.) *An Anthropology of Names and Naming*. Cambridge: Cambridge University Press: 178–199.

Benston, K.W. (1982). '"I Yam What I Am": Naming and Un-Naming in Afro-American Literature'. *Black American Literature Forum*. 16 (1): 3–11.

Black, M. and Coward, R. (1998). 'Linguistic, Social and Sexual Relations: A Review of Dale Spender's Man Made Language' in D. Cameron (ed.) *The Feminist Critique of Language*. Abingdon: Routledge: 111–133.

Craven, C. (2007). 'A "Consumer's Right" to Choose a Midwife: Shifting Meanings for Reproductive Rights under Neoliberalism'. *American Anthropologist*. 109 (4): 701–712.

Daly, M. (1985). *Beyond God the Father*. Boston, MA: Beacon Press.

Giddens, A. (1996). *Modernity and Self-Identity*. Cambridge: Polity Press.

Hockey, J, Meah, A., and Robinson, V. (2010). *Mundane Heterosexualities*. Basingstoke: Palgrave Macmillan.

Keene, M. (12th September 2012). 'What Should We Call Me? Changing My Name as a Feminist Choice'. Available at: http://apracticalwedding.com/2012/09/changing-your-name-to-your-partners-last-name-as-a-feminist-choice/. [Accessed: 28th January 2013].

Leonard, J. (1990). *Naming in Paradise*. Oxford: Clarendon Press.

Livingstone, D.N. (2003). *Putting Science in Its Place*. Chicago: Chicago University Press.

Majkut, K. (18th May 2012). 'Why Do Bride's [sic] Take Their Husband's Name?' Available at: http://thefeministbride.com/history-of-name-change/. [Accessed: 28th January 2013].

Mills, C.W. (1940). 'Situated Actions and Vocabularies of Motive'. *American Sociological Review*. 5 (6): 904–913.

72 *Power, politics, and naming*

Mills, S. (2003). 'Caught Between Sexism, Anti-Sexism, and "Political Correctness": Feminist Women's Negotiations with Naming Practices'. *Discourse and Society*.14 (1): 87–110.

Pateman, C. (1988). *The Sexual Contract*. Stanford, CA: Stanford University Press.

'Sandra Fluke Cartoon Creates Controversy of Its Own'. (8th March 2012). *The Huffington Post*. Available at: http://www.huffingtonpost.com/2012/03/08/sandra-fluke-cartoon_n_1333404.html. [Accessed: 6th January 2016].

Schimmel, A. (1989). *Islamic Names*. Edinburgh: Edinburgh University Press.

Scott, M.B. and Lyman, S.M. (1968). 'Accounts'. *American Sociological Review*. 33 (1): 46–62.

Shipman, T. (3rd January 2013). 'How Feminism is to Blame for the Breakdown of the Family, by Left-Winger Diane Abbott'. Available at: http://www.dailymail.co.uk/news/article-2256850/How-feminism-blame-breakdown-family-Left-winger-Diane-Abbott.html. [Accessed: 24th January 2013].

Smart, C. (2012). *Personal Life*. Cambridge: Polity Press.

Spender, D. (1998). *Man Made Language*. London: Pandora Press.

Stepto, R. B. (2009). 'Introduction' in *Narrative of the Life of Frederick Douglass* (author Frederick Douglass). Cambridge, Massachusetts: Belknap Press: vii-xxviii

Thwaites, R. (forthcoming). Making a Choice or Taking a Stand? Choice Feminism, Political Engagement, and the Contemporary Feminist Movement. *Feminist Theory*.

'Who is Lucy Stone?' n.d. Available at: www.lucystoneleague.org. [Accessed: 24th January 2013].

Wintour, P. (3rd January 2013). 'Diane Abbot Outlines Plan to Curb Fast Food Shops'. Available at: http://www.guardian.co.uk/politics/2013/jan/03/diane-abbott-fast-food-curb [Accessed: 24th January 2013].

6 Maintaining the status quo?

Love, heterosexuality, and emotion work[1]

'Love' is a concept for which we have only one word in the English language, and this word has to encapsulate a great deal. It is a term which is defined in myriad ways, and is often linked with sexual desire (Hendrick and Hendrick, 1992: 5). Much of social, political, and economic policy is based on the 'natural' heterosexual relationship (see for example, Griffin, 2007): an idealised relationship, certainly within Western societies. Marriage is a pivotal moment in a person's life and is meant to join love and lust together in a public, legal celebration.[2] It remains both an individual and a collective experience (Mansfield and Collard, 1988: 30–31) though, as I shall show, name retaining attempts to control the public element of marriage.

Within the institution of marriage, women are expected to do a great deal of the care work for children and partners, as well as the housework, and continue to do this to a greater extent than men (Maushart, 2003). The unmarked and seemingly unnoticed quality of this unequal physical and emotional labour has been commented upon in previous studies (Mansfield and Collard, 1988: 35). As Askham's study (1984) shows, a movement into more structured roles occurs on marriage as stability is needed to maintain the relationship. In more recent work, such as Hockey et al. (2010: 179–180), men showed more awareness of the constructed inequality of labour in marriage and were attempting to come to terms with the inequality of emotional labour especially, but women remain the 'self-defined guardians of their families' emotional lives' (2010: 18). Mansfield and Collard's finding that performing traditional gender roles within marriage confirms 'normality' for those involved continues to have resonance (1988: 53). The 'emotional labour' (Hochschild, 2003a: 7) within relationships is rarely counted as work by those within the relationship itself, but is nevertheless an important contributor to its smooth running – work performed in the main by women. I wish to consider the unequal nature of love and particularly 'emotion work' (Hochschild, 2003a) in marital relationships in this chapter, and how naming decisions become a part of this work.

As Beasley et al. argue (2012: 1), the research on heterosexuality often focuses on the bad rather than the good, presenting it as either dangerous or dull. I do not want to argue that heterosexuality is a 'monolithic source for the inculcation and doing of heteronormativity' (Beasley et al., 2012: 2) or that there is never any pleasure or agency for women within this institution. However, the practice of

74 *Maintaining the status quo?*

name changing does not provide a highly progressive perspective on heterosexuality, showing instead a great deal of emotional labour on the part of wives and an element of exploitation of the idea, and feeling, of both love and commitment by husbands and others. Name retaining may well be a genuine attempt to change this situation, but it remains a small change on the margins of the norm. The ultimate day-to-day happiness of the vast majority of my participants with their decision is a crucial point to remember, and certainly not in every case do they feel subordinated by or to their husbands; however, the process by which they made their decision to change names and the assumptions surrounding the norm do not suggest egalitarian thinking processes or practices.

Name changing is seen as a sign of the woman's commitment to her marriage and is an encouraged practice in the British setting; as I have already shown, it remains the norm (Valetas, 2001: 2). The women who changed names often situate this action within a narrative of true love and true commitment. They take their action to be a symbolic sign and expression of these feelings, yet rarely comment on the unequal nature of this contribution. When situating their action within this narrative, women often implicitly or explicitly accept that name changing *should* be the woman's action. In so doing they manage two things: gendering who must do the public work of love and commitment, and masking the inequality behind the name change as ritual. The idea of giving up a part of selfhood as a sign of a woman's love for her husband is an ingrained idea. Name retainers also accept the ideal of love as egalitarian, but their thoughts and actions around names show an attempt to thwart the patriarchal nature of name changing and have the symbols of marriage live up to their egalitarian ideal. They attempt to control who knows they are a wife by refusing this public symbol of wifehood, and redefine ideas of love, marriage, and wifehood by retaining their name. I will discuss these ideas within this chapter, using empirical data, but first I will turn to the gendered structure of love and the ways in which this is justified.

Gendering love; gendering commitment

Love is not removed from social context (Jackson, 1993: 202) and should not be seen as too sacred, mystical, or biologically based to be exempt from sociological and scholarly scrutiny. It is a foundational emotion within modern society – our 'secular religion' (Beck and Beck-Gernsheim, 2004: 184), but the emotion is not an egalitarian one, and it works within a patriarchal social context: women do more 'love work' than men do, but this is hidden behind stories of biology, naturalness and free choice. In this section, I will examine the kinds of gendered work involved in love relationships and the stories used to keep this looking 'natural'.

Love stories: biology

The most powerful way of describing love is as a timeless, biological emotion, felt to be 'natural' (Johnson, 2005: 6). These stories around love paint it as an emotion women are 'naturally' more invested in: women are meant to be more

Maintaining the status quo? 75

in tune with their emotions and more willing to settle down and have children. Human behaviour is often justified in terms of animal behaviour, as love is seen as so 'natural' and 'hard-wired'. In scientific discussion of 'mate choice', it has been noted that the female of the species chooses her mate based on particular characteristics, and that, following Darwin, both sexes evolve characteristics which will appeal to the opposite sex (Fisher et al., 2006: 2173).

In these discussions, love is a part of biological processes which control the progression of evolution and are responsible for how we act and, in a fundamental way, who we are. This kind of discourse *fixes* gender and gendered behaviour. There are, of course, more nuanced discussions of the *intersection* of biological processes and society (e.g. Reis and Collins, 2004), but even these often ignore the *gendered* implications of their findings. Reis and Collins point out that young children identify with caregivers who provide for their physical and psychological security, but do not mention the probable gendered differences in identification and relationship that gendered care work will produce (Reis and Collins, 2004: 234). The kind of caring love they describe has an important gendered element. The social and historical context of love is therefore highly significant.

Instead of thinking of love as a natural basis from which behaviours and roles flow, we should consider it as a justification for social structures and norms. Love itself is a socially constructed emotion, based on gendered inequality, as I will go on to show. I will first consider the Western basis for the construction of unequal love by considering significant religious, philosophical, political, and ritual aspects, before briefly returning to the pervasive modern narrative of 'choice' and its part in maintaining the status quo in gendered relationships.

Unequal love

Love, Simon May argues, is the modern religion: 'no less attractive to the diehard atheist than to the agnostic or believer' (Simon May, 2011: 3). He claims that, within a Western context, the Hebrew Bible and Plato provide us with the most influential ideas about love to this day. However, he argues that the influence of the Bible has skewed human love into an unrealistic emotion in which humans have interpreted their own love as akin to God's love – unconditional and eternal (Simon May, 2011: 4). This is unmanageable for humans, he writes, as it is in fact a 'most conditional and time-bound and earthy emotion' and we have made it 'labour under intolerable expectations' (Simon May, 2011: 5). Love is about rooting oneself in the world and finding meaning for existence, particularly in a world increasingly sceptical about God; we need little else to feel completely at home (Simon May, 2011: 36).

The inequality of love is there from its first definitions. Love between God and worshipper is far from equal: the one owes their very existence to the other. The imagery of inequality continues in the many references to the relationship between Christ and his followers as bridegroom and bride, in which the woman is told to submit to her husband: 'Wives, submit to your husbands as to the Lord, because the husband is the head of the wife as also Christ is the head of the

76   *Maintaining the status quo?*

church – he himself being the saviour of the body. But as the church submits to Christ, so also wives should submit to their husbands in everything' (Ephesians 5: 22–24). Here marriage is used as the exemplar of unequal love, in which one party must be submissive, and this party is to be the woman (stemming back to the Creation myth). God and creation, husbands and wives, are set up as unequally, but perfectly, in love – in fact, their relationship is only sound if this element of inequality is present and understood.

Within Plato's *Symposium* the most highly valued of loves is that between an older man and a youth, in which the young man is most definitely the lesser in an unequal partnership of education and sex (Plato, 2005). In Plato we also find the first discussion of completion of oneself through another (without a heterosexual bias), the ability of love to bring out the best in the lover, for love to allow one to see the whole person in their beauty – physical, intellectual, spiritual – and to see others as valuable in a fundamental way (Plato, 2005). Between these two sources, we have the basis of modern conceptions of love in the Western world: as wonderful, transcendental, eternal, unchanging, and satisfying basic ontological needs, but also, *in the exemplars*, as unequal.

In more mundane everyday relationships we can see this inequality being learned: the child–parent relationship calls for total dependence of the one upon the other. The parent is meant to love but also discipline, meting out violence as chastiser when deemed necessary. The child learns that this kind of violence/discipline is a part of 'unconditional love' – the person with power in the relationship has the right to behave this way *because* they are the more powerful and that this is not only acceptable but recommended and taken as another example of a kind of 'true love'. This love is also dependent upon space – set within the home such love is acceptable, but no one outside the home has a right to use violence against the child as a sign of love. Both the relationship and the space of domesticity regulate what kinds of 'loving' behaviour are acceptable. The way we learn about love as children is as inherently unequal: it includes chastisement, and possibly violence, and this is most particular to domestic, familial relationships.

It is true that our marriage ceremony calls for life-long commitment: unchanging, constant connection with one other person until death. More recently this commitment has been conflated with life-long *love* also: modern marriage should be founded on love, almost to the exclusion of everything else. In discussing migration and mobility, Bauboeck (2012) commented that cross-border marriage is allowed when couples prove their *love* for one another. They have to show love through particular state-sanctioned means: photos, letters, and emails, for example. 'Marriages of convenience' are looked upon as appalling and underhand, but Bauboeck points out that this idea is very recent in its conception, as many people married for money, status, position, or in other words, convenience, in times past (Bauboeck, 2012).

Cross-border marriage shows how important an emotion love has become in proving genuine connection and relationship. It is state-sanctioned and state-approved, via particular tokens or 'proofs'. Couples originating from within one state may also have such 'proofs' of love for one another, along culturally acceptable lines, and often use marriage as the ultimate declaration of love for the other person. Love is an increasingly powerful justificatory message and has been put to good use in the debate around same-sex civil partnerships and marriage (see Woo, 2007). States may sanction and encourage marriage through tax-relief, and in doing so confirm their commitment to love within heterosexual couples and their families as an important socio-structural story. Such interest is, of course, not disinterested nor egalitarian, but neither is the emotion of love itself: hierarchy, tension, and power are built into the emotion we describe as 'love'. Being in love and looking from the inside out, as it were, to this claim, may make it seem preposterous, but this is a part of the 'masking' of the inequality that is inherent in love.

Studies from the 1970s and 1980s showed that, despite apparent changes in the socio-economic position of women, the inequality between husbands and wives persisted (Bell and Newby, 1976: 166) and that women continued to have their ideas and desires around timing of children and work overruled by their husbands (Leonard, 1980: 242–243). Though we are now more than 30 years on from these studies, their comments continue to ring true: more recent research has found that women's earning capacity does not necessarily relate to their power within the marriage as spouses look to preserve gendered expectations and minimise possible anxieties or arguments when a woman earns more than her husband (Tichenor, 2005). Following traditional role patterns remains common, though couples will often *say* they are acting in an equal manner.

The marriage ceremony is designed to differentiate maleness and femaleness (Leonard, 1980: 265) and, however people try to reinvent it, its symbols can and do continue to be interpreted in traditional ways, fixing values in people's minds and (re)creating group norms (Leonard, 1980: 265). Indeed, involvement in such rituals and ceremonies 'may cause people to feel particular sentiments, to accept norms and concepts, and to objectify and confirm certain social roles' (Leonard, 1980: 265). Symbols are important as they 'are, literally, effective' (Leonard, 1980: 265); paying attention to a symbol may be tantamount to accepting it (Leonard, 1980: 266). This adds to ideas of what is and what is not acceptable and correct.

In the case of name changing, following this ritual and changing this symbol of selfhood emphasises the idea that this is the most acceptable practice for women and that other naming ideas are problematic; maintains a separation between men and women in terms of their behaviour and action; suggests that women's selfhoods should be more turned towards family; and upholds the historical connection to the subsuming of a woman's identity into and under a man's. This connection, historically publicly and legally accepted, remains alive in terms of gendered relations and expectations. It therefore remains a symbol for a wider patriarchal system of gendered hierarchy, however the women in my study who changed their names actually feel about their own actions.

78   *Maintaining the status quo?*

Choice

The final narrative is one of choice, which I have already explored, but is worth reiterating here: the narrative of free choice maintains the idea that women change names with no other regard than for their own feelings and wishes. This ignores the many and pressing structural pressures and indeed the social ease there is in women changing last names, as well as the difficulty involved in following other paths. This does not add up to free choice, and this chapter should add to the evidence that naming decisions are not made with purely one's own heart in mind.

We can see then that love is created unequal and the discourses surrounding it are justifications for this inequality. Such arguments ignore the importance of gendered love to managing work within a patriarchal society. Love includes care and nurturance work, as well as putting others before oneself. Women do a great deal of this 'love work' within their families. This means others are catered to and cared for by women. It saves the state a great deal of money in terms of care being done within the home. Yet this is all hidden and masked behind the word 'love'.

'Love work' and 'love power'

The work involved in love has been discussed in part by Hochschild, through her concept of 'emotion work' (Hochschild, 2003a). To this I want to add my own terms: an element of 'conspicuous commitment' and call the whole (emotion work and conspicuous commitment) 'love work'. The emotional work of women conducted under the label of 'love' is a form of 'love power' which men have over women and can use to exploit them (Jónasdóttir, 1991: 17). Before exploring this, I will outline Hochschild's arguments as a reminder of her seminal work in this area.

Hochschild divides 'emotion work' into the private and professional, and within her definition of the 'private' falls the relationship between husband and wife. However, I would argue that marriage actually crosses the boundaries between these two definitions as both part of the private world and a highly public institution, meaning elements from both sides of her discussion are relevant. She argues that within institutions 'various elements of acting are taken away from the individual and replaced by institutional mechanisms' (Hochschild, 2003a: 49). In other words, roles are created for people to fill within institutions; within marriages there are normalised roles for men and women, with duties and responsibilities to be taken on. She goes on to argue that 'Many people and objects [are] arranged according to institutional rule and custom' and that the institution in this way becomes 'a director' and will 'alter the relation of actor to director' (Hochschild, 2003a: 49).

The institution of marriage has a history and its examples can be seen in the married couples women and men see around them growing up: not following such 'stage directions' in terms of behaviour is difficult. To re-emphasise a point made in the introduction to this chapter, falling into such roles and following the 'rules' of marriage is seen to *confirm* normality (Mansfield and Collard,

Maintaining the status quo? 79

1988: 53). People therefore, to a greater or lesser extent, *act* within marriage to ensure their sense of normality (both private and public) is confirmed, and name changing is one way of achieving this by following expectations: a technology of the married self. As Hochschild notes, institutional techniques for deep acting can be pervasive in 'suggest[ing] how to imagine and thus how to feel' (Hochschild, 2003a: 49).

'Deep acting' is a method of acting in which actors use their own real life experiences, feelings and memories to recreate a particular emotion on stage or screen by genuinely coming to feel that emotion, but Hochschild uses this idea when examining and describing everyday emotional experience. People will use past emotions, the daily 'props' of life around them, and their own abilities to manage their emotions, to come to feel in a particular way (Hochschild, 2003a: 42–43). Such management entails an understanding of the social expectations of how to feel and how to act in a given situation and to manage emotions to fit. On the day of marriage itself, and throughout married life, 'the formal rules that prop up an institution set limits to the emotional possibilities for all concerned' (Hochschild, 2003a: 53).

Marriage is meant to be built upon love – an all-consuming, passionate love, which is at the same time companionate and unconditional – and couples work to try and make it so, or at least make themselves feel that is what they are experiencing. Everyone within marriage must surely have to act at certain points in such a life-long commitment, but as Hochschild argues, women are more likely to act in this way than men because of their lower social status (Hochschild, 2003a: 57), meaning they need to work harder to find respect and credibility in everyday interactions. Rebecca Erickson's study found that women saw emotion work as an integral part of their work within the family and as a part of showing love; men saw it as a part of their interpersonal relationship with their wife and did not define it as central to their sense of self (2005: 348). Within an institution such as marriage, built on inequalities of status, within a wider patriarchal context of gendered inequality, women do more 'emotion work' than men; yet it often goes unnoticed and is usually accepted as normal, and even showing innate, unchangeable differences between women and men. As Hochschild notes: 'the deeper the bond, the more emotion work, and the more unconscious we are of it. In the most personal bonds, then, emotion work is likely to be the strongest' (Hochschild, 2003a: 68). Marriage is one such deep bond.

Such emotion work includes, in Hochschild's words, 'affirming, enhancing, and celebrating others' (Hochschild, 2003a: 165). Or, Erickson's definition, which is more specific to the marriage bond: 'Offering encouragement, showing your appreciation, listening closely to what someone has to say, and expressing empathy with another person's feelings (even when they are not shared) – day after day, year after year' (Rebecca Erickson, 2005: 338). Hochschild shows in her description how self-effacing such work is, with one self turned towards the glorification of another (here the idea of a 'secular religion' becomes particularly pertinent); while Rebecca Erickson argues that emotion work is repetitive, time-consuming, and difficult.

80   *Maintaining the status quo?*

Name changing is an act of just such emotion work, though it also contains another element of 'conspicuous commitment'. Such commitment is no private act between two individuals; instead it is a public proclamation, directed toward society at large and a matter of display. Name changing is a form of declaring wifehood and lack of availability to others. For some participants, it was also a way of claiming respectability and/or status, for example:

> At the time of marriage I had a baby out of wedlock and didn't want to rock any more boats by not changing my name – I wanted to be accepted and respectable.
>
> (P28: name changer)

> When I changed my name I took on a new identity as a married woman which I still feel very positive about. I feel my name gives me status in society and also confirms me as both my husband's partner and the mother of my children. I am proud of our identity as a family.
>
> (P61: name changer)

Putting the feelings of others before their own is a gendered framing rule (Hochschild, 2003b: 99) – women *should* put others before themselves, as it is women's role to care for other people first. This frame has been applied by my participants to their situation. They feel they *should want* to please others; this is a way of being seen as respectably feminine. For those who were ambivalent about these rules of feeling (their initial emotions did not fit with the framing rules) they most often used 'deep acting' to find contentment with their name change: working on their own emotions until they fit these rules.

Other people also worked on participant emotions. Husbands in general expected wives to change names: either both spouses had accepted this is what would happen and there was no discussion, or there was a discussion, and it was made clear that the woman should change her name, usually using very emotional means. For the close to 20 per cent of participants whose husbands became 'very upset' at the suggestion of their wife *not* changing, there was a significant pressure then placed upon them to do so. Usually the woman would accept the social and feeling rules in place for her and change her name. This act is then described as an act of love and/or a free choice.

Participants' work on feeling is therefore gendered, and it is a part of a wider social context of gender inequality, and of course what is/can be felt or even imagined to be felt relies on this social and historical context. The narrative of sacrificial 'true' love itself (subordinating oneself to one's partner), the gendered nature of this sacrifice within heteronormativity, and the idea of loyalty to one person are the context in which, despite other changes in women's position within society, the feeling of love inspires traditional actions on the part of women. Keeping one's name goes against this context, while name changing follows social and feeling rules. For those women who felt an initial ambivalence towards name changing they were caught between rules and their own feelings, but deep acting could secure adjustment and contentment with the name change; along with the important contentment of others. Of course women have agency and some did not

Maintaining the status quo? 81

do this deep acting, remaining ambivalent or unhappy; some acted to take their old name back. They were however a very small minority.

This appropriation of women's love by men – and indeed women and men of extended family and friendship groups – has been called 'love power' (Jónasdóttir, 1991). It is clear in the cases of conflict between spouses over names that love is being used to shape women's decisions and force them to conform to an idea(l). This use of love is exploitative: shoring up masculine identity and dominance of the family unit, while subordinating women's identities to these aims. I would argue that this is also happening in the cases of the name changers who did not question their change at all – the social gendered contexts of 'love power' have been accepted in a deep way by these participants and the 'love power' is implicit rather than explicit. To put this mostly theoretical discussion into context, I will now turn to the words of the participants themselves.

Name changers and the love narrative

Over 41 per cent of the 75 name changers (31 participants) in my study spoke explicitly of love, commitment, and pride in their marriage being connected with their name change: it was a significant justification narrative for name changing. The idea was that 'true love' and 'true commitment' were shown through this gesture:

> I decided to take on my spouse's name because I felt it would be more of a commitment to our marriage on my part. Proud of it.
>
> (P34)

> Wanted to 'complete the full marriage and change my surname, it made me feel more connected to my husband. . . . [wanted to show] my love and commitment by changing my name.'
>
> (P54)

> I loved my husband, it was nice to take his name.
>
> (P69)

The gendered asymmetry of this supposed gesture of love and commitment was rarely brought up by my name-changing participants; the idea of giving up a part of selfhood as a sign of a woman's love for her husband is an ingrained idea.

Participant 21 spoke a great deal about love and commitment within her interview, and the transformative effects they had upon her life. Describing her own feelings about sharing a name with her husband she said she enjoyed being close and feeling like a team together against the world. Marriage had brought her a great deal of security and a newfound self-esteem; she spoke of it in ecstatic terms:

> Everybody said . . . 'nothing changes when you get married', but my whole world changed, everything changed, it was amazing, for the better, [husband] says the same as well, it just makes you feel stronger, I don't know if it makes

you . . . makes you trust more, I don't know, this bond which just intensifies and . . . it just makes you more secure as well, with yourself, with your relationship, with everything else going on . . .

(interview data)

The name symbolised this new happiness and security and P21 was extremely pleased with her decision, despite previous reluctance to consider name changing. Yet it had taken marriage to bring this transformation about, and in this, P21 reflects a great deal of research into (heterosexual) women's desire to be married and achieve a sense of higher status and security through being loved by and loving a man (see, for example, Langford, 1999).

There were five explicit mentions of status in the survey by participants using the love narrative. For example, P61 said she wanted to be married to have 'the status of a married woman and be . . . Mrs'. She put this down to being a 'traditionalist' and wanting to be seen to be a part of a 'legal partnership'. Participant 62 also commented that changing her name '[conferred] a status and the sense of being in a relationship' which at that time in her life were highly significant. These women are both highly educated and have achieved a great deal on their own, but they still looked to the status of 'wifehood' and attachment to a man in marriage. Interviews brought out less explicit mentions of status, with women often unable to quite formulate this feeling into words. For example, P21 said:

Well, I think it makes us equal that we have the same name so that's a good to start with and the fact that we're Mr and Mrs kind of makes us . . . I don't think I'd have had Mrs if I'd kept my name. Mrs [OFN], no that doesn't sound right. I wouldn't have felt equal, I would have still felt lower . . . not lower, that's the wrong word but I would have felt . . . I dunno, it just puts you on an equal footing having the same name.

The feeling of being in some way unequal becomes apparent in this account, in which she cannot bring herself to accept that she felt 'lower', but that there was some inequality without the name change. These participants referred to the 'equality' of Mr and Mrs SameName and being seen by the outside world as a partnership. This suggests that, in a society in which there is gender inequality and women are on the lower end of the hierarchy, women look to access male power and prestige through marriage to feel that they have achieved a new status and can somehow use the gendered power their husband has accrued.

Further to this, and in agreement with Simon May's thesis of rootedness (Simon May, 2011), participants referred to a sense of security, commitment, and self-esteem coming from the name change:

Proud to have my husband's name; makes me feel wanted.

(P83)

There's a sense of security in being able to call myself 'Mrs Married Surname'.

(P115)

Maintaining the status quo? 83

Such positive rootedness in the world through the love of a partner can be wholly transformative. Participant 112 had been badly bullied at school, and her name was used against her. On marrying, she was delighted to 'embrace the future and move away from the past' by changing her name to that of the person she loved. The name change allowed her to move on and become someone she prefers – someone happier and more confident. Participants 95 and 113 also spoke of similar events in the survey: P95 said 'at the time it made sense' because she wanted to move away from the unhappy period of bullying and focus on a happier future, while P113 wrote:

> I hated my maiden name. I'd been bullied throughout school and, to me, [OFN] sounded odd and disjoined. . . . I got my degree with that name so it's still part of who I am, but I still don't like saying it or using it.

At the time of marriage these women found the possibility of moving their self-hood on through their partners and the transformative love that was being offered to them, using marriage and name changing as the legal and symbolic means of cementing this alteration. Love is transformative. It can change a system of belief, a lack of self-esteem, a feeling of insecurity or instability. However, the fact the loving response of women to this transformation is to give up a part of their selfhood raises questions about the gendered nature of this transformative power. Women expressing their feelings of being somehow lesser, and requiring a status boost, shows the wider patriarchal context in which name changing works: women's selfhoods are not considered as important as men's.

This can be further observed in accounts from just under 22 per cent of the 75 participants who changed names when they mentioned feeling that not to change names would have been problematic in terms of how they themselves, or their partners or families, would have viewed their commitment to the marriage:

> If I hadn't changed my name I would have felt like I was holding back from my marriage.
>
> (P2)

> It would have been like hedging your bets or not expecting the marriage to last [to retain].
>
> (P44)

> His family would have seen it as a serious snub not to change.
>
> (P111)

The above quotes show women attempting to 'do' love, commitment, and marriage appropriately: their 'love work'. My idea of 'love work' is similar to Hochschild's 'emotion work', except that is also encapsulates my concept of 'conspicuous commitment'. As Hochschild argues, women are more likely to do 'emotion work' than men, predominantly because of their lower status within society *as women* (Hochschild, 2003a: 162). This work 'affirms, enhances, and

84 *Maintaining the status quo?*

celebrates the well-being and status of others' (Hochschild, 2003a: 165). In caring, nurturing, listening, pre-empting, and actually putting the needs of the man first, women act to affirm, enhance, and celebrate men's well-being and status above their own: names are another part of this work. The name changers in my sample have internalised the idea that love and commitment equal a particular set of actions and acquiring of symbols *on their part*, and that this does not necessarily need to be reciprocal. In fact, their very attachment to their partner can be questioned if they do not follow the accepted gender rules around name changing – they may even question it themselves, as with P2. As part of their 'love work' they pre-empt and divert possible anger or discontentment from others by changing names, often with little regard for their own feelings. The feelings of their husbands and families are pushed to the fore in doing the appropriate 'love work'. In Cancian and Gordon's (1988) paper on emotion norms in marriage they note that 'self-help' and therapeutic guides to the 'marital emotional culture' are directed towards women (p. 310) and that women are expected to uphold the marital relationship – this emotional labour is divided along gendered lines (p. 311).

The political and patriarchal realities of this intimate relationship are unpalatable when love is meant to be a genuinely egalitarian emotion and when marriage is meant to be based 'solely on feelings of reciprocal love and thus be independent of external considerations' (Honneth, 2004: 142). Thus, most discussions of marriage, justice and love by the classic theorists ignore the negatives and the possible abuses within such an intimate relationship, and certainly ignore the gendered differences. These classic formulations of marriage have been crucial to law makers debating whether this intimate institution should ever be intervened upon. Hegel, for example, wrote that '[t]he union can be expressed fully only in mutual love and assistance', downplaying any interjection by the state (Hegel, 2008: 85).

As Honneth has argued, Hegel formulated the tension between justice and love as

> wherever in families rights that have a legal characteristic are put forward by a member, the moral substance of familial life has already been destroyed; for the relationships between the various members normally consist not in the exchange of rights and duties but in the mutual guarantee of care and attention.
>
> (Honneth, 2004: 152)

Hegel's model does not determine what and how many rights and duties are to be exchanged and does not put emphasis on them being equally reciprocal at all, but just that an expression of a need should be enough to have it satisfied by care. The problem is that Hegel's notion can restrict the needs of one member of the group to satisfy those of another (Honneth, 2004: 153), and ignores the fact that women do more care work than men. 'Love work' is done to an unequal extent by women.

Women 'do' the public signs of being in love and committing to a relationship to a greater extent than men. Men are usually allowed a great deal more freedom than women in choosing whether these signs are appropriate for them. It is here that names fit in: women are expected to show they are in love and 'off the market'.

In a supposedly individualistic society, women continue to act in a highly relational manner towards their husband and (future) children, sacrificing a part of their own selfhood for the wider family. This act is seen as loving and as showing commitment. The 'love work' of affirming, enhancing, and celebrating men rather than women requires women to deny their own self while affirming his (through using his name and getting rid of her own), enhancing his sense of selfhood as a husband with a (symbolically at least) dependent wife, and celebrating his selfhood by using his name and adding a link to his lineage and family tree, rather than her own. She 'conspicuously commits' by moving away from her own family (symbolically), becoming a part of his, and continuing that line. She must, as part of her gendered 'love work', think carefully about the feelings of others when she comes to marry: changing her name is a symbol of love and commitment and a way of ensuring her husband and his family feel valued and deferred to over her own.

Men do not have to show their love or commitment in this way, and do not face condemnation for retaining their own symbol of selfhood. Women do more 'love work' and are expected to demonstrate their love and attachment more publicly proving their status as 'wife' and their dedication to that one unit and no other: referring back to historical property laws around legal, biological heirs. Name changing, its symbolism and connotations, are a part of this 'love work'. Women are demonstrating how 'truly in love' they are; a story which may seem romantic, but hides the gendered inequalities of this submersion of self. All of this is gendered work that women do and men do not. Loving gestures are not egalitarian, and neither is love. Thus far I have spoken about the name changers and love, but where does the hypothesis of unequal love stand when applied to the name retainers?

The name retainers and love

The name retainers made no mention of love as a part of their decision. Their justifications for retaining their name focused on individual selfhood, feminism, and attachment to the lineage of their birth family (all of which are discussed in other chapters). The conspicuous commitment of the name change was a step too far for them – they had married and shown their love for and commitment to their partner through this act. This was perceived to be enough. They wished for love in marriage to be equal – adhering to the narrative of egalitarian love – and felt that name changing represented inequality. I will discuss these ideas in more detail below.

Nineteen name retainers (70.37%) were explicitly critical of the name-changing norm, speaking of it as unequal or unnecessary – usually citing the fact that women were expected to do something men were not:

> Why should women do this and not men? It is unequal and no one's business.
> (P85)

> [I]t is wrong that a woman's name badges her at any and every time in her life as belonging to a particular man.
> (P88)

86 *Maintaining the status quo?*

With discussion of inequality, feminism was also raised by the name retainers as a reason for not changing names, with 12 participants (just over 44%) citing feminism generally, women's studies courses, or explicitly using feminist discourse to reflect on how this norm represented men 'owning' women, or to reflect on the patriarchal history of the name change more generally. As well as discussing their sense of coherent and continuing selfhood as significant (see Chapter 8), these were the most significant reasons given for retaining names: feminism and an active dislike of the norm, two reasons that are closely linked. The more critical and even political reasoning of these women contrasts with the generally romantic and holistic reasons of love and unity given by name changers. Instead of love there was confusion, anger, criticism, or indifference to a norm name retainers did not want to follow. When asked in interviews about love and the idea that name changing shows 'true love' and 'true commitment', name retainers refused this idea, claiming that names did not express a person's love or dedication to another and that there were other, more important measures of these emotions. Marriage may still express love, but name changing does not.

Marriage, despite its unequal history, has been entered into by these women, but the idea of using obvious symbols to connect themselves to marriage publicly has been refused. Name changing, for the majority of these women, was explicitly pointed to as a symbol of inequality, but marriage did not have this stigma. This raises some interesting questions about narratives around marriage, as well as how name changing/retaining connects with the public world. I will explore these before investigating versions of heterosexuality to try to understand where participants are situating themselves within this organising principle.

Pervasive marriage; pervasive love

Participants have all married at some point in their lives and have therefore accepted the idea of marriage as an important symbol of their commitment and love. As P61 said, 'marriage itself' shows love and commitment. This narrative was rarely discussed in such explicit terms – only, in fact, when I asked about commitment and love pointedly with the five name retainers I interviewed. As with name changers then, love and commitment as shown through the act of marriage was assumed to need no articulation, but was instead taken for granted. It was the name as symbol that was viewed differently.

In my call for participants, I asked for women who had been married at some point in their lives; hence I implicitly asked for people who had accepted the idea of marriage; however, I had participants who had separated, divorced, and been widowed, and the idea of marriage as a symbol of love and commitment was not questioned. Though ideas of what marriage meant and what was to be expected from partners varied to some extent, participants were united in their belief that marriage showed love and commitment, whether they married in the 1940s or in 2011.

Cancian and Gordon argue that women in the 1940s were urged to be realistic about marriage and keep expectations low to avoid disappointment; while women in the 1960s were urged to talk about feelings and express love, with a large dose of deep acting recommended to change internal feelings (Cancian and Gordon, 1988: 315–316). This 'therapeutic model' continues to be relied upon today, though theories of modern reflexive selves suggest deep acting may be less acceptable to individuals content to move on when relationships become unsatisfying.

My participants do not easily reflect this research. For participants married in the 1940s, the more pragmatic and distanced terms in which they discussed their marriages came from the time that had passed between their husbands' deaths and the research taking place. One participant discussed how her husband had experienced what is often called 'love at first sight' when he saw her, assuring himself that she would become his wife. She herself did not feel this immediate recognition, but was shortly also wrapped up in this romantic narrative. I quote this (wonderful) story at length below to illustrate this point:

> I was going to a rather eccentric poets' party . . . given by a rather eccentric man and his very eccentric sister and . . . I got to the front door and as the door opened a man came out who was, literally my oldest friend, I mean we'd been babies together in India . . . and he said 'don't go in there, don't go, come and have dinner with me, it's awful!', so I was just about to leave when the host arrived and of course he said 'oh how lovely to see you' you know, so of course I couldn't go, so I walked into a room in this poets' party and my husband, he said that as I walked into the room he thought 'that's the woman I'm going to marry'. I, well . . . he was with another friend and in actual fact I rather fancied the other friend! . . . I travelled a lot at that time so I didn't see [husband] for quite some time but we happened to have a mutual friend so we met again in the house of this mutual friend and then . . . we were engaged within a week! I remember him saying 'I knew I'd meet you again', which was all very nice.
>
> (P7; interview data; name changer)

This does not suggest a lowered expectation of marriage, but a close adherence to a narrative of 'true love'.

It is also hard to suggest that younger participants are less pragmatic about their marriages. Women who had married in the 1970s and 1980s (and therefore should fit into the 'therapeutic model' of marriage) reflected on the sometimes difficult realities of their long relationships, coping with, for example, alcoholic and/or depressed partners, periods of separation, serious mental and physical abuse, and the death of children.[3] Apart from – and thankfully – the participant who had experienced sustained physical and mental abuse from her partner, these women had remained with their husbands. There was no sense of walking away from the marriage because it was difficult, but instead every attempt was made to keep it going. Though participants who had married in the 1990s and 2000s did mention the possibility of divorce ending their relationships – therefore accepting that marriage is no longer necessarily forever – there was no flippancy about this

88 *Maintaining the status quo?*

statement; instead it was perceived as an absolute last resort when all other methods had been tried to save the marriage. I could not perceive any sense of Bauman's modern individual, unable to make lasting relationships and unwilling to sacrifice anything of themselves to that relationship to sustain it (Bauman, 2003). Instead, the idea of love and life-long commitment was so utterly accepted by all participants that it was hardly mentioned.

Such silence is instructive. My participants are clearly from a historical period in which the importance of love to marriage is accepted and, perhaps, seen as increasingly important as other ties of family standing and duty become less significant. It also shows how pervasive the narrative of love as egalitarian and fulfilling actually is. As we make sense of our lives through the important narratives of today, we all look to our 'secular religion' (Beck and Beck-Gernsheim, 2004: 184) to help form coherent stories of selfhood and life narrative: love as narrative is used to justify certain actions, to the extent that it no longer needs to be openly narrated, but becomes a silent, assumed, culturally acceptable basis for these acts. The inequality of love and heterosexual relationships is not recognised or is 'forgotten' by participants; 'forgetting' must occur to allow the relationship to continue and for the narrative to have and give meaning (Anderson, 2006: 205), whether they changed their names or not. For the name retainers, marriage could be accepted, but changing names could not.

Refusing the name as symbol of love

The name as a symbol of selfhood is taken by name retainers to be too personal to change: for example, P40 felt it was so personal that even marriage was not a sign she had known her husband long enough to change such a sign of selfhood:

> I hadn't known my husband long enough to change to his name.

It is too deep a sign of selfhood to relinquish. Further to this, it is taken to be an obvious sign of marriage and wifehood and not something name retainers want to 'buy into'. They see the presentation of themselves to the world as 'wives' as unnecessary:

> Why should I present myself to the world as married? Men don't have to do this.
>
> (P46)

The name change is not a sign of love and commitment, as marriage is, but a sign of unequal gender relations – for some this makes it the very opposite to a sign of love, and working against this norm is the clearest way of displaying equality:

> It made our marriage one of equals, right from day one.
>
> (P16)

Maintaining the status quo? 89

The name retainers then, have a rather different idea of love than the name changers, and a different idea of what being a wife means. Love for them does not entail the merging of identities symbolised in the name change – they had been made a team by marriage and did not need any further public symbols of togetherness. They wanted to make sure the world saw them 'not purely [as] a wife' (P96); for some this was part of enjoying the confusion name retaining engenders in others:

> I also get a perverse delight out of explaining my decision to people and challenging their notions of wifehood.
>
> (P12)

Participant 12 has clearly reflected deeply on the symbolism of the name and its connections with ideas of 'proper' wifehood and heterosexual coupledom. To repeat, not all name retainers saw their decision in this way, but the majority did. As P44 (a name changer) said

> If you want to get rid of all symbols of marriage maybe that says something about how you feel about the married state and your acceptance of it and how you feel others perceive it.

Her argument is sound: the name retainers want to rid themselves of this particular symbol of marriage and its connotations, and therefore how others may perceive them because of it. They do not refuse all symbols of marriage, and have clearly accepted the 'married state' itself, but have refused to be entered into public discourse as 'Mrs Married Name'. The name acts as a relational connection between public and private worlds and these women do not wish to be known necessarily as wives. They see marriage as an *aspect* of their life, and indeed a rather private one between them and their husband: '[it's] no one's business' (P85). These women are attempting to privatise their commitment: the opposite of the 'conspicuous commitment' enacted through the name change. They are refusing this aspect of love work.

Beck and Beck-Gernsheim (2004) have argued that love is losing its rules and that we must all choose how to create love within individual relationships. In this way, it is increasingly privatised. I would also argue that there is more fluidity around certain aspects of love than before, but I do not consider this phenomenon to be quite as advanced as they do. Other authors have argued that the privatisation of family life has ensured that little attention has been paid to the amount of work women do within the home (Luxton and Fox, 2009: 15–16) and that this system of gendered labour is rarely questioned because of its private status (Worts, 2009: 325). Privatisation appears only to have had bad consequences for women.

However, this attempt by my name-retaining participants to privatise their commitment is an attempt to both thwart and play down their move against the norm. In privatising their commitment to the married state by refusing the shared name as a public symbol of wifehood and 'true love', they attempt to take control of

90 *Maintaining the status quo?*

how they are perceived by the public and to control the connotations of wifehood that come along with marriage. In so doing they refuse the definition of 'true love' and 'properly committed wife' set up by the norm, while at the same time attempting to keep their marriage as an *aspect* of their lives which will not necessarily be publicly known or discussed. Names, these participants assert, are not important to love, but instead are important to selfhood. Love may be relational, but selfhood is seen as individual and should not be changed, threatened, or compromised by the name change. They situate this attempt at changed selfhood, for the most part, within a feminist discourse of gendered inequality, but love remains free of political connotations. Hence, marriage can be entered into, but names must not change. Marriage, they contend, need not be a public institution, needing outward scrutiny and support, but a fully private and purely personal relationship: this brings the relationship as close to Giddens' idea of the 'pure relationship', which has only an 'internally referential system' (Giddens, 1996: 6). Commitment is not quite pre-supposed, as Giddens suggests, but needs few public statements and symbols; in fact, it is better without them. Therefore, there is not a dominant trend towards this kind of relationship in my data, but a minority of participants who could be described as coming close to this idea.

The discussion thus far has displayed a rather traditional view of heterosexuality and what roles men and women play within it; however, this change in the definition of 'true love' and 'true commitment' from a wife, which the name retainers discuss, is a way of restructuring what it is to be 'properly' heterosexual.

Heterosexualities

Hockey et al. (2010) discuss the concept of hegemonic heterosexuality, a concept that is not fixed, and is situated within a specific cultural and historical context, but that gives meaning to heterosexual lives and a kind of yardstick from which to measure normality (Hockey et al., 2010: 180). Many varieties of heterosexuality come under the institution's 'umbrella' (Hockey et al., 2010: 180) and name changing/retaining divides up two versions of what it is to be heterosexual and live a heterosexual selfhood.[4]

Hockey et al. explore the way in which heterosexuality is naturalised and '*made to disappear*' (Hockey et al., 2010: 6. Emphasis in original). It is constructed continuously, but also performed continuously and creates its own norms and ideals (Hockey et al., 2010: 6). Name changing on marriage is – within Britain – one such heterosexual ideal, regulating women and men along gendered lines of what it is to be heterosexual, to be a wife/husband, to love, to be committed, to show all of this publicly, and what kinds of behaviour to expect from a partner. Those women who change names reach out to this particular ideal, which is a part of our hegemonic heterosexuality at present.

Name retainers are pushing at this idea of hegemonic heterosexuality and attempting to redefine wifehood along a less public line, in which the selfhoods of women are preserved through the continued use of their own name. For them, heterosexuality continues to structure their lives as they marry and become wives, but they play down the public aspect of this, attempting to keep marriage and love firmly between them and their husband. Removing the public aspect from such a highly public institution as marriage is, at present, extremely difficult. Along with the gendered aspects of power, particularly in reference to naming, and to be discussed in relation to gendered selfhood in Chapter 8, the action of name retainers is perceived by the general other as strange – it is an attempt to undermine a patriarchal norm, redefine wifehood, keep marriage and love purely private matters, and maintain/justify the maintenance of selfhood through name retention. It is a new version of heterosexuality, which points towards a reflexive modern self, but as yet is lacking in credibility and is hard to achieve. It is certainly not the free choice of Giddens' (1996) reflexive modern agents.

The action the name retainers take can perhaps best be summed up by the term 'quiet subversions' (Beasley et al., 2012: 67). This type of subversion occurs when a person departs from a norm of the more 'traditional' heterosexual relationship, with the example that Beasley et al. (2012) use being long distance relationships. Instead of following the norm of cohabitation when forming a committed (married) heterosexual relationship, these couples have decided to/must remain apart. Despite the fact this arouses suspicion about their commitment to each other (2012: 70), most couples express their happiness with living a rather unconventional heterosexual life (2012: 82).

The subversion arouses suspicion from others, requires justification, and requires planning and active thinking on the part of the couples involved. This kind of subversion is therefore very similar to that of the name retainers in my study, who have departed from the norm by retaining their names though they have married in the 'traditional' manner (as opposed to continuing 'just' to cohabit). Equally they have to be able to justify their actions in a way name changers do not, and their actions can arouse suspicion in others, who question their commitment. 'Quiet' does not mean participants were not vocal about their reasons for retaining – indeed they were expected to account for it in a way name changers were not. Instead it brings into focus the fact that, despite choosing an unusual path in one area of the institution of marriage, the name retainers in my study have otherwise followed 'traditional' routes – heterosexual marriage and monogamous love. Name retaining is recognised as a genuine possibility for women on marriage, though it remains a possibility little taken up and therefore a relatively difficult decision to make. This makes it a 'quiet subversion': a small but significant action going against the heteronormative grain.

The last name is a connection between couples, but is one that can be extended to children and wider family. Understandings and perceptions of family are also significant to discussions and decisions around names. The next chapter will examine this issue in detail.

Notes

1 With thanks to Inter-Disciplinary Press for their permission to reuse my original chapter from one of their edited collections, with citation: Thwaites, R. (2014). 'Love Stories: Naming Decisions and Narrative in Contemporary Britain', in S. Petrella (ed.) *Doing Gender, Doing Love: Interdisciplinary Voices*. Oxford: Inter-Disciplinary Press: 193–217.

92 *Maintaining the status quo?*

2 This book focuses on heterosexual marriage and name-changing practices. See Stocker et al. 2014 for more on homosexual (male) partnerships and naming decisions.
3 These themes came out during the interview process when women perhaps felt more able to go into something so personal once they had met me. They also had more time to expand upon these themes.
4 I sampled for heterosexual women, but two participants openly told me they were bisexual, and there may be others who did not desire to reveal this information; however, being within such a heterosexual relationship is to be organised by heterosexuality. Indeed, heterosexuality is an organising principle even for those who do not live in heterosexual relationships.

All Bible quotes taken from *The New English Bible*. (1970). Oxford University Press/ Cambridge University Press.

References

Anderson, B. (2006). *Imagined Communities*. London: Verso.
Askham, J. (1984). *Identity and Stability in Marriage*. Cambridge: Cambridge University Press.
Bauboeck, R. (2012). 'From Migrants to Citizens – and the Other Way Round: Migration and Mobility in the European Citizenship Constellation'. Unpublished paper presented at Goethe University, Frankfurt.
Bauman, Z. (2003). *Liquid Love*. Cambridge: Polity Press.
Beasley, C., Brook, H., and Holmes, M. (2012). *Heterosexuality in Theory and Practice*. Abingdon: Routledge.
Beck, U. and Beck-Gernsheim, E. (2004). *The Normal Chaos of Love*. Cambridge: Polity Press.
Bell, C. and Newby, H. (1976). 'Husbands and Wives – The Dynamic of the Deferential Dialectic' in D. Leonard Barker and S. Allen (eds.) *Dependence and Exploitation in Work and Marriage*. London: Longman: 152–168.
Cancian, F.M. and Gordon, S.L. (1988). 'Changing Emotion Norms in Marriage: Love and Anger in U.S. Women's Magazines since 1900'. *Gender and Society*. 2 (3): 308–342.
Erickson, R.J. (2005). 'Why Emotion Work Matters: Sex, Gender, and the Division of Household Labor'. *Journal of Marriage and Family*.67 (2): 337–351.
Fisher, H.E., Aron, A., and Brown, L.L. (2006). 'Romantic Love: A Mammalian Brain System for Mate Choice'. *Philosophical Transactions: Biological Sciences*. 361 (1476): 2173–2186.
Giddens, A. (1996). *Modernity and Self-Identity*. Cambridge: Polity Press.
Griffin, P. (2007). 'Sexing the Economy in a Neo-Liberal World Order: Neo-Liberal Discourse and the (Re)Production of Heteronormative Heterosexuality'. *The British Journal of Politics and International Relations*. 9: 220–238.
Hegel, G.H.W. (2008 [1821]). *The Philosophy of Right*. New York: Cosimo Classics.
Hendrick, S.S. and Hendrick, C. (1992). *Romantic Love*. Newburg Park: Sage.
Hochschild, A.R. (2003a [1983]). *The Managed Heart*. Berkeley, CA: University of California Press.
Hochschild, A.R. (2003b). *The Commercialization of Intimate Life*. Berkeley, CA: University of California.
Hockey, J., Meah, A., and Robinson, V. (2010). *Mundane Heterosexualities*. Basingstoke: Palgrave Macmillan.

Maintaining the status quo? 93

Honneth, A. (2004). 'Between Justice and Affection: The Family as a Field of Moral Disputes' in B. Roessler (ed.) *Privacies: Philosophical Evaluations*. Stanford, CA: Stanford University: 142–161.

Jackson, S. (1993). 'Even Sociologists Fall in Love: An Exploration in the Sociology of Emotions'. *Sociology*. 27 (2): 201–220.

Johnson, P. (2005). *Love, Heterosexuality and Society*. Abingdon: Routledge.

Jónasdóttir, A. (1991). *Love Power and Political Interests*. Örebro: University of Örebro.

Langford, W. (1999). *Revolutions of the Heart*. London: Routledge.

Leonard, D. (1980). *Sex and Generation*. London: Tavistock Publications.

Luxton, M. and Fox, B. (2009). 'Conceptualizing "Family"' in B. Fox (ed.) *Family Patterns, Gender Relations*. Don Mills: Oxford University Press: 3–20.

Mansfield, P. and Collard, J. (1988). *The Beginning of the Rest of your Life? A Portrait of Newly-Wed Marriage*. Basingstoke: Palgrave Macmillan.

Maushart, S. (2003). *Wifework*. London: Bloomsbury.

May, S. (2011). *Love: A History*. New Haven, CT: Yale University Press.

Plato. (2005). *The Symposium*. London: Penguin.

Reis, H.T. and Collins, W.A. (2004). 'Relationships, Human Behaviour, and Psychological Science'. *Current Directions in Psychological Science*. 13 (6): 233–237.

Stocker, R., Hardy, S., and McKeown, E. (2014). 'A Novel Gay "Right" of Passage: Constructing Ceremonies, Conveying Meaning and Displaying Identities through Men's Civil Partnerships', in S. Petrella (ed.) *Doing Gender, Doing Love: Interdisciplinary Voices*. Oxford: Inter-Disciplinary Press: 219–247.

Tichenor, V.J. (2005). 'Maintaining Men's Dominance: Negotiating Identity and Power When She Earns More'. *Sex Roles*. 54 (3/4): 191–205.

Valetas, M.-F. (2001). 'The Surname of Married Women in the European Union'. *Population and Sociétés*. 367: 1–4.

Woo, J. (2007). 'Sexual Stories go to Westminster: Narratives of Sexual Citizens/Outsiders in Britain'. Unpublished PhD Thesis, University of York.

Worts, D. (2009). '"Like a Family": Reproductive Work in Co-Operative Setting' in B. Fox (ed.) *Family Patterns; Gender Relations*. Don Mills: Oxford University Press: 325–342.

7 'Displaying' and 'doing' family

Genetics, social connection, and respectability

As Luxton and Fox (2009: 3) have argued, the word 'family' is often used with an assumption that its meaning is uncomplicated, though in fact defining the concept can be difficult and complex. The Office for National Statistics defines families as being started 'when people form partnerships or marry or when they have children' (Macrory, 2012: 1). The Oxford English Dictionary gives several definitions of family, showing how the word has changed in use over time, but also how difficult it is to accurately describe this grouping in the present day (see *Oxford English Dictionary Online*). There are political discourses surrounding 'the family' and from the political Right a narrative of maintaining 'family values' (Grice, 16th July 2013). When used by politicians, it becomes clearer that 'family' can have a myriad of meanings, sometimes with highly political overtones. What we have called family in Britain has changed over time and can be defined differently, depending upon context. However, the nuclear, heterosexual family, connected by genetics, continues to be a dominant conceptualisation of 'normal' family life and still underpins much political and economic policy (Griffin, 2007). The family name is one way of displaying and 'doing' family (Morgan, 2011) within contemporary Britain; it is a process of 'kinning' (Nordqvist, 2014: 271) which has the potential to be both fixed and creative (Mason, 2008). It is also one way of delineating and keeping track of families in Britain by the state: the norm of one family unit sharing one name delineates relationships of care and protection. This family is often presumed to be a biological, heteronormative one and, when not possible, this remains an ideal to strive towards, rooted by its name into past, present, and hopefully future too. These issues will be discussed in more detail below, starting with the importance of genealogy and the name's place in creating a lineage.

A genetic lineage

'The family' can be traced back in time through its genealogy, indicated most commonly through a family tree. This kind of tree pictorially represents genetics, heterosexual relationships, and gendered relations, with female 'lines' frequently seen as secondary to the male lines which 'continue'. Female lines are seen to 'end' on marriage, as the family name does not get passed on but instead 'dies' as the woman takes on the name of her new family. In fact, despite the continued genetic connection passed from the female line to her children, the lack of a name being passed on comes to take on more significance, with participants in my own sample describing themselves as 'the end of the line'. Therefore, names appear to trump genetic connection in the British context of family creation, despite the social and personal significance of genetic connection between family members. This means that even when genetic connection cannot be established the norm of one name in one family can signify these connections in place of genetics.

Genealogy makes blood ties meaningful (Kramer, 2011: 385). Genealogy as a pastime has been justified as a means to know about oneself *in the present*, as we are all made up of those who went before (Mason, 2008; Kramer, 2011: 385). Genealogy is a line between past and future, situating individuals and giving them a history; a person sees themselves as meaningfully 'in time' – placing oneself in a family tree is a temporal placement (Kramer, 2011: 386). Yet it can almost provide immortality, as the line stretches on after death and descendants remember the life of the dead person (Kramer, 2011: 386). The dead still play a role in personal life and behaviour. Traits and habits which are related to the dead person can be seen as part of identity creation in the living – or as a burden of expectation. The dead are felt to 'reappear' through the living in how a person looks or acts. Social death is expected to come with biological death, and yet it would seem this is not always the case (Kramer, 2011: 392): people live on in the looks, mannerisms, and viewpoints perceived as meaningful for the relatives left behind.

However, genealogy is not necessarily considered a positive thing; a sense of self is not always to be found in one's lineage, especially when the people of the present view this lineage as meaningless history (Kramer, 2011: 387). Indeed, being clear about one's genealogical background could actually close off possibilities for 'creative imaginings of past realities' and the possibilities this can leave open for selfhood (Kramer, 2011: 387). Biological bonds, after all, can be seen as 'random' and 'alternative forms of sociality can be equally important' – close friends, for example (Kramer, 2011: 387) – and this most especially when the historical bonds of a lineage are distant and no longer emotionally meaningful for the living. Creating meaning through imagination is key.

Nordqvist's work (2014) on reproductive technologies and lesbian couples building families is pertinent here. The new forms of family that are created by the possibilities opened up by reproductive technologies are of increasing interest to sociologists (Finch and Mason, 1993; Mason, 2008; Nordqvist, 2014), and the area of kinship affinities is also increasingly being studied (within families created by reproductive technologies and beyond) (for example Finch and Mason, 1993; Mason, 2008). The parents in Nordqvist's study (2014) used imagination and creativity, as well as more scientific and biological connections to consider, imagine, and create kinship affinity. This could be done by parents trying to find sperm donors with similar physical characteristics to them or similar interests, seeing, for example, musicality to be something which could be genetically passed on. They tried to ensure their children would feel rooted within their families by creating kinship narratives around their origins, as well as creating particular types of connection between donors, biological parents, and social parents, whether that

96 'Displaying' and 'doing' family

meant fully involving donor fathers or allowing them limited or no access to allow the role of the 'social' parent to take precedence over any idea of a biologically connected parent. The imagination used, in response to unusual origin stories and potential family form, worked in tandem with a knowledge of what 'normal' families look like to create suitable kinship affinities for children so that they felt rooted and involved in meaningful relationships.

As Mason argues (2008), there are a variety of different ways in which sociologists can think about kinship and the meaningfulness of kinship affinity. She argues for four axes of kinship affinity: fixed; negotiated, creative; ethereal; and sensory (Mason, 2008). Naming is a form of kinship affinity which can seem fixed and 'given' but has many possibilities for creativity and negotiation, and therefore stretches across the first two categories Mason outlines. Names can be given and shared in traditional ways, continuing norms of kinship and intelligibility, but they can also be used to created normative looking families where, biologically, they may not exist; furthermore, they can be used to create all sorts of new and varied family and kinship connections. Family is about those in the present who are close to an individual and are meaningful in some way and names are a part of displaying that to both self and others. Fitting oneself into a family can be seen as a highly collectivist activity, in which relational bonds in the present (as well as links with past and future members of the family) are sought to be kept alive. Yet, there is also a narrative of finding the *self* within the family, which is a more individualistic stance.

I want to analyse how participants understand this process of family creation and the forming of a family identity, in both its relational and individualist aspects. Who is meaningful and what makes them so varies, but biology is an important part of the story within the Western context. Yet, as Edholm argues (2009: 22–23), biology is 'socially defined' and even those prohibited by incest taboos from forming relationships has changed over time and between societies. My participants are British and live within a context of shared understandings of what counts as biological and what relationships are acceptable or otherwise. However, their conception of family is not always related to biology, and even when it is this does not mean their relationships with biological kin reflect the ideal bonds of care, love, and support which are often seen to flow 'naturally' from blood ties. Some participants questioned the idea that names can be a marker of family in a time of rapid social change, or as useful in making sense of their own (childhood) experiences; however, this did not mean they were totally averse to attempting to use names to define their own family unit as adults. Some participants spoke of names as the clearest and easiest way of defining families; others were less convinced that names were significant at all.

It is this varied and complex construction of family and family identity that I want to consider in this chapter and how names are a part of displaying and 'doing' this unit which remains so foundational to British society and its organisation. Participants linked practices of naming with children and other family, and described how they created their idea of 'the family' and what family means to them. Names hold an important place in these discussions but the story is not straightforward. I will explore ideas of biological and social family in my sample, how participants 'do' and display family, respectability, and how children fit into naming decisions.

Names: biological or social?

In constructing family, it became clear that biology and heritage (or lineage) as markers of familial links were complex ideas for participants and that names were an important part of their understanding and expression of how they viewed their 'true' family. This came across in both name retainers' and name changers' accounts. For example, P53 (name changer) discussed how her father left her when she was five and that she felt no connection to him or his name at all. This link, though biological, was not emotional or 'alive' for her in any way, and changing her name finally removed the last connection to a man she did not know and who was not part of her life. Participant 40 (name retainer) felt that because her father was adopted and had no biological 'roots', she should keep his name and make sure she played her part in ensuring *he* felt rooted. Implicitly she was suggesting that she would build a lineage for him, using the name as the social sign of this lineage, and that she would build it through her own biological connection to her father and her children.

The conflation of biology and lineage can be seen in this account: P40's father does have genetic 'roots' somewhere but he does not know them so this link is not alive to either him or his daughter. Equally though, the people who raised him are not mentioned or considered as 'rooting' him in the world: this has to be done by his daughter and her children through their *biological* link. Though I speculate when I say her father's name would not be that of his biological parents as an adopted child, it is likely he is carrying the name of his social parents – despite their lack of ability to 'root' him, according to this participant, that name is nevertheless the start of a biological lineage. The disruption of biological lineage can be smoothed over by the name.

Further to this, the reactions of family groupings added to the complexity of biological understandings of family versus the social connection of names. When women changed names participants spoke of feeling 'claimed' by their in-laws – not all of them appreciated this! Participant 43 (name changer) spoke of her irritation at feeling claimed, while P62 (name changer) found to her 'disgust' that her family felt they could tell her she was no longer one of them after marrying and changing her name. Though this was half in jest, P62 found it unsettling and said it was because her family is 'quite patriarchal' and thought about 'these things' in a traditional manner.

The flip side of this is when participants were pleased to be seen as more a part of their husband's family, to the extent that they spoke of taking on his heritage in becoming a part of his lineage. Participant 97 (name changer) spoke of being close to her husband's family and linked to their genealogy after her own parents passed away: she considered her own line as a 'dead-end', despite having given birth to a child who is genetically a part of her own biological lineage. Her own

98 'Displaying' and 'doing' family

line symbolically died with her parents; she then changed names and felt she lost her last symbolic and public connection to them – her husband's line has taken precedence and is real in a way her own is not. The name change displays the end of one line and the continuation of another.

Participant 120 (name changer) spoke of becoming a part of her husband's Scottish heritage and being proud that she and her children now share in it: she felt she had no real roots to speak of in any particular geographical location, having moved around a lot as a child, and said, 'I like the idea of having Scottish heritage.' The name provided this social and symbolic link and showed complete acceptance of her by his family. Though she herself has no immediate genetic link to Scotland she has taken on that heritage and talks about it as if it were her own. For these participants the social and symbolic link of the name to people and places has come to be as, if not more, significant than biology as we usually understand it in Britain. The social relationships formed by marriage and name changing have come to take on a biological significance, as if the lineage they have joined truly does run in their blood.

Straightforward acceptance of biological connection as understood in the British context and direct mapping onto names was, however, also a major theme. Name retainers in particular spoke of the connection with paternal grandparents, fathers, and other family members on their father's side:

> I wanted to keep my father's name. . . . I'm proud of it. The name [and the family] are famous in the French Caribbean and even in France.
>
> (P1: name retainer)

> My dad died in 2009 and I wanted his name to continue . . . grief has made me reconsider a lot of things.
>
> (P51: name retainer)

Family members were often inspirational figures rather than people participants had known: P88 (name retainer) said there were many 'strong women' on her father's side and, in her interview, P96 (name retainer) spoke of the link back to the Suffragette movement that comes through her name: 'there's the background of that name which I could trace back to the Suffragettes which is important to me.' It was not therefore purely a connection with their father, but with the wider paternal family; this had inspired a close affinity with that last name and its history and name retainers did not want to be parted from this. The name for these participants is valuable and is therefore a positive signifier; names lacking in positivity lack value (for some participants after divorce, for example) and can therefore be discarded.

However, just over 50 per cent of name changers noted feeling connected to their (birth) family history, so this feeling of connection was not necessarily lost once the name changed (see Figure 7.1). And, both changers and retainers noted feeling close to their mother's side without a naming link: family is, of course, about more than just names.

'Displaying' and 'doing' family 99

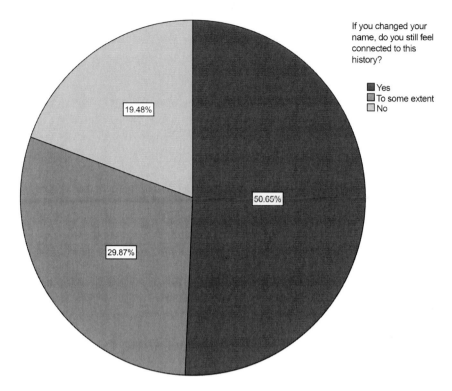

Figure 7.1 Whether name changers still feel connected to their birth family history (Percentage)

'Doing' and displaying family

In Chan's description of family practices in Hong Kong some ideas of how modern families are constructed come to the fore: participants spend time on both paid and unpaid (care) work, invest heavily in child-rearing, and spend time with nuclear and extended family groups (Chan, 2012). Chan's participants were no longer close to their partners, but it can be assumed that if partners were still close spending time together would be important to their idea of family too.

Other forms of family creation are also viable when relatives and partners do not offer the support and emotional bonding necessary: large networks of friends, for example, may provide an exciting and rewarding way of creating a kind of family (Chan, 2012: 35–36). Many varieties of family are possible and Britain is seeing increasing diversity in family forms created, for example, through divorce and remarriage. However, this may contrast with how 'doing' family is described and what is actually aspired towards: despite the reality of different family forms and possibilities for who could be included under the banner 'family', the desire to adhere to the norm and display a certain form of family remains. This form of family may be perceived to be the most 'proper' or respectable, which will be discussed further below.

100   'Displaying' and 'doing' family

My participants reflected this divide between the norm and the possibilities. In interviews, I asked a variation on the question 'what says "family" to you, other than names?' and participants talked around ideas of spending time together, sharing memories, and also biological connections in a genetic sense:

P21: Emm, being together I suppose, sticking up for each other, yeah, yeah . . . covering up for each other I suppose, if one of us has got in trouble, one of them being drunk and having to sneak them into the house without mum and dad noticing, that kind of thing! So, I'd say teamwork really . . . but equally with mum and dad, I've supported mum and dad quite a lot and they've supported us, so yeah I'd definitely say being a team . . . (name changer).

P100: . . . spending time together and therefore having the memories, yeah, yeah . . . and I would say that for me the the . . . particularly the blood relationship is important, that whole blood is stronger than water kind of thing . . . (name changer).

There are various ways of 'doing' families (Morgan, 2011). However, in a time of rapid social change, a variety of family forms are proliferating and my participants mention their awareness of these forms of family becoming more normal and everyday. Participant 113 (name changer) wrote of how 'society can deal with different names now' and P85 (name retainer) notes that there are now 'three names in my family' and that she expects sharing a name to become less common. This kind of comment can then be juxtaposed with the desire by just over half of my participants to agree that name sharing in families is either 'very important' or 'quite important', and with the fact that most women in my study did change their name (75 out of 102) (see Figures 7.2 and 7.3).

The narrative of proliferating family forms has given rise to the idea that the importance of sharing one last name in a family is in decline. Yet participants continue in large numbers to adhere to the norm. The numbers and the qualitative data do not correspond in my study, and the question is why?

Klett-Davies claims that family forms are indeed proliferating. She gives evidence of a great deal of research pointing towards this fact, and says:

Children are routinely raised in 'complicated' family structures. Families now include a mix of cohabiting parents, stepfamilies, single-parent families, those in civil partnerships and those in living apart together (LAT) relationships as well as the 'traditional' nuclear formation.

(Klett-Davies, 2012: 122)

New Labour pushed for more recognition of other family forms, not just the heterosexual couple with children (Klett-Davies, 2012: 123), but right-wing stories of the 'state-dependent single mother' are commonplace (Grice, 16th July 2013): social anxieties are displaced onto scapegoat groups, and the gendered, sexualised, classed, and arguably raced figure of the single mother is an easy target.

'Displaying' and 'doing' family 101

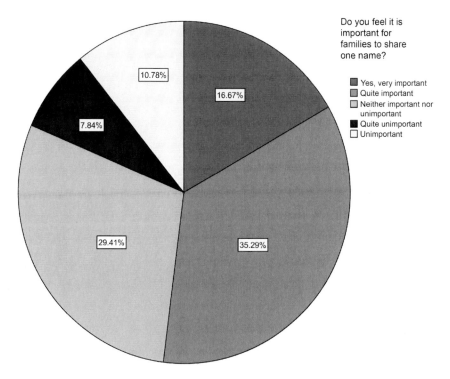

Figure 7.2 To what extent participants think it is important to share one name within a family (Percentage)

Instead of investigating the poverty of single mothers in terms of gender or other social positionings, women are urged instead to marry and maintain their children within wedlock. Tensions over new family forms are visible.

Participants in my study reflect this tension. Participant 27 (name changer) noted that she had worked with families with several names due to the break-up of the stable, married, nuclear unit and that the family link was 'lost a bit'. Participant 36 (name changer) felt children would be singled out if they did not share a name with their parents, believing the way to show you are a unit is to share a name – for her varied forms of family, symbolised by various names, are a problem, certainly for children who may be asked to account for the situation. This last participant's observation does not suggest an ease with new family forms – if people (in her comment, children) must routinely justify their behaviour there is no sense of the normalisation of diversity. Also, to refer back to Figure 7.2 on sharing one name within a family, my participants in general were happy to allow 'others' to do as they wished, but 'for themselves' wanted to change names and share a name within the family unit. The divide between 'us' and 'them' was clear.

Names and family forms are intimately connected and the two are often conflated – names are even used as a shorthand to refer to varied family forms with,

102 *'Displaying' and 'doing' family*

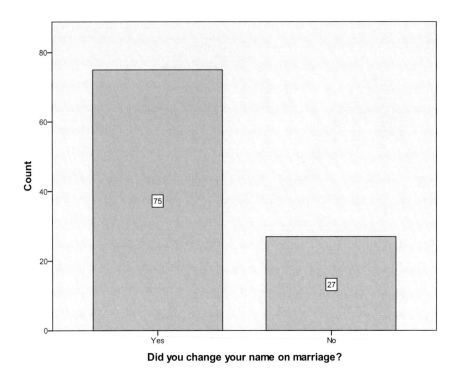

Figure 7.3 Whether participants changed names on marriage (Count)

for example, P68 (name changer) wanting 'everyone in my grown-up family to have the same name as a sign of togetherness'; she felt she did not belong anywhere in her 'split family' as a child as she did not share a name with everyone. Having a different name from other family members was a painful experience for this participant as she was often called to account for it and therefore had to experience the pain of her parents' separation every time she did so. Her different name was both painful in itself – as it symbolised her feeling of not belonging – and because it was connected to the wider pain of her parental break-up. As sharing a name is such a significant part of displaying the 'correct' family form in Britain, it is unsurprising that the two are connected so intimately. It is a means of 'doing' and displaying family (Morgan, 2011), and the 'right kind' of family at that; names can recreate ideas and practices in a dialectic process.

Using this line of argument, I claim that what is considered the 'proper' family form – heterosexual, married, nuclear unit – at this historical moment is reflected in the sharing of one name. Though family forms may be changing and diversifying, there remains a certain unease around this change. Names therefore connote the family form which is considered ideal. In this way participants' attempts to create what would look like biological links through the social connection of

'*Displaying' and 'doing' family*   103

names makes sense: biological relationships, as we understand them in Britain, are the ideal family relationship and attempting to construct them out of names is an attempt to claim this ideal. The norm of sharing one name also feeds into the unease with new family forms – people are discouraged from innovation (see Chapter 9 also). They are also discouraged because of the stigma which remains a part of not adhering to the norm.

Respectability and the naming norm

Skeggs argues that heterosexuality is associated with respectability, and that certain types of positioning are therefore distanced from this normative form of sexuality: 'Black and White working-class women *and* the lesbian' (2001: 118. Emphasis in original). Therefore, equal access to heterosexuality's respectability is not possible: some women will find they must work to maintain it even if they define as heterosexual. This is equally true for those who transgress the norms of heterosexuality, though those with class and racial privilege could, arguably, cushion themselves from the stigma to a greater extent than those without such privilege. As Skeggs notes, heterosexuality

> is where subject positions such as mother, wife, girlfriend, are defined and institutionalized through a process of iterability, a regularized and constrained repetition of norms, a ritualized production, into which we are implicated on a daily basis. . . . Heterosexuality is continually given legitimacy through its repetition and through the silencing and delegitimation of any alternatives.
>
> (2001: 120)

The naming norm in Britain acts as one of these repeated norms, itself part of the larger ritual of marriage – the taking part in which, my data show, remains the most acceptable route as an adult looking to commit to another person and, especially, to raise children. When women do not follow this norm their respectability can be called into question, as will be outlined below.

Participant 76 shows how tension arises when, on the one hand not being married or having children outside marriage is believed by the participant not to be a moral problem, while on the other stigma continues to exist and pressure to conform is felt. She said she felt 'no compunction' at having had her child without being married and that her husband did not feel strongly about marriage either, but that it was such a 'step change' for her life course (becoming a mother at 39) that she felt she *should* get married. There was no other explanation for this than the feeling that such life changes should prompt marriage. It appeared that societal pressure was impacting upon this participant and, whatever her political views and her rational level of feeling that conforming to social norms was not important to her, she felt it necessary to marry.

Interestingly, this participant describes her actions in terms of her child – her *child* wanting her to marry and, eventually, all use one name for the sake of schools. She said that if her child had wanted her to legally change her name, she

104 *'Displaying' and 'doing' family*

would have. However, her child was very small and unable to make such decisions. Instead it would appear that social norms of heterosexual respectability came into play for this participant: she therefore married and used her husband's name while her child was young.

Participants who retained names experienced reactions which questioned their feminine respectability, in terms of acting as a wife 'should', through questioning their love and commitment, as has been discussed in the previous chapter. However, there were further examples of questioning respectability coming from those working within institutions, showing the ingrained nature of connecting one-name-one-family with respectability:

> I was told on coming to the UK that it would be easier for benefits etc. if I have his name.
>
> (P63: name retainer)

> [Using his name at school and for the NHS] to save confusion and to prove my kids are mine.
>
> (P84: name retainer)

> I will use his name in [schools/doctors] if there are emergencies and they have assumed, as it's easier for them.
>
> (P96: name retainer)

The confusion – and sometime pointed remarks – that participants encountered encouraging them to share names with their husbands acted as reminders that, in the UK, one name is normal and understandable. It is also, of course, related to the fact that children are generally given the father's last name. The *intelligibility* of families depends on adherence to this norm. Stepping outside the norm requires explanation and can engender judgement. Women are questioned as to their relation to their children, and their lives are made difficult by this institutional confusion. This was more noticeably a problem for women with children who did not share names: it was the lack of a clear social connection between mothers and children that was especially problematic.

The mother–child relationship is made intelligible by the shared name. I would argue, in fact, that the bureaucratic system has been set up in response to this practice as our society has become more dependent on paperwork. This has cemented the norm into daily life at a time in which the norm could in fact begin to be challenged. Not to fit into these bureaucratic boxes is to be a problem, both in the sense of causing the authorities problems in registering a person and in the sense of being unusual and therefore difficult. Respectability comes from *not* being unusual and difficult, and from fitting into bureaucratic forms. It would appear that the institutions of modernity, and the associated organisational bureaucracy, regulate which naming decision many women make, how they then form a sense of self from that name, and how gendered power relations are (re)created via these practices (see more on bureaucracy in Chapter 9).

The reality of this questioning and the worry over it certainly push women who might otherwise keep their own name or who have been ambivalent about the naming norm to change names. Participant 30 (name changer) is an example of a person who has come through this particular process of decision-making.[1] She noted that her baby had been the 'catalyst' for this change, as one name 'creates more of a family' and it was important the three of them be united. She worried over the change because 'I'm a very independent person and want to keep my own name as it is my identity from before marriage', but also wants to 'feel I am starting my own family and feel that having my husband's name will help with this'.

Her OFN had close and emotional connections to her family in the north of England who had 'influenced everything I am today'. As a sign of this feeling of independence and 'identity before marriage' she is not going to change her name at work: 'I've made a reputation for myself . . . it's a major part of my life and very important to me' (this separation of work and home will be discussed further in the next chapter). Nevertheless, having a baby has meant that this name could no longer encompass her identity once she became pregnant: somehow her own name was now inadequate and her husband's name would be able to give her a sense of 'starting my own family'. Becoming a mother and being recognised as such was significant enough for P30, and others like her, to change names despite an earlier decision to retain.

Participant 51 (name retainer) suggested that 'children not having their father's surname is a more unusual decision than a woman not taking her husband's name' and, from the evidence in my study, she seems to be correct as eleven of the eighteen name-retaining women who had children had given their children their husband's name. Five women in my sample did, however, give their children their name, and two double-barrelled. Participant 3 (name retainer) noted giving her children her name 'especially because I was unmarried', though she had always wanted to give her children her name. It is clear that, though the decision remains unusual, it is not impossible by any means to do new things with the names of children. This does not, however, make the reactions many women experience from loved ones and institutions less meaningful and the fact that those retainers considering having children made comments such as 'having children might make me reconsider my decision – or we'd both have to' (P101: name retainer). These comments show the one-name-one-family idea has an imaginative and emotional pull beyond marriage.

Though most participant accounts implicitly discussed respectability, P28 (name changer) *explicitly* mentions respectability. She had given birth to her first baby before she married and spoke of the stigma surrounding that event and how it ensured her name change: 'I wanted to be accepted and respectable.' At the time of her marriage (1970s) she said that name changing was 'normal and expected' and that she gave it no real thought. She said that in the 1970s there was little discussion of naming decisions on marriage and 'a great deal of stigma attached to women who had a different name to their husband or her children'. Marriage and name changing ensured her respectability: following the norms and 'making up'

106 'Displaying' and 'doing' family

for her past 'unacceptable' behaviour helped her to regain a sense of stability and respect from those around her.

Participant 28 did marry in the 1970s, and the stigma of a child born before marriage was greater at this point in time. However, that stigma has not completely disappeared. The most respectable and normalised course of action remains marriage and name changing before having children. My participants, whatever their decision, generally wanted to be married before starting a family:

> Emm, well to be honest we probably would have been quite happy just continuing to live together but we've both come from stable families so, em, felt that, em, marriage was quite important really and we wanted children and although I wouldn't have minded not being married when we had children our preference was to be married so I guess that's why we did that. It was the catalyst to start thinking about it, it wasn't the only reason, but if we're thinking of having children then hold on we need to start thinking about getting married as well . . .
>
> (P24: interview data; name changer)

The justifications for this action were usually around stability for children. Marriage is connected with stability and responsibility (Askham, 1984) and provides a certain framework of care, resources, and public recognition from which it is socially acceptable to build a family. Despite other possibilities for family formations in which one could raise a family, participants preferred to marry and raise their children within this setting: the importance of traditional heterosexual rituals remains in place. The significance of stigma and respectability also remains in evidence: transgressing the norms of heterosexuality is an act of distancing oneself from its respectability (see Chapter 9).

The respectability of heterosexuality rests on a number of things: ideas of sexuality generally as 'uncivilised' and needing to be rigidly policed, displays of independence as unfeminine, the othering of those who transgress norms, and the social shame placed upon acts and agents of transgression. Skeggs (2001: 121) has claimed that displaying any form of sexuality was equated with being 'other' through colonial discourses about the 'uncivilised', 'baser' races in colonised countries – nature, lack of cleanliness, and base instincts being set up in opposition to civilisation, cleanliness, and restraint. Skeggs argues that white working-class women were also connected with this 'impurity' and sexuality in opposition to white middle-class women, during the nineteenth century (2001: 122).

Though her argument remains true, from this investigation it can be argued that the desire to be respectable and removed from conceptions of 'base' sexuality is also important for middle-class women. Middle-class women are also positioned on the negative side of such binaries as listed above due to their being women. They are not cushioned from the need to be perceived as respectable by their class position – they instead must look to maintain strict codes and appearances of respectability so as not to lose this (class) privilege. To be seen to be sexual remains a difficult position for middle-class women to inhabit, as much as working-class women. My sample is, in the main, middle class:

'*Displaying' and 'doing' family* 107

they are highly educated and in professional jobs. Yet their class privilege does not enable them to ignore codes of respectable femininity. The intersections of gender and class here are highly important. Nearly three-quarters of my sample followed the normative rules of heterosexuality, remaining connected to their respectability.

The place of children in naming decisions

The importance of mother–child relationships in accepting the norm have been briefly touched on, but this was such a significant theme for women considering name changing that it deserves closer attention. Women generally looked to their future and familial identity when name changing – they considered the future children they may have and thought very positively about them sharing a name. One name would bind them together as a family unit, giving them all a sense of camaraderie and of being part of a team, and children would feel secure and safe in the knowledge they were part of a family. Some women felt, from their own childhood experiences, that sharing a name was significant to a child's development in terms of feeling safe and happy. Naming children with anything other than one name was generally deemed too complicated for the child and others to cope with – and indeed, it seems that more than one name in a family *is* too hard for many institutions to cope with, though not necessarily for children themselves, as will be seen below.

The pull of one name in a family – a 'family name' – is very strong (see Figure 7.2). Women discussed wanting to share a name with their children, changing names after their children were born, or loving the feeling of pride they had in knowing they shared a name with their children:

> Felt happier with my name as time went on, but especially once my children were born.
>
> (P9: name changer)

> I only changed my name after having children. I wanted a 'family name'.
>
> (P11: name changer)

> I wanted to share my name with future children.
>
> (P19: name changer)

It seems one-name-one-family continues to be an important public symbol of what makes a family. Finch argues that names 'map family connections' and 'constitute . . . family relationships' (Finch, 2008: 710). It is also seen as something which helps children to feel secure enough to build up a sense of themselves within the family:

> [Helps children] 'understand who they are and where they come from'. [It gives them] 'security and self-esteem'.
>
> (P61: name changer)

108   *'Displaying' and 'doing' family*

[The children] feel a sense of identity from it.

(P83: name changer)

These viewpoints reflect what Nordqvist (2014) found in the creation of families using reproductive technologies, where families which may be seen as unusual or new in formation attempted to ensure a process of kinning was followed which would provide children with a sense of belonging and security within the family. Genetic connection, resemblances, capabilities, and capacities may be some of the ways of displaying this connection, but names are also significant markers of this, particularly within the British context.

In fact, many women felt so strongly about this 'kinning' they would retain their husband's name even after divorce to provide that security and continuity for their children. Participant 23 (name changer) felt sharing a name was 'right' so that her 'children felt we were all a family' and security was to be maintained by her keeping her name after divorce, while P26 (name changer) kept her husband's name for her son's sake, despite making her feel she is still a part of her husband's life. This is another example of women putting the feelings of others before themselves (Woodhouse, 1988: 380) – here the security of their children must come before their own desires and wishes, however detrimental this may be to the woman's own health (Day Sclater, 1999: 180).

The idea that children do feel a sense of security from the shared name can be seen in some descriptions by the women of their own childhoods. Participant 31 (name changer) did not want her own children to face the questions she did about why she had a different name from the rest of her family; P68 (name changer) came from a '"split" family as a child' and 'wanted everyone in my grown-up family to have the same name as a sign of togetherness'. Some participants expressed annoyance at the idea of children having to 'explain the unexplainable' (P33: name changer) if parents did not share a name. Participant 33 continued with the idea that children like to belong and fit in and that it is unfair on them to be expected to face questioning about their name. This argument assumes the norm of women changing their name is correct and unchangeable, and that women who decide to step outside of it are putting their children in a highly uncomfortable position. It is an argument which continues the stigma attached to name retaining. It suggests that women who truly care about their children would not put them in this position for the sake of their own interests, playing on cultural ideas of motherhood and sacrifice. These (normative) arguments are a powerful statement in defence of the importance of belonging to sense of identity – both individual and familial.

Belonging

There was a desire to belong to a new family unit of one's own making in my sample. Participant 18 (name changer) spoke of one name making you feel you belong somewhere and P120 (name changer) noted that she likes and enjoys 'belonging to a family' and is very happy to be part of the strong family heritage which her name symbolises. Other participants reflected upon the move from their birth

'Displaying' and 'doing' family   109

family to that of their own family. Participant 31 (name changer) felt she did not belong in her original family and puts this in part down to names and what they symbolised for her. Her father left when she was young and had no contact with her after that; when her mother remarried she was left with her biological father's name and was the only one to have it. She felt left out and wanted to rid herself of it and be a part of her own family, all sharing a name. She considers her original family name merely the name of the man her mother was married to at the time of her birth and nothing more. For other participants, this sense of movement from the single to the married state brought about some sense of separation from their parents, siblings, and other birth family because they had moved into a new couple identity, which name changing reflects.

Belonging can be utilised 'as a concept that allows for a person-centred, dynamic and complex approach . . . that understands people as active participants in society' (Vanessa May, 2011: 367). Belonging can be used to examine the interrelatedness of self and society (Vanessa May, 2011: 367) and has been defined as 'a sense of ease with oneself and one's surroundings' (Vanessa May, 2011: 368), central to identity (Weeks, 1990). It is about recognising what an individual has in common with some and what separates that individual from others. In a state of belonging, we can be completely ourselves (Vanessa May, 2011: 368). Belonging connects the individual and the social, and this is significant because

> our sense of self is constructed in a relational process in our interactions with other people as well as in relation to more abstract notions of collectively held social norms, values and customs.
>
> (Vanessa May, 2011: 368)

Shared understandings of the group, who makes it up and how people within it behave, can be claims to belonging: this certainly suggests an idea of family. The question remains, however, where these collective rules come from. The decisions about who 'we' are, are usually made by those with power and therefore belonging has its own power hierarchy (Vanessa May, 2011: 369). Vanessa May provides a cultural example of ethnic minorities in Britain having their claims to be British rejected (2011: 369), and in my own research, I found that the idea of belonging may be shattered when decision-making around identity is taken out of the hands of the individual: the women who had not been consulted about their thoughts on their own name as children were the ones left confused and unhappy. Belonging is a political and collective concept, as well as an individual one; it is emotional for someone wanting to feel at home and political when trying to claim 'space and . . . recognition' (Vanessa May, 2011: 369). If individuals are not involved at every level of decision-making around their own identities and sense of belonging they may come to feel insecure.

Rowe argues that any sense of belonging is dependent upon positioning, saying '[l]ikewise our belongings are conditioned by our bodies and where they are placed on the globe' (Rowe, 2005: 36). The sense of belonging engendered by the sharing of a name with other family members is therefore entirely culturally dependent: people in other countries will have other ways of showing their inclusion in a group and will be dependent on them for a sense of security and feeling at home. Rowe (2005: 16) argues that love is conditioned by these positionings: what and who we value is a part of where we live, while the fact displays of love are policed along cultural lines has been shown in the previous chapter.

The relational nature of selfhood is built up within conditions of racialised, sexualised, gendered (and so on) positionings – this includes who we desire to set up a family with, the kinds of people we may want our relatives to be, and the ideas we will pass onto children. Families are enmeshed in webs of power. Sharing a name therefore encircles a family grouping, bordering off their particular position and displaying to the world their sites of (or lack of) privilege; names help to create and display units of organisation within society. However, this belonging is an entirely constructed feeling and as such relates back to the feeling work mentioned in the previous chapter: there are socially scripted ways of coming to feel a sense of belonging, which is, in itself, a socially constructed feeling.

Belonging is a part of the everyday when it works, so 'to belong' is really to not have to consider it (Vanessa May, 2011: 370). It is when we become aware of going about our daily routine and feeling a sense of unease and/or disruption, that we feel a lack of belonging (Vanessa May, 2011: 370). Vanessa May contrasts this concept with Bourdieu's *habitus*: Bourdieu's concept shows how people feel a place is 'natural' through habit and use, whereas the concept of belonging allows theorists to understand how and why people can be in an everyday and familiar setting but feel estranged from it (Vanessa May, 2011: 370). Belonging is 'bound up with being able to act in a socially significant manner that is recognized by others' (Vanessa May, 2011: 372), and one name in a family continues to be a socially recognised norm.

However, belonging was not discussed as a wholly good thing by participants, and some questioned the ability of name sharing to create a sense of belonging at all. Participant 27 (name changer) wondered whether a mother keeping her own name could actually be 'a positive influence on children's abilities to maintain their individual identities'. However, she still maintained that, within the system we have today, sharing a name in a family is important. The question arises as to what children themselves think.

Hayley Davies' work on what Australian children think of their family name shows that children are aware there is often more than one name within a family – many of them live in step-families or have half-brothers and sisters – and that different surnames do not necessarily mean 'not family'; however, it also shows that children still subscribe to the assumption that women will change their names on marriage and children share the names of their fathers in societies where this is normative practice (Davies, 2011: 559). This assumption remained in place despite even their own name having been changed over the course of their life due to a mother's remarriage (Davies, 2011: 559). The children participating in Davies' study show the tension between the norm of one name signifying a family and their knowledge of the fact families are now more fluid: they cite other factors

'Displaying' and 'doing' family   111

such as laughing and talking easily with one another as a sign of family which can override the lack of a shared name (Davies, 2011: 561). However their interactions show that they expect 'full' siblings to share a surname, but understand that those who do not share a surname may still be part of a wider family or kin network (Davies, 2011: 561).

This research shows that children have a nuanced understanding of names and family connections/relationships – the (adult) idea that children need to share a name with parents and siblings to feel part of the family is not true in any straightforward sense. Children, as Davies' argues (2011: 555), remain the recipients of adult decisions around their names in most cases, and it is the parents who are investing the most in naming their child, what that name represents, and who they are visibly connected to through that name. However, children are a part of the wider patriarchal framework and re-iterate the assumptions of patronymic naming practices and the heterosexual familial imaginary, whatever the fluid situation of their own families (2011: 567): *real* – in the sense of 'fully biological' – families should be connected by name. The place of children in the decisions of the women in my study was shaped by their own experiences as children, their ideas about belonging, and thoughts about the necessity of being intelligible as family in the public domain, as understood in British society. To reiterate, others – including the generalised other or society – play a large part in ideas of family and belonging.

The significance of one name for name retainers

For women who retained their name the descriptive statistics show a large number of this group feeling it is neither important nor unimportant to share a name (see Table 7.1).

When looking at the written comments in conjunction with the numerical data, it becomes clear than many of these women were struggling with the tension between their own ideology and the belief that sharing a name can bring a family

Table 7.1 Whether it is important to share names by naming decision (Count)

		Did you change your name on marriage?		Total
		Yes	No	
Do you feel it is important for families to share one name?	Yes, very important	16	1	17
	Quite important	32	4	36
	Neither important nor unimportant	18	12	30
	Quite unimportant	5	3	8
	Unimportant	4	7	11
Total		75	27	102

112 *'Displaying' and 'doing' family*

together – the patrilineal norm. Participant 5 (name retainer) said that ideologically she would say sharing is not important; however she can understand it practically. Participant 76 (name retainer) said that it is quite important to share a name and she feels her child was affected by this once she started nursery. A small number of participants noted that not sharing a name with their husband could become more of a problem for them if/when they have children (see Figure 7.4). As P3 stated, it is often the event of having a child which pushes women to change names even if they are not keen to do so for themselves. It seems that this norm is strong enough to make even those women who have decided to retain their names on marriage agree it is useful in promoting a sense of togetherness, belonging, and making things easier for those 'others' outside when they come to have children.

The desire to look like a close family who belong to one another in a symbolic and public way causes tension in the thoughts of these name-retaining participants, though of course has not yet brought the majority of them to change names. The reality though, that their decision is often ignored in the face of other people finding a family name by which to call the entire unit, shows how the norm can be upheld by other people in spite of the woman making a less usual decision. Her individuality is subsumed under the wider group identity, which stems from the husband/father.

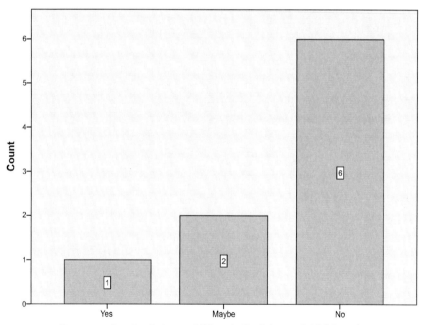

Figure 7.4 Childless name retainers considering having children in the future and impact on their naming choice (Count)

'Displaying' and 'doing' family   113

There were other women though who found sharing a name to be completely unimportant and even stressed their own experiences as displaying this, either in their own families now or when they were children. Participant 48 (name retainer) sums this up neatly saying '[families are] collectivities of people with all sorts of relationships.' She grew up with a brother with a different name and with foster siblings and truly believes what you call yourself 'shouldn't matter a jot'. It is only important to 'feel your own name, whatever that might be'. As P48 notes, it is often other people who make this important. Only P16 expressed her certainty that sharing was entirely necessary and highly important, but she was in the position of her husband having taken her name and her children having that name as well (see Chapter 9). She was the only participant to express such certainty over the norm, though perhaps in part because her situation was very unusual: despite following the accepted and expected pattern of everyone in a family sharing one name, it is her name which is shared.

Name-retaining participants were far more likely to have given children their name or a double-barrelled name than the women who changed their names (see Figure 7.5 for what name retainers did with their children's last names).[2] For P12

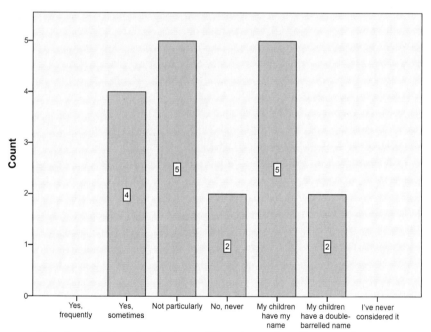

Figure 7.5 How name retainers felt about not sharing a name with their children (including count for those who do share and double-barrelled children's names) (Count)[*]

* The pilot study I carried out suggested women would be more likely to give their children their husband's name even if they retained their OFN themselves, hence the wording of this question.

114 *'Displaying' and 'doing' family*

(name retainer) it was important that her children have her name 'since I did all the work in producing them'. The couple double-barrelled their surnames as her husband wanted the children to have his name too. She feels this is not ideal and believes that children should have their mother's name as 'fathers often contribute so little, or are off the scene.' She argues that it makes 'little sense for children to have their fathers' names'. One woman had double-barrelled her child's name, but later her husband said he felt it would make their daughter think he did not recognise her so they changed their daughter's last name to only her father's. Double-barrelling remains an uneasy option for some: they feel it can portray a lack of togetherness and, in this case, a lack of love and recognition, despite the fact it would appear to be the most inclusive option. I discuss double-barrelling further in Chapter 8.

It could be argued that name-retaining participants are more individualistic than their name-changing counterparts: they look to their own set of desires and their own future before considering that of a family or wider group identity, and in that sense, come close to Bauman's descriptions of the more selfish later modern actor (Bauman, 2003). However, I would argue that these women had often considered future children and a family identity and their part in the creation of this unit. They felt either that they obviously biologically and in a very primal and basic way 'owned' and were connected to their children so did not need to share names (biology trumping the social role of names); or they showed their connection through the social link of sharing *their* name with their child; or they double-barrelled to give a more inclusive and balanced name to reflect the roots their child had, and in so doing they were actually considering a wider, family identity and inclusivity for their child. The fact one-third of the name retainers (9 out of 27) did not have children could actually be down to age, and most of them noted thinking about having children in the future – and this, as noted, could be a point at which they reconsider their naming decision. Children and the importance of being seen and understood as a family clearly have a significant impact on women's naming decisions.

Conclusion

The name links people to others. It acts as a connection between private and public worlds. It can express ideas of biology, social connection, love, and care, or be an uncomfortable reminder of relationships now lost or meaningless. The name cannot stand alone, but is made important by what it represents – and what it represents, and the significance of this, are socially constructed. It is a part of our social fabric in terms of how we organise and understand those around us and we try ourselves to produce these understandings by using names strategically as part of a process of 'kinning' (Nordqvist, 2014). It is brought to life by real relationships and the important, meaningful connections it represents and as such is significant to selfhood, the theme for the next chapter. As P113 (name changer) states:

> My name does represent me but only because I've built up friendships and relationships with people who identify me with emotional feelings and

moments in their lives. My name identifies me in an ID sense but I've made [my] name live and breathe and exist in the wider world by using it.

Notes

1 At the time of taking part in the research P30 had not finalised her name change, but she was in the process of completing it and made her desire to be considered a 'name changer' clear.
2 The name-retaining participants who gave their children their husband's name in the main seemed unconcerned about this as they felt it was obvious they 'owned' their children (biologically), but were irritated by increasingly being called by their husband's name themselves once children came along.

References

Askham, J. (1984). *Identity and Stability in Marriage*. Cambridge: Cambridge University Press.

Bauman, Z. (2003). *Liquid Love*. Cambridge: Polity Press.

Chan, A.K. (2012). 'Doing Family, Contesting Gender and Expanding Affinity: Family Practices of Married Women in Hong Kong'. *Families, Relationships, and Societies*. 1 (1): 25–41.

Davies, H. (2011). 'Sharing Surnames: Children, Family and Kinship'. *Sociology*. 45 (4): 554–569.

Day Sclater, S. (1999). *Divorce: A Psychosocial Study*. Aldershot: Ashgate.

Edholm, F. (2009). 'The Unnatural Family' in B. Fox (ed.) *Family Patterns, Gender Relations*. Don Mills: Oxford University Press: 21–28.

Finch, J. (2008). 'Naming Names: Kinship, Individuality and Personal Names'. *Sociology*. 42 (4): 709–725.

Finch, J. and Mason, J. (1993). *Negotiating Family Responsibilities*. London: Tavistock/ Routledge.

Grice, A. (16th July 2013). 'Conservatives Prepare to Get Tougher Still on Teenage Single Mothers in Crackdown on Benefits'. *The Independent*. Available at: http://www.independent.co.uk/news/uk/politics/conservatives-prepare-to-get-tougher-still-on-teenage-single-mothers-in-crackdown-on-benefits-8710047.html. [Accessed: 17th September 2013].

Griffin, P. (2007). 'Sexing the Economy in a Neo-Liberal World Order: Neo-Liberal Discourse and the (Re)Production of Heteronormative Heterosexuality'. *The British Journal of Politics and International Relations*. 9: 20–238.

Klett-Davies, M. (2012). 'A Critical Analysis of Family and Relationships Policies in England and Wales (1997–2011)'. *Families, Relationships, and Societies*. 1 (1): 121–131.

Kramer, A.-M. (2011). 'Kinship, Affinity and Connectedness: Exploring the Role of Genealogy in Personal Lives'. *Sociology*. 45 (3): 379–395.

Luxton, M. and Fox, B. (2009). 'Conceptualizing "Family"' in B. Fox (ed.) *Family Patterns, Gender Relations*. Don Mills: Oxford University Press: 3–20.

Macrory, I. (2012). 'Measuring National Wellbeing: Households and Families, 2012'. Office for National Statistics Report. Available at: http://www.ons.gov.uk/ons/dcp171766_259965.pdf. [Accessed: 9th October 2012].

Mason, J. (2008). 'Tangible Affinities and the Real Life Fascination of Kinship'. *Sociology*. 42 (1): 29–45.

May, V. (2011). 'Self, Belonging and Social Change'. *Sociology*. 45 (3): 363–378.

Morgan, D.H.J. (2011). *Rethinking Family Practices*. Basingstoke: Palgrave Macmillan.

Nordqvist, P. (2014). 'Bringing Kinship into Being: Connectedness, Donor Conception and Lesbian Parenthood'. *Sociology*. 48: 268–283.

Rowe, A.C. (2005). 'Be Longing: Toward a Feminist Politics of Relation'. *NWSA Journal*. 17 (2): 15–46.

Skeggs, B. (2001). *Formations of Class and Gender*. London: Sage.

Weeks, J. (1990). *Coming Out: Homosexual Politics in Britain from the Nineteenth Century to the Present.* London: Quartet Books.

Woodhouse, L. (1988). 'The New Dependencies of Women'. *Family Relations*. 37 (4): 379–384.

8 Names, (gendered) self, and society[1]

As Brown argues, 'Few topics engage our attention more completely than the way we think and feel about ourselves' (Brown, 1998: vii). The self is a point at which 'questions of ontology, knowledge, and value' intersect (Meyers, 1997: 1). Selfhood matters: both how one perceives oneself and how one is perceived by others. Most significantly, as Meyers argues, how individuals think of and narrate the story of their self impacts on their wider perspective on the world, 'opening up social, intellectual, and aesthetic possibilities and concomitantly limiting imagination and action' (Meyers, 1997: 1). Identity is complex and made up of a myriad of intersecting strands including gender, class, ethnicity, nationality, and sexuality, and can be related to both the local and wider social situation (Rahman and Jackson, 2010: 156). Identity is about 'who we are and who we perceive others to be' (Rahman and Jackson, 2010: 156), but does not encompass all the things selfhood can, including 'emotions and desires, or personal attributes . . . which do not necessarily give rise to enduring identity labels'. There is a slight difference in these terms and to what they refer; here I will use them to maintain the distinction as outlined by Rahman and Jackson. The self is social, influenced by the politics and socio-economic position of society in general and the self's own personal circumstances (which are in turn related to one another): we are shaped by past and present selves and societies, and we look to mould selfhood in a particular way for the future.

Discussion of the self has been ongoing, at least since Plato, with the idea of the 'core self' remaining significant in philosophy and in the cultural imagination: this self is one which has a central core that does not change, but which influences the person throughout their life, being the very basis of who they are. However, other ideas have arisen. Mead's self, for example, is dependent on context and other people, their thoughts and opinions (1964: 218). The self in Mead's theories is the social, dialectical, experiential self – constantly changing with the new experiences of the immediate 'I' – attempting to form itself into a kind of coherency (Mead, 1964). Mead is a modern theorist (as opposed to postmodern), but he is well aware of the contextual nature of the self; a self which is in process and changes with new experiences, rather than being fixed.

Gergen goes further suggesting that it would be 'much more fruitful to speak of multiple conceptions' of the self (Gergen, 1971: 20). He argues that Western

118   *Names, (gendered) self, and society*

cultures still speak of, and therefore imaginatively construct, the self in terms of singularity when actually this is a misleading way of articulating the self, as we can construct ourselves differently in different situations, sometimes using contradictory representations (1971: 19–20). The growth of the idea of fragmented selves, which can never be considered whole, Gergen situates within postmodernism, as the modern ideas of linearity and progress have been destabilised (Gergen, 1991).

Unlike Gergen, however, I do not argue that this historical period is 'postmodernity', preferring to consider it 'late modernity' (Giddens, 1996). The idea of fragmented selves has grown up *within* modernity. A non-unitary self with no single, fixed core can be traced at least to David Hume during the Scottish Enlightenment; Hume thought of the self in terms of 'bundles of sensations, perceptions and thoughts piled on top of each other' (Hood, 2012: ix). As modernity has progressed, ideas of linearity and progress have been challenged and a singular description of self – though still having a strong imaginative pull on the articulation of (Western) selfhoods – is not the only narrative which can now be utilised, and the fluid or fragmented self has gained considerable philosophical credence. Despite this, coherence when telling one's life story remains significant and indeed crucial to making sense of one's experience to both the self and others.

The self has always been an important topic of discussion for feminists investigating the gendered social world, as this expression of personhood and autonomy has often been denied to women or repressed under gendered inequality. Feminist philosophers have entered the debates on what the self 'is'. Chodorow (1981) argues for the relational self, cared for as a child by adults and building a sense of self from these initial interactions; Kristeva (1987) sees the self as discursively created and non-unitary, working between 'feminine' semiotics and 'masculine' symbol; and Butler (2004) charges that the self is illusionary, created from discourse and repeated actions and norms. Young (1997) has argued for the displacing of the masculinist narrative of the independent self, who needs no one to sustain it and would be shamed by asking for help. This self is really an illusion, Young argues (1997: 124), and the interdependency of selves should be celebrated, legislated for, and used as a narrative for the construction of self in the imagination.

The tendency for feminist scholars of the self to move away from the philosophical tradition of the unitary and singular self can be seen as a part of the project of giving women voice to their experiences and not seeing these experiences and life tasks as secondary to the projects of men. The universalised singular self of classic philosophy has been seen to hide a masculine identity and to exclude the realities of women's lives. The depiction – and historical reality – of the dependency of women on men and the connection of women with caring for others and the messiness of everyday life (Gordon, 1990: 115) was used to argue for their lack of strong individual selfhood and to ensure they were kept out of political and other powerful positions within society (see, for example, Rousseau, 1979). The gendered inequality and the material restrictions which flowed from this unequal organisation of society were not recognised by theorists of political philosophy, and were generally argued away as biological and 'natural' (Rousseau, 1979; see also Lister, 1997). Women's selves were to remain within certain strictures and roles and masculinist narratives of independent and linear selfhood were the only acceptable forms. It is therefore unsurprising that feminists have argued for the fluid and creative self when, they theorise, women's lives are more cyclical than men's with the events of childbirth, care work, and the attendant periods away from paid work (see Gordon, 1990).

Participants in this study reflect the complexity of selfhood in the many ways in which they engage with their own selves and the influences of those around them: names are a way of representing the self to the world as well as a symbol around which the person can build up their identity and therefore interact with the creation of a life narrative. The ways in which names are engaged with in Britain are gendered, in that women are *expected* to consider discarding one name at particular life turning points which impacts heavily on selfhood. In this way, women engage with names and selfhood in a particular way – by this I do not mean to suggest all women engage fully and thoughtfully, as they may unthinkingly follow a particular path, but they will become aware of the consequences of their decision as it plays out in their life. It is also not to suggest that men do not engage with names, but that their engagements are not as *expected* by society or as necessarily connected with the life change of marriage. Naming practices are a 'technology of the self' (Foucault, 1988): they regulate behaviour, differentiate between men and women to organise our society along gendered lines, and are a means of displaying certain qualities to others (loving, committed, adult, wifely, etc.).

I will first analyse how participants think about their own self in connection with their last name, as either 'core' or 'fluid', in both positive and negative terms, before turning to the dialectic between self and society in the building and making of a sense of selfhood. Between these two sections, I will argue that my participants are not spontaneously producing selfhood narratives, but are doing so to make sense of themselves as social actors within a particular society and to be intelligible to others within that society also; their choice of narratives is not random but comes from socially acceptable and credible options. I will also explicitly discuss a gendered identity emerging through thought processes around names and the decisions women take.

Core selves, fluid selves; positive and negative aspects

In answer to the statement 'Names are important to a person's sense of identity', nearly 52 per cent of survey respondents chose 'agree' and 31.4 per cent choose 'strongly agree'. In the qualitative sections of the survey, the data showed that most had found that after marriage a period of re-adjustment was needed to re-think the self: that should not imply a purely negative re-adjustment but a process of taking on a new role and processing new reactions to this. Ultimately 73.5 per cent of the 102 participants felt either 'positive' or 'quite positive' about the decision they had made with their name. However, the process of coming to this sense of positivity was not always straightforward; at pivotal life stages a person's selfhood comes under consideration: marriage is one such stage. Three-quarters of the women in my study came to be positive about their naming choice, but had complex thoughts around both the positive and the negative aspects of marriage, wifehood, and identity; the name was used to display their positivity and/or reconcile tensions (though some of my sample remain ambivalent or unhappy about their naming choices and continue to deal with this every day).

Feminist analyses of heterosexuality have shown how important this institution is to providing people with a sense of adult status (Hockey et al., 2010: 133). The rites and rituals of heterosexual lives remain important for a sense of order and stability in people's lives; they provide a framework for making meaning out of life events (Hockey et al., 2010: 137). Heterosexuality is 'a largely silent principle of social organisation' (Johnson, 2005: 5), but a significant one, and the highly valued and visible rite of marriage remains powerful. Marriage has always been an important rite of passage (Mansfield and Collard, 1988: 52) though for younger women with more educational, career, and financial options, the importance of marriage as a marker of adulthood may have diminished and become one of a series of possible markers. This is a question that should be tested by further research: in a neoliberal Britain, post the 2008 financial crash, with the rise of 'generation rent' (Osborne, 2015), unable to buy their own house, and therefore either spending years renting or even staying with parents, buying a house may be a less viable adult status marker. This, when coupled with the developing 'precariat class' (Standing, 2011) who find stable, long-term work with in-built benefits increasingly hard to find, may actually mean marriage is becoming a more significant marker of adultness once more.

The generational differences were clear in my study: participants in their late forties and older explicitly wrote or spoke about their perception of marriage as a marker of adult status. The name change marked this move from single to married; proof of the rite of passage which women have undergone. This positive change was mentioned by 21.3 per cent of name changers who felt marriage and name changing – becoming 'a wife' – were signs of adulthood. They talked of looking for stability and security, of thinking about having children, about feeling they should commit to someone: all ideas connected with responsible adulthood:

> I was 25 at that stage and probably felt I should commit myself to somebody.
>
> (P68; interview data; name changer)

> It was grown-up to change your name and be Mrs.
>
> (P4; name changer)

Changing your name was a public sign of marriage, along with the change in title, and this change symbolised becoming an adult and a person bestowed with status via the marriage ceremony and the creation of a new family unit: this is one example of the name as a technology of the self, regulating behaviour and being used to display certain qualities to the world, here namely responsible adulthood. The fact that for this to be achieved women have to connect themselves to a man via

Names, (gendered) self, and society 121

his name and the heterosexual institution of marriage generally went unnoticed by participants and when it was mentioned it was as a relic of the past:

> seems strange to have to make a choice between your husband's name and your father's name – a *relic* of a male dominated system which recognised descent through the male line with associated inheritance and succession issues.
>
> (P44: name changer)

Participant 44 pointed out that her decision should not be interpreted as her being subservient to her husband or a denial of feminism, but as 'what you did in working class families then [1980s]'. She feels that society has moved on and people may interpret her actions incorrectly, yet she argues that getting rid of all signs of marriage is not the best course of action – she was happy to be married and this is one sign of her commitment. Signs and symbols of this newly achieved status remain important. In Britain there remains an expectation that women will marry, become wives, and display this publicly through the name (and title) change – and following these rules brought a large number of women respect and happiness. In day to day discourse as 'a wife', which the name change symbolised to other people, they found connotations of adulthood, responsibility, stability, and respect. This could all be encapsulated within a fluid and adaptable narrative of selfhood, adjusting to life changes and new experiences.

Other name changers' narratives focused more on fragmentation and compartmentalisation of their lives. Participant 52 changed her name on marrying, but kept her original family name at work. For her, marriage had not been an important goal; it was perceived as a means of tying a person down to a boring life, without freedom. In fact, for P52, marriage was seen as provincial and representative of the kind of thing one's parents would do. However, on meeting her now husband, this quickly changed and within 6 months, they were engaged. The decision to change her name was, however, more protracted – it seemed to reach down deeper into her ideas of selfhood and her values than the act of getting married:

> Having . . . wrestled with this big thing, having a major ideological and personal shift from anti-marriage to pro-marriage and then hey, why not go the whole hog . . . why not cap it all off with the name . . . and then I couldn't quite bring myself to do it because . . . because I mean I'd been single, well I mean not single but not married, until I was 32 and that's quite a long time to be your own person and I'm [Original Family Name], everyone knows me as this, that's me, my work life, everything I've published, that's me . . . all of the things that gave me my identity – my primary source of identity before was always my career – and if anyone does know me it's as [Original Family Name], that's me! I'm not going to give all that up. It took me a while to figure out I could keep my name at work and change it in my personal life.
>
> (P52; interview data; name changer)

122 Names, (gendered) self, and society

In this account, P52 reveals the struggle to re-envisage her new self after marriage. She feels that marriage has re-orientated the sources of her sense of selfhood and self-worth, but aligning this with her past career-focused self does not appear possible. Her original family name represented this career-orientated self, and P52 looked for a way to publicly display the changes in her life without dismissing her old name and the connotations of success and personal achievement it held. However, these must be compartmentalised for the contradictions she understands to exist between the categories of 'wife' and 'worker' to be managed. This extract from her interview illustrates this point:

R: Is Ms a positive thing for you?

P52: No, I'd rather not be anything. It's sort of innocuous isn't it? The thing is, I want to avoid being a Mrs at work. Oh no. It's horrible isn't it!

R: (laughter; surprised) Why, explain, explain! Why horrible?

P52: Oh, imagine. It's all those, all those lingering things that I associate with old-school versions of marriage. Mrs Such-and-such. It's like a lesser, lesser-than . . .

R: . . . But being a Mrs in your personal life you don't feel . . .

P52: Oh yeah, really good. When you're ordering shoes or something and it's 'is it Miss or Mrs'. I always say 'Mrs'! (sweeps her hair back in a proud gesture) (laughter)

R: Oh, so that's really interesting, so it really has completely different connotations for you?

P52: Completely! Even, as I say, ordering shoes, like I don't really care what Barretts think of me, but I'll still very proudly tick the Mrs box on the thing, I love it, it's great! That Mrs [Married Name] I'm very grown-up, mature adult and everything! Especially when you go and stay in hotels and things, that declaration of Mrs (claps hand together). I think, I revel in it! I think it's brilliant! Mrs, it's really good, but then imagine here, oh it would be awful, I mean, it wouldn't really, but I've got that lingering 'it would undermine my authority as a credible academic to be attached to someone else, an adjunct to someone else.'

In one context, Mrs Married Name is a source of joy, a sign of adulthood and maturity; in another it would represent a lack of success, a lack of authority, a lack of credibility, and a symbol of being merely an appendage of another person. This divide in selfhood for P52, is strictly observed. Her narrative of selfhood is one of compartmentalisation – in one part of her life she is one kind of person, and in another she has a different sense of what she values and represents to the outside world. Her selfhood is fragmented, divided up between the situations of work and home, and separate names have become a symbol of this and a useful way of managing the contradictions. The enjoyment of the separation of selves into work and home was highlighted by P52's narrative, but can also be found in another 12 participant accounts.

Renaming forces a re-thinking of oneself and a re-identification with husbands and the new family unit being created – adulthood, wifehood, and moving away from the family of childhood. It is a very relational move: the self in connection with others (husbands, children), and this self must change and adapt to new roles. In a supposedly individualising Western society (Giddens, 1996; Bauman, 2011), the relationality of this move may seem surprising. As Beck and Beck-Gernsheim argue (2010: 74), women continue to be connected more with others through their care work and these responsibilities allow them less chance to act out the fully individualised self. However, as Young argues (1997: 124), full individualisation may well be an illusion.

The narrative of the fluid and adaptable self of the late modern period is a useful way of describing and justifying the changes taking place: both name change and changes in sense of self. However, compartmentalisation may be necessary to resolve tensions between roles and ideas of self as women struggle between modern individualism and more relational positions: this is a fragmented selfhood. This modern narrative of selfhood – fluid or fragmented – is being used to make a traditional and still highly relational decision coherent in a supposedly individualising society.

For name retainers there was a positivity in the *continuity* of naming they experienced. Keeping their names confirmed their identities on marriage and renewed their sense of commitment to this identity:

> [I wanted to] retain my prior identity using the name I had used all my life.
>
> (P46: name retainer)

These narratives of selfhood require an idea of identity as linear, continuous, and unbroken, for ontological security to be maintained: 22 of 27 name retainers (nearly 82 per cent) discussed the importance of the continuity of selfhood through retention of their name. Though these women would probably not, if challenged, agree they had not changed throughout their lives, they require a justification for not changing names in a society geared towards this. The most positive and socially acceptable reason in an individualising society is one which holds out the person's sense of selfhood as fundamental: each individual person deserves to have their life's narrative respected. Women who work against the grain can use a narrative of linear selfhood – an accepted philosophical idea – as well as the present-day narrative of the importance of the individual, to justify their name retention and in this way keep a positive and continuous sense of self. Although the linear, core self narrative has been criticised by feminists as refusing change and not representing women's lives and experiences, my participants use it in a very particular way to thwart a patriarchal norm.

For many of my name-retaining participants it was the historical connection of name changing to subsuming women's selfhood that made the idea anathema. Participant 46 wrote that changing her name seemed 'too enormous' when considering the history of the name change (e.g. women as property and loss of individual identity in law). While P85 questioned why women should make this change and not men: 'It's unequal and no one's business.' In fact, just over 44 per cent of

124 *Names, (gendered) self, and society*

my name retainers saw their action as a feminist decision. Hence they were using a *masculinist* narrative of selfhood to defend a *feminist* decision.

If going against the prevailing norm in any situation can be seen as a 'deviant' decision, then name retainers can be seen to be acting 'deviantly'. Those acting deviantly, it has been argued by Scott and Lyman (1968: 62), are more often called upon to account for their actions than those who conform. This was borne out by my study. The name changers used the narrative of fluid or fragmented self, but implicitly. Name retainers on the other hand were prepared to defend their decision explicitly and used the narrative of core selfhood to do so:

> The thought of becoming someone else terrified and outraged me.
>
> (P12)

> Wanted to get married not lose my identity.
>
> (P37)

> . . . changing my name would be such a shift in my mind-set about how I view myself, so I look at other people who've changed their name and sort of think 'why have you done that, you've got rid of your *actual* name?'
>
> (P51; interview data)

Name retainers appear then to remain a part of the long-standing philosophical discussion of self in terms of a core, fundamental self. These narratives also fit in with the late modern, individualistic idea that the individual has a right to have their selfhood respected and their life goals unhindered or hampered by others. In this way the name-retaining participants perhaps most closely resemble the late modern self of the theorists of individualisation. This individualistic self maintains its own goals as paramount and looks to safeguard itself rather than act in a more relational manner. As most name-retaining participants had children or were planning to have children, this is not to suggest they actually do less care work or have less interest in this, but that they adopt and make use of the late modern individualistic narrative that the self should have a certain freedom from others and their demands.

More negatively, however, this narrative of naming denies the relatedness of selves as outlined by Mead (1964) and Gergen (1991): instead one is seen to act alone on one's own life path. To use Gergen's framework, in valorising the individual and their personal aims and actions, theories of individualisation suggest a highly modern approach (rather than postmodern). It also prevents name retainers from easily articulating change. However, the justification for acting in a more individual than relational way requires the *credibility* of the narrative of linear selfhood and the importance of the individual. It is a very useful way of expressing a confidence and contentedness with selfhood and, as an accepted narrative of self formation, a rational means to justify working against the norm. Furthermore, it provides the coherency central to ontological security (see Mead, 1964; Giddens, 1996). There is a complex – and sometimes contradictory – tension

Names, (gendered) self, and society 125

between the narratives used by my sample, the history and assumptions of those narratives, and the traditional or modern state of the naming decision made. However, it was clear that 'deviant' name retainers needed to pay particular attention to how they justified their actions in a way those making a traditional naming choice did not.

Justifying your self: norms, deviancy, and their vocabularies

Forming a coherent narrative of self is pressing: when we do things which are unusual for us, we have to find an excuse or a way of explaining our actions (Hood, 2012: xii). The overarching narrative of our lives needs to make sense, both to ourselves and to others. The act of telling a life history is an act of storytelling (Atkinson, 1998: 1). We use stories to make our lives understandable to ourselves and others (Atkinson, 1998: 1), and these have a unilinear direction, relying on people understanding this conception of time and the ideas that stories therefore have beginnings, middles, and ends (Polkinghorne, 1995: 8). It is through these narratives that we create that coherent life story deemed so important and necessary; without such a coherent story subjects are open to diagnoses of madness (Wilkinson-Ryan and Westen, 2000: 540).

Janet Askham's study on identity and stability in marriage shows some of the pressures married couples face, both in terms of what roles they must take on and what expectations are placed upon them to account for themselves positively (Askham, 1984). Her study found that a certain number of gendered role constraints were placed upon men and women in marriage and that these were accepted by married couples: these role constraints meant that possibilities for developing selfhood were curtailed (Askham, 1984: 186–187). The institution of marriage is connected with stability and responsibility: the building of (particular kinds of) families. It provides a certain framework and set of expectations: people are expected to speak of their married life in certain, socially acceptable ways. As Askham argues, marriage is not about varying different identities but of an expected one; the qualities her participants spoke of as having been developed in them because of marriage are 'common to the married' (1984: 185). If couples want to show themselves to be 'normal, respectable, moral people: namely those who are married' (Askham, 1984: 142) then they are urged to account for themselves in particular ways. Marriage is generally seen as a social good, and this is the *vocabulary* to which participants in that institution are meant to adhere. Admitting marriage is anything otherwise can be very painful, difficult, and embarrassing.

The vocabulary of marriage must then fit into an overall life story and, as I have outlined above, participants fell into roughly two groups, each with a particular life narrative. It is these two overarching ideas of selfhood which are utilised by participants in my study. Name retainers were *more likely* to appeal to a narrative of core, unchanging selfhood than name changers; name changers on the other hand could justify their decision using ideas of flexible and adaptable selfhood, which made the seemingly traditional decision up-to-date and creative. The

126   *Names, (gendered) self, and society*

tensions here are clear, but participants nevertheless used these narratives to justify their decisions, implicitly or explicitly, and from them formed a coherent story about themselves. This need to account – to the self and others – for decisions around marriage and selfhood suggests Giddens' theory that relationships are becoming increasingly inwardly referential (1996: 6) is not fully correct. Participants continue to need to justify themselves to others and consider the thoughts and wishes of others as they do so.

To repeat, certain vocabularies in institutional situations are acceptable, other vocabularies are less or unacceptable, and when an agent uses any such set of vocabularies they are 'influencing others' and themselves (Mills, 1940: 907) as to what accounts and actions are in/appropriate. These vocabularies are a form of social control, upheld as 'normal' by the generalised other or society (Mills, 1940: 908). Whenever and to whomever a person has to account, they must be able to make a coherent story based on rules, expectations, and final action. Breaking away from the naming norm is to act 'deviantly' and certainly requires more frequent and considered accounting than following it (Scott and Lyman, 1968: 62).

The self as a whole in Mead's theorisation (see Mead, 1974) is the social, dialectical, experiential self – constantly changing with the new experiences of the immediate 'I' – attempting to form itself into a kind of coherency. The sense of coherency and constancy that can be engendered by forming an understandable narrative is, I would argue, a means by which to create a sense of ontological security (Giddens, 1996). It provides a sense of stability, a base upon which a person can say they have founded themselves, a set of values which they can see as unchanging and as integral to themselves. This much needed ontological security masks the constant flux and change of selves, the shifting levels and layers of selfhood, which reform and re-gather, much like the moving and changing of Rose's pleat theory (Rose in Budgeon, 2003: 44).

Bloom and Munro (1995) discuss the humanist idea of the core self as *refusing* the 'possibilities of changes in subjectivity over time' and masking the many important roles gender and other social positionings play, as well as 'language, social interactions, and pivotal experiences' (p. 100). The core self has been perceived as limiting, particularly by feminists; the non-unitary idea of subjectivity can be read as part of a transformational politics, in which selves can always change, re-orientate themselves to the world, and in this way anything and everything can change (Bloom and Munro, 1995: 100). This idea is obviously appealing to a transformational politics as people are never beholden to a core, set self. However, these two narratives of core, unchanging self and fluid self, are both used by participants and are appealed to to help justify particular decisions around the name. They are narratives; they are tools. They are useful in making sense of whether to change a name or not and the impact on selfhood this may have, as well as in explaining this to others in an acceptable way.

The self and the social community: the reactions of others

The importance of other people in shaping our sense of self cannot be underestimated. As Gergen has said 'We appear to stand alone, but we are manifestations

Names, (gendered) self, and society 127

of relatedness' (1971: 170). Other people shape 'self-definition, self-regulatory processes, and personality' (Andersen et al., 2002: 159). However, it is not only particular other people who shape our sense of self but institutional practices and the generalised other. To return to Mead, the generalised other is the social community in which each self acts and from which it makes sense of norms and communal standards and values (Mead, 1964: 218): there is a process of constant interaction between individuals, institutions, and the social community to construct selfhood. Before turning to investigate specific reactions to name changing or retaining, I wish to dwell briefly on the more general importance of names within wider society and how they are used by others to 'place' participants in terms of race, nationality, and class. Participants found the specific name they have, the way it sounds and its connotations, could have real and material impacts on their lives.

Participant 66 has one parent from Syria and one from Britain. Her first name is a common British, female name; her last name reflected her Syrian ancestry and connection with that culture. Before marriage she enjoyed the balance of the two names, feeling they displayed connections with both cultures, while also suggesting to others her Muslim beliefs. She took on her husband's name when they married and has mixed feelings about this decision: she does not appreciate looking like 'a 100% British woman'. She had some pressure from her in-laws to change her name, but also recognises the importance of name sharing in UK culture, so appreciates the idea of her and her children sharing one name. She has also experienced racist reactions to having an Arabic name in the past: '[I have suffered] some mild discrimination in the UK because of my Arabic name – especially in airports – and on these occasions I am happy to have an English name.' Participant 66 used her OFN to display cultural and religious connections. She feels that, to an extent, this has been erased from her public persona since her name change (she uses her Arabic name as a middle name, but this is often ignored on official forms, etc.) and dislikes the cutting off from her Syrian heritage that this entails in her everyday life. Her full name before marriage placed her in a way she appreciated and felt truly represented her. The change on marriage has made her look '100% British', something she does not identify with and would rather her name did not symbolise.

However, this married name has its advantages within Britain and when moving between national borders. The power of the norm in Britain – via parents, her partner, and the example of those around her – has encouraged her to accept the importance of changing her name and sharing one name with her children; specifically, her husband's name. The Islamic culture P66 identifies with does not have a history of women changing their names on marriage (see Schimmel, 1989), but the cultural importance of it in Britain has been enough to sway P66 to conform to this pattern of gendered naming. Further to this, the impact of world events, economics, politics, and power imbalances have impacted upon her. When moving between national borders, the cultural capital of being British is useful. Currently British people are able to move fairly freely around the world, often without visas, or with visas that are free and easy to obtain. The accrued capital here is significant, but is gained by a complex mix of historical

128 *Names, (gendered) self, and society*

and present-day circumstances, many of which have grown from racism and imperialism.

Participant 66 lies at a point of intersection between all of the above. She has the accrued cultural capital of being British, but until recently also attracted racist stereotyping and discriminatory treatment because of her Arabic last name. The power of the name as symbol is so great that taking on her husband's last name has ended this discrimination: her ethnic and cultural heritage have been masked by this change and hence her problems have disappeared. This example shows not only how facile and puerile racist assumptions are, but equally how significant a name can be in terms of placement within society (historical, present day, economic, political), the treatment one can expect to receive, and one's chances for moving across borders.

'Deviant' identities are contextual. Participant 7 was one of my older participants, putting herself in the 76+ age bracket. In my interview with her, we spoke of the significance of national identity and the discomfort one can feel when placed differently to how one would wish. Participant 7 married in the 1940s and lived through the Second World War. However, her birth name was German in origin. When attempting to join the naval service for women, she was taken aside and told 'there's a problem with your name. It's German you see' (P7; interview data) and then questioned about the loyalty of her father to the British state. Then, recently, at a party with friends of her generation at which her brother attended and their German name was revealed, one of P7's friends turned to her and said 'oh, so you're German are you!' (P7; interview data). This interaction left P7 feeling uncomfortable. She was aware she was surrounded by friends who felt similarly to herself about the Second World War and the fighting with Germany. Participant 7 is British – her birth name reveals a connection with Germany that comes from many generations before her – however, the name had the power to make her friends look at her a little differently, however briefly, and push her into the uncomfortable position of being identified with Nazi Germany. She said to me during her interview:

> You know, lots of people still have problems with German names and well . . . let me confess to you, so do I. I mean, when you've been through a war . . .

To a modern reader this is perhaps difficult reading, but for a woman like P7 and her friends this period in history is a part of their lived experience. The impact of this interaction was therefore real and unpleasant for her; her birth name was used to distance her from her own national identity. Her married name has ensured this discomfort is rare for P7; she has been able to distance herself from the connotations of a German name that may arise in the minds of her contemporaries and place herself as British. She was 'glad to get rid of' her birth name. However, I should note that P7 went on to say:

> I went to Berlin for the first time three or four years ago as I'd never wanted to go before. Of course once I got there I thought it was wonderful!

Names, (gendered) self, and society 129

Finally, the increasing nuances of class division within Britain (Savage et al., 2013) are reduced in the discussion of names to more overt symbols of class background. The double-barrelled or hyphenated name came under a great deal of criticism from participants, who labelled it 'pretentious' (P44; P82), 'over the top' (P24), 'excessive' (P47). Others worried they were too complicated for forms or for their children to then hand on to the next generation: P100 labelled them 'a nightmare', while P107 said double-barrelling was 'too complicated'. Participant 120 wrote that double-barrelling 'seemed wrong to me. . . . I thought it would betray my class identity (!)', while P115 bemoaned the growth in double-barrelling, seeing it as a middle-class aspiration which she thought 'slightly daft'. My participants were selected to be those who had chosen the norm of name changing or had gone against it completely, so their reactions are no doubt a part of the sampling process and different ideas are likely to have emerged with a hyphenating sample. Nevertheless, these reactions reveal an interesting relationship with the idea of double-barrelling for those who do not choose to do so.

The historical connotation that double-barrelled names have in Britain is with the upper classes. This has been discussed in recent years in Conservative Party circles, in which concern was expressed that candidates may seem distant from the electorate because of their classed names (Fleming, 2009). My participants in the main reflect this connection of double-barrelled names with the upper classes. This accounts for P120 stating, if slightly self-consciously, that she would not have wanted to 'betray her class identity' and P44 and P82 seeing such names as a sign of being pretentious. Participants 24 and 47 further this argument by seeing the exercise as simply too much: double-barrelled names are unnecessarily showy. Participant 115 sees the growth in hyphenated names as a part of the middle classes aspiring to be more like the upper classes and thinks it unnecessary and rather silly.

Theories of classed capital (see e.g. Bourdieu 2010 [1984]) argue that 'high' culture is a part of upper-class life; art films, for example, are infrequently accessed by lower class people as they are not a part of their 'cultural repertoire' (Barnett and Allen, 2000: 161). My sample cannot be defined as 'lower class' as it is made up of predominantly middle-class, well-educated women, yet there was a definite attempt to set themselves apart from the 'pretentions' of the double-barrelling upper classes. Gunn argues that taste, culture, and morals have always been a part of class – in fact they were part of constituting the concept (Gunn, 2005). The evolving middle class in England (late eighteenth to twentieth century) taught its children to behave respectably (Gunn, 2005: 59) and attend the 'subscription library, assembly room, literary and philosophical society, scientific association, and so on' (Gunn, 2005: 51). Women were the prime 'bearers of class', having to show off their classed accomplishments (playing the piano) and correct choice of furnishings and fashions (classed consumption) (Gunn, 2005: 55). Middle-class behaviour revolved around self-control and the working of the mind (Gunn, 2005): attention to dress was important, but not to excess, and the work of the middle class was solid and worthwhile, but not manual. This set the middle class against both the upper and the working classes, with the working classes seen as

130   *Names, (gendered) self, and society*

those who did the practical work and were 'the bone' of society; the upper classes were described as 'the belly', consuming and speaking, but not necessarily adding to society as the middle classes – 'the mind' – did (Gunn, 2005: 53).

These class divisions were mostly born out of the nineteenth and twentieth centuries, but their remnants can be seen in the discussion around names arising from my sample. The upper classes are still defined as rather unpractical, more interested in aesthetics and frippery than they should be – double-barrelled names are 'too much', 'excessive' and unnecessarily complicated and therefore in bad taste for the middle and working classes. However, as P115 comments, there remains an attempt to aspire to be of a higher class and the growth in a practice associated with the upper classes may reflect this. There can be other readings of the growth of hyphenated names however, such as wanting to symbolically display equality, but my sample was, in general, against the practice and therefore saw it in more negative terms.

These examples show the role names have in communicating certain thoughts and ideas to other people about the person they are dealing with. Names can be used to place people within a social hierarchy and the consequences of this can be highly political, as already discussed in Chapter 5. A further example of this is a study done for the Department of Work and Pensions to test discrimination levels in recruitment practices in British cities. They found candidates with 'white names' were favoured over ethnic minority candidates. Of the 106 white candidates, 68 per cent received a positive response; but out of the 310 ethnic minority candidates just 39 per cent received a positive response (Wood et al., 2009: 31). This test had been designed to remove all other markers of ethnicity except the name, and these names were chosen to be easily identified with a particular ethnic group, as well as minimising the possible effects of other structures such as gender, and having all candidates equal in terms of qualifications and experience (Wood et al., 2009: 16). This shows that names convey a great deal of information with which other people process and classify that person, in this case as worth employing. The decision to change or retain a name was frequently political; whether or not participants intended it to be, the reactions of others proved they had taken a politically significant step.

Name retainers experienced a wide range of responses from individuals around them and in their dealings with institutions such as banks, doctors, and schools: 29.6 per cent of these women explicitly mentioned reaction of some kind from family, friends, or institutions. Participant 14 for example noted in the survey that no one she knew had any problem with her decision, and P1 and P6, for example, found their husbands to be in support. Husbands of name retainers were, overall, supportive of wives' decisions to keep their own name; three men in this group changed their last name to their wife's as having one name was very important to them for their idea of family cohesion. Participant 16 noted that she had experienced a wide variety of responses from 'upset or confused to admiring' – her husband has changed his name to hers and her son also shares this name. Participant 16 is an interesting example of a self working against the grain; her story reveals that if it were purely family unity that was important in name changing, the shared name could easily be the woman's. Her case shows that there is resistance to this idea within Britain and in so doing highlights many assumptions working underneath the naming practice: gendered social hierarchal order is symbolised and maintained in the name (see Chapter 9 for more).

Participant 70 (name retainer) noted, other people do not understand you 'belong to each other' as married couples are conceived of as one unit, sharing a (man's) name. Explanation of relationships has to follow when the normalised pattern has been broken: people are confused by the move against the gender order and unsure how to cope with its significance. This confusion has led to some name retainers using their husband's name in schools and at doctors to 'save confusion' (P84: name retainer) and to ensure everyone knows that they are the mother of their children. The fact a name carries so much significance in the UK, to the extent that to share a name means a woman will be accepted almost without question as the mother of a set of children, is a real pressure on women. An individual's own wishes may well be subsumed under and into the social norm of the community when such implicit *and* explicit pressure is being put on them by family, relatives, and institutions. Changing names becomes the simplest and most efficient way of dealing with *other* people and not confusing their ideas of social/gender order and power. The institutionalised practice of name changing, in particular, is a part of creating a *gendered identity.*

Gendering identity

British society, as elsewhere, remains organised in part by the social construction of gender. Femininity and masculinity 'shape people' (Holmes, 2009: 36) and our society is organised and made intelligible by and through gender. In this way gender shapes selfhood – understanding oneself, other people and institutions, as well as the 'generalised other' (society) is done in part through gender. As Peterson and Runyan (1999) argue, gender is a lens through which we see the world. This lens 'colours' all of our interactions and makes them make sense only through our understandings of gender. In the case of my study, gendered identity came clearly to the fore in discussions over whether a woman would change her last name (see further examples in Chapters 6 and 9).

My participants, if arguments arose, were more likely to accept their husband's wishes and change their name. It would appear then that feminine submission is also a part of selfhood within coupledom and marriage and that women are used to the idea of a 'proper' couple meaning one in which their identity will be, symbolically at any rate, subsumed under a man's (see also Chapter 6). In order to make a coherent narrative of selfhood the women can construct this change in terms of love, unity, commitment, and cohesion. However, few questioned their husband's commitment, love, or desire to form a unit despite his name retention – it remains a man's prerogative to refuse such an identity change, but is something expected of women.

It would seem that a certain kind of masculinity remains bound up with marriage and the symbolic dominance of the family through the shared name. This

132   *Names, (gendered) self, and society*

symbol of patriarchal relations remains intact, with a male head of household subsuming the identity of his wife under and into his own. The fact name changing continues to be the dominant trend shows that this patriarchal assumption continues to hold sway. The institutionalised nature of name changing ensures a continual re-production of gendered selfhoods in which women are encouraged to give up a part of their wider selfhood for their husband and children in particular, as well as the generalised other of society, as a part of keeping the gendered social order intact. The history of patrilineal property rights and men dominating the family may be historical in a legal sense, but the shared patrilineal last name ensures this situation continues in a more subtle form. The strong reactions of others when the status quo is upset by name retention, or by men taking their wives' names, clearly exposes the gendered status of name changing and the underlying patriarchal power relations. The name retainers are, from this point of view, working against some very serious societal pressure. Participant 100 (name changer) attested to this in her interview:

> [O]ne of my friends didn't change her name for quite a long time after she got, after she married and I was always very careful to check I addressed things properly to her and I don't think other people were, I considered it important to me, just like I consider it important if people are a medical doctor or a PhD doctor I always put Dr on rather than calling them Mrs X. But in the end she cracked, she sort of gave up, you know, when she had a child she just sort of gave up, classic case, she thought 'this is too much like hard work' and she couldn't be bothered with having a separate, maintaining, having separate name anymore, so em, yeah, so she, she did, so I know very few people, and most of the people I know, and these are all people who have degrees by and large and I really, apart from [husband's] sister I don't think . . . I can think of any . . . body who's kept their maiden name when they've got married, which is really quite surprising, it's slightly scary actually, surely someone should have managed it! I mean [friend] probably held out the longest . . .

Conclusions

As Mead's theories (1964) describe, the self is created within a dynamic relationship between past and present experience, other people, institutions, and the wider society. The ways we then justify our actions – the vocabularies we use – must make sense to this socially situated self and its others. The name-changing norm organises women into gendered, heterosexual units, specifically designating them as *married* women. This re-thinking of the self as married is complex and names become a part of how women think of and present themselves to the world, both positively and negatively. Life narratives must include and make sense of the decisions surrounding marriage and participants use either the narrative of a linear self or a fluid/fragmented self to do this. Name changers can talk about their identities as creative, flowing and changing, allowing the moment of change or adaptation in the name change to sit within a high modern narrative of multiple selves. The name retainers are, however, more restricted and cannot discuss themselves

Names, (gendered) self, and society 133

in terms of growth and change, but must use the idea of (masculinist) linear, core selfhood to justify their deviance from the naming norm, which will need to be accounted for to make sense to others. This long understood philosophical idea has a credibility that is useful when attempting to thwart a patriarchal norm.

Gendered identity is (re-)produced through name-changing practices and, for those who did not change, their decisions upset the order so completely that they must account for their decision time and again as others attempt to make them intelligible. Many women entered into a symbolic relationship of submission within marriage by following the pattern of subsuming identity under that of the 'authoritative representative' (Bourdieu, 1991: 106) of the family – their husband. The male prerogative not to change names would appear to be bound up with a particular masculine identity as family head and the dominating, authoritative presence in the hierarchical heterosexual family. This kind of masculinity was called into question by a woman considering her own identity over that of her husband/new family and the result was emotional upset, anger, and argument. Femininity calls for acceptance and maintenance of these male feelings; masculinity does not call for the reverse. Gendered ideas of power, dominance, and credibility continue to be bound up in naming practices related to marriage and the very way in which people build up and think about their sense of self at a pivotal life turning point.

The final chapter in this book will turn to investigate in more depth the transgression of not following the naming norm and the impact this has on lived lives. It will explore how British society is organised around the naming norm, with the bureaucracy designed to uphold it acting as a disincentive to non-traditional naming forms and social organisation.

Note

1 With thanks to Policy Press and the editors of *Families, Relationships, and Societies* for their permission to reuse material from my article printed by them in 2013, with citation: Thwaites, R. (2013). 'The Making of Selfhood: Naming Decisions on Marriage'. *Families, Relationships, and Societies*, 2 (3): 425–439.

References

Andersen, S.M., Chen, S., and Miranda, R. (2002). 'Significant Others and the Self'. *Self and Identity*. 1: 159–168.

Askham, J. (1984). *Identity and Stability in Marriage*. Cambridge: Cambridge University Press.

Atkinson, R. (1998). *The Life Story Interview*. London: Sage.

Barnett, L.A. and Allen, M.P. (2000). 'Social Class, Cultural Repertoires, and Popular Culture: The Case of Film'. *Sociological Forum*. 15 (1): 145–163.

Bauman, Z. (2011). *Liquid Modernity*. Cambridge: Polity Press.

Beck, U. and Beck-Gernsheim, E. (2010). *Individualization*. London: Sage.

Bloom, L.R. and Munro, P. (1995). 'Conflicts of Selves: nonunitary subjectivity in women administrators' life history narratives' in J. Amos Hatch and R. Wisniewski (eds.) *Life History and Narrative*. London: The Falmer Press: 99–112.

134 *Names, (gendered) self, and society*

Bourdieu, P. (1991). *Language and Symbolic Power*. Cambridge: Polity Press.

Bourdieu, P. (2010 [1984]). *Distinction*. Abingdon: Routledge Classics.

Brown, J.D. (1998). *The Self*. Boston, MA: McGraw-Hill.

Budgeon, S. (2003). *Choosing a Self: Young Women and the Individualization of Identity*. Westport, CT: Praeger.

Butler, J. (2004). *Undoing Gender*. Abington: Routledge.

Chodorow, N. (1981). 'On the Reproduction of Mothering: A Methodological Debate'. *Signs*. 6: 500–514.

Fleming, A. (1st December 2009). 'Double-Barrelled Names: Not just for Tory Toffs'. *The Guardian*. Available at: http://www.guardian.co.uk/politics/2009/dec/01/double-barrelled-names-tories. [Accessed: 14th June 2013].

Foucault, M. (1988). 'Technologies of the Self' in L.H. Martin, H. Gutman, and P.H. Hutton (eds.) *Technologies of the Self*. London: Tavistock Publications: 16–49.

Gergen, J.K. (1971). *The Concept of Self*. New York: Holt, Rinehart and Winston.

Gergen, J.K. (1991). *The Saturated Self*. New York: Basic Books.

Giddens, A. (1996). *Modernity and Self-Identity*. Cambridge: Polity Press.

Gordon, T. (1990). *Feminist Mothers*. Basingstoke: Palgrave Macmillan.

Gunn, S. (2005).Translating Bourdieu: Cultural Capital and the English Middle Class in Historical Perspective'. *The British Journal of Sociology*. 56 (1): 49–64.

Hockey, J, Meah, A., and Robinson, V. (2010). *Mundane Heterosexualities*. Basingstoke: Palgrave Macmillan.

Holmes, M. (2009). *Gender and Everyday Life*. Abingdon, Routledge.

Hood, B. (2012). *The Self Illusion*. London: Constable.

Johnson, P. (2005). *Love, Heterosexuality and Society*. Abingdon: Routledge.

Kristeva, J. (1987). *Tales of Love*. New York: Columbia University Press.

Lister, R. (1997). *Citizenship: Feminist Perspectives*. Basingstoke: Palgrave Macmillan.

Mansfield, P. and Collard, J. (1988). *The Beginning of the Rest of your Life? A Portrait of Newly-Wed Marriage*. Basingstoke: Palgrave Macmillan.

Mead, G.H. (1964). *On Social Psychology*. Chicago: The University of Chicago Press.

Mead, G.H. (1974 [1934]). *Mind, Self, and Society*. Chicago: The University of Chicago Press.

Meyers, D.T. (1997). 'Introduction' in D.T. Meyers (ed.) *Feminists Rethink the Self*. Boulder, CO: Westview Press: 1–11.

Mills, C.W. (1940). 'Situated Actions and Vocabularies of Motive'. *American Sociological Review*. 5 (6): 904–913.

Osborne, H. (17th November 2015). 'Generation Rent: Only 26% of Young Adults Will Be on Housing Ladder by 2025'. *The Guardian*. Available at: http://www.theguardian.com/money/2015/nov/17/generation-rent-young-adults-housing-ladder-2025. [Accessed: 30th March 2016].

Peterson, V.S. and Runyan, A.S. (1999). *Global Gender Issues*. Boulder, CO: Westview Press.

Polkinghorne, D.E. (1995). 'Narrative Configuration in Qualitative Analysis' in J. Amos Hatch and R. Wisniewski (eds.) *Life History and Narrative*. London: The Falmer Press: 5–23.

Rahman, M. and Jackson, S. (2010). *Gender and Sexuality*. Cambridge: Polity Press.

Rousseau, J.-J. (1979). *Emile or on Education*. New York: Basic Books.

Savage, M., Devine, F., Cunningham, N. Taylor, M., Li, Y., Hjellbrekke, J., le Roux, B., Friedman, S., and Miles, A. (2013). 'A New Model of Social Class: Findings from the BBC's Great British Class Survey Experiment'. *Sociology*. 47 (2): 219–250.

Schimmel, A. (1989). *Islamic Names*. Edinburgh: Edinburgh University Press.

Scott, M.B. and Lyman, S.M. (1968). 'Accounts'. *American Sociological Review*. 33 (1): 46–62.

Standing, G. (2011). *The Precariat: The New Dangerous Class*. London: Bloomsbury.

Wilkinson-Ryan, T. and Westen, D. (2000). 'Identity Disturbance in Borderline Personality Disorder: An Empirical Investigation'. *American Journal of Psychiatry*. 157: 525–541.

Wood, M., Hales, J., Purdon, S., Sejersen, T., and Hayllar, O. (2009). 'A Test for Racial Discrimination in Recruitment Practice in British Cities'. Department for Work and Pensions. Research Report No. 607.

Young, I.M. (1997). *Intersecting Voices*. Princeton, NJ: Princeton University Press.

9 Accounting for transgression

One of the most stark contrasts between the name changers and the name retainers was the need name retainers felt to have some account for their naming decision, something which would to some extent satisfy the queries of others. It was clear other people had asked for such accounts, which name retainers had to be ready to provide. They may well have thought a great deal in advance of their marriage about this issue and known they would not change, or simply had to come up with a story at the time as questions began to be asked, but they were prepared with justifications. These justifications of feminism, a different kind of heterosexuality and 'true love' not based on the joining of identities, a strong sense of linear selfhood, and important links to family and experiences through the name they were born with have been explored throughout this book. This chapter is instead dedicated to exploring the reasons why accounting for the unusual act, the act going against the grain, the *transgression*, needed such careful accounting, and in doing so will examine the wider phenomenon of having to account for one's transgressions in a society with rules, norms, and boundaries for thought and action.

What is a transgression?

There are a number of different ways of describing and defining transgression, across a continuum of 'bad' acts. Transgression is a complex term, which has a number of connotations relevant to the naming act; the naming act interacts with ideas of transgression in complex ways also. First, to define transgression, I agree with Eli Adams when he says, transgression is

> not a radically alien or "unimaginable" phenomenon, but is a constant, central presence of our imaginative lives whose authority can be felt in the intensity with which it is resisted and regulated both by individual agents and by larger social and discursive structures.

> (1993: 208)

This definition of transgression fits particularly well with the naming act. Retaining one's name on marriage is not alien in contemporary Britain or unimaginable,

Accounting for transgression 137

in the sense that one knows it is a possibility, even if some women may feel it is 'unimaginable' for *them* to retain their birth name. Nevertheless though, to retain one's name remains an unusual and, to some extent, threatening idea in terms of the gendered social order and is therefore resisted and regulated by individuals and by the structures to which Adams refers. The marriage ceremony makes the changing of a woman's name easier than it does for a man, along with most of our bureaucracy, which usually encourages and validates the name change for women. I will explore these themes in more detail below, but will first spend some more time examining the name retain as transgression and looking at the reactions experienced by my participants from other people.

The reactions against name retainers, seen throughout this book, show that not following the norm *is* a transgression. It is a move away from the social and gender order, with masculine identity and authority challenged and the make-up of families made almost unintelligible. It calls into question how we as a society understand 'proper' femininity through 'respectable' marriage and, usually, motherhood. Without the social link of the name a great deal more work has to be done to establish relations and categorise people. The stigma (and even shame) of having family formations outside the nuclear unit and not all sharing one name is certainly a great deal less significant now than in the past. However, I would claim that, judging by the reactions against name retainers and the continued adherence to name changing and sharing, it continues to exist and is connected with the display of unrespectable heterosexuality which transgresses norms. In fact, the name retain is one of a number of 'quiet subversions' (Beasley et al., 2012: 67) of heterosexuality, as discussed in Chapter 6; though the name retain does have the power to stretch beyond 'quiet subversion' to induce much more hostility and anger. It is a transgression which produces a wide range of emotional reactions, revealing how deeply engrained in our gendered social order names are, how meaningful the act of name changing continues to be, and just how significant it can be when a woman transgresses this norm. As Adams says, the 'intensity' of its authority can be felt.

Reactions to transgression

Acts in our society have meaning – without this meaning they will become useless and defunct. This idea of acts follows the symbolic interactionist school (for example, Mead, 1964; Goffman, 1990 [1959]): interaction is what our society arises out of and without meaningful actions and interactions there can be no intelligible social order. I therefore argue that what we continue to *do* in our society continues to have meaning to us. The name change continues to be the prevalent action for women on marrying and therefore continues to have meaning to society. Women changing their name to that of their husbands has social meaning, wider than the individual couple. That meaning is explored throughout this book, but it is worth taking a moment here to consider that meaning and try to encapsulate at least some of it as it will help to put the reactions of others in their context.

138   *Accounting for transgression*

In a patriarchal society, in which particular standards of gender – a power relation – are mapped onto bodies defined as male and female, particular acts are expected of men and women which the 'other' group is excluded from: naming rituals are one of these actions. The name-changing ritual has a patriarchal past, based on the idea of women being subsumed into their husband's identity and losing their legal status as individuals (Pateman, 1988). The name change is no longer so explicitly connected with this but remains a gendered act, encouraging women to give up a part of their identity for their husband, coupledom, and presumed, new family. This encourages identification with this new family and gives the husband's identity a dominance over the identity of the family, certainly in public, but also in private as the woman and any children come to think of themselves as 'the Browns'. The family identify is simplified to this one symbol and in a society geared to perceive one family name as easy to deal with and understand, it becomes so in a lived and real way. The name change therefore continues to have gendered and unequal overtones and, as will be seen below and in the other chapters in this book, is taken as a sign of a woman's submission to her husband and the 'proof' of her love and commitment, which her husband is not expected to provide.

Name retainers experienced this reminder of the ongoing meaning of the name change in the reactions they received to their naming decision. The gendered meaningfulness of the name change continues to be very important to the ordering of our society, particularly in terms of gender and gendered roles. The reactions to name retainers showed them plainly that they had transgressed this order and would need to be able to account for such unusual action. Nearly 20 per cent of all husbands became 'very upset' at even the *suggestion* of their partner not changing names. This often led women, however ambivalent they felt about changing, to accept their husband's wishes. Participant 95 (name changer) wanted them both to change to a new name but 'my husband was very against this.' She felt that changing was 'a simple thing to do to make him happy.' Husbands became emotional at the suggestion of their wife-to-be not changing names, taking it as a 'personal slight' (P82: name changer). It would appear that some men continue to feel strongly about sharing a name, yet apart from the minority of men in the name-retaining group who changed to their wife's name, they refused to change their own name to achieve this goal. Indeed, as seen in Chapter 4, sometime the male parter would even suggest not getting married when the idea of name retaining was raised.

To clarify, the man in the couple *assumed* names would be changed, but when his partner raised the fact she was considering not changing the ensuing discussion produced strong emotional reactions from the male partner. Refusal to change appears to be a male prerogative: 'He refused to change his' (P11: name changer). This refusal did not in any way mean the discussion about the *woman* changing her name was closed: as 75 per cent of women in my sample changed names the discussions ensuing from a woman suggesting she might not change her name usually ended in the man's adamance winning out.

For the 18.5 per cent of name retainers who did not have their husband's support in retaining their name, the process was an uphill battle. Some of these examples have been highlighted above, but are worth reiterating here. Husbands sometimes deeply resented the family party being called by their wife's name, and some wives had to make sure this never happened to ensure husbands' feelings were not hurt. P8's (name retainer) husband and his family wanted her to change and she had to stand up to the pressure. He wanted them to share but would not take her name, instead using emotion to attempt to force her to change her mind: he said any children they had would be affected (presumably negatively), she was disrespecting his family, and that her mother had changed her name so she should follow her example. He did not take her suggestion to change to her name seriously. Participant 48 (name retainer) also had to cope with strongly emotional statements: her family and his were *very* disapproving of her decision and thought she was ' "making a point! And "being modern!" ' Her husband's brother told her husband ' "well I wouldn't settle for any of that." ' She continues to receive cheques made out to her in her husband's name – a *highly* common theme for name retainers. These general reactions show that name retaining remains a difficult decision that suggests a threat to an established, gendered social order. This can be seen even more explicitly in the case of P16.

In the survey, P16 (name retainer) wrote of always having felt proud of both her names, first and last, as they were symbolic to her as a part of her self. The idea of changing had always angered her and she questioned why this should have to happen. Participant 16 uses the narrative of a core and unchanging self to justify her naming decision – she has kept a stable and reassuring sense of connection with her self and her past throughout her life and has never had to feel the disjuncture she takes name changing to be. As stated above, she experienced a wide range of reactions when people heard about her naming decision.

The reactions P16 has received however, respond to the realisation that it is *her* name which is shared; the confusion, upset, or admiration are all engendered by this fact. The suggestion from this reaction is that she has upset some kind of expected order, as otherwise the fact she *shares* a name would not be problematic. And of course she *has* upset an expected order in firstly retaining her name and secondly using it as the dominant symbol of the family unit, which is expected to be the male partner's. The representative of the group has the power to speak for it and all of its individuals as one person (Bourdieu, 1991: 106). Historically this was the role of the husband and father and, with the common last name such a priority for the presentation of family cohesiveness, this power appears to continue, though in a less obvious form.

Bourdieu claims that the authority of a person within society is cemented by particular rites of passage, and marriage is given as a specific example. Marriage produces a number of sexual divisions between men and women and masculine and feminine, each boundary entirely arbitrary but made to look natural (Bourdieu, 1991: 118). Once these rites have become recognised and normalised however their 'symbolic efficacy' acts on reality (Bourdieu, 1991: 119). By subsuming women and men under one name, this practice engrains and emphasises the gendered power within marriage and society more generally: a social order is maintained and innovative ways of dealing with the last name and family groupings are legally and socially discouraged. However, P16 has managed to do just

140   *Accounting for transgression*

that, and therefore inspires reaction where, had she changed to her husband's name, there would have been none.

When seen in light of the context above, the comments from the 15 participants who *changed* their name and who felt that life would just be easier with a shared name can be well understood:

> I just didn't want to be asked why all the time.
>
> (P35: name changer)

> Life is more straight forward and less confusing in financial, legal, and social terms.
>
> (P44: name changer)

> It requires less explanation.
>
> (P71: name changer)

There is nothing in these quotes to suggest that these women had been told explicitly to change their name, but their understanding of social norms and values is clear. As actors within a society encouraging this norm because of its gendered meanings, they are well-versed in what behaviour is expected of them without much, or any, explicit encouragement. They show an understanding that transgressions need to be accounted for. We are all social selves who are a part of our social order; choices are not made free from this context.

Talking about transgressing

When discussing their reasons for not changing names, participants are involved in a sort of accounting – accounting for their own actions and for the social order. The vocabularies we use to justify our life choices and actions are significant and not chosen at random, but learned as part of being an intelligible social actor who makes a space for themselves within society. As accounting was a much more explicit need for name retainers, it will be their accounts I focus on here: their transgressive accounts and how they attempted to justify this act of going against the grain. By 'justify' I do not necessarily mean 'make palatable to those who disagree with them', but instead to make understandable and intelligible. Their justifications may actually be highly incendiary to those who disagree with them and, as discussed earlier, feminism as a justification can be particularly inflammatory as it asserts women's rights to space, power, and authority over themselves.

Certain vocabularies of motive around institutional situations are acceptable: as described in Chapter 6, love is presently one such vocabulary in the institution of marriage. Other vocabularies are less acceptable or unacceptable, and when an agent uses any such set of vocabularies they are 'influencing others' and themselves (Mills, 1940: 907) as to what accounts and actions are in/appropriate. These vocabularies are a form of social control, upheld as 'normal' by the

Accounting for transgression 141

generalised other or society (Mills, 1940: 908). Whenever a person has to account, and to whomever, the person must be able to make a coherent story based on rules, expectations, and final action.

Garfinkel took this idea of accounting further than Mills, arguing that rules are not seen as organising principles in themselves but that they require to be meaningful to social actors; social actors must be able to find the action and the end point of the rule socially meaningful and intelligible (see Rawls, 2002: 43). As Garfinkel (2002: 172) argues, social order must be accountable and actors must be able to use appropriate vocabularies to make it so. Scott and Lyman (1968: 62) have argued that 'deviant' situations are those which need accounting for. Breaking away from the naming norm is to act 'deviantly' and certainly requires more frequent and considered accounting than following the norm.

However, I do not want to fully remove agency from my participants. Heritage has argued that norms only '*tend* to bind' and that agents will be aware of their parameters; those who depart from the norm are those willing to 'stand or forestall the consequences' (Heritage, 2008: 118), and the name retainers are willing to do this. The above-quoted participants, who discuss how problematic they saw retaining their name to be and therefore decided changing was for the best, show how difficult it can be to contemplate 'standing' or 'forestalling' the name-changing norm. They do not want to be held to account. As Mills noted (1940: 907) 'acts often will be abandoned if no reason can be found that others will accept' and P74 (name changer) shows this thought process in action: 'no compelling reason not to [change names]'. If we cannot make a meaningful case to others – justify and account for ourselves well enough – then we may have to abandon the choice we were going to make. Not only does this show once more how limited 'free choice' really is, but it also explains how norms continue to hold such power over us all, and just how difficult it can be to go against them. Therefore, as possibilities of different forms of action drop by the wayside, increasingly limited forms of action and social organisation become reality. The name change holds its foremost position in contemporary Britain for all of these reasons.

Following the norm is to have made sense of rules, expectations, and actions. Name changers must be able to understand the connection of names with intelligible families, for example, and be able to act on that to account for their conduct if necessary. The major difference is that following the norm uses a vocabulary which continues to be widely accepted and is therefore often unspoken. Silences speak, in fact, about power (see Chapter 3). In this way, Scott and Lyman's discussion (1968) of deviancy and accounts still stands: the 'deviant' are called to account far more often and more deeply than the 'normal'. As P70 (a name retainer) states, it is hard to make other people understand you 'belong to each other!' For her, it is other people who make names problematic. The actions of name retainers are looked at as individual and personal steps, often, as P70 shows, problematic ones which require an explanation, while the norm is allowed to fade into a collective background and goes relatively unquestioned; the justifications unspoken and often mysterious and intangible.

142 *Accounting for transgression*

The entirely constructed ease which sharing a name provides for families – after all, other countries function well without this norm – and the reactions to even the suggestion of name retaining correspond to Eli Adams' (1993) description of the intensity of resistance to anything other than the norm. The transgression against normative heterosexuality and against the domination of masculinity will create a level of stigma. Hence, to avoid this stigma and to be properly feminine women will hold to the norms of marriage and naming practices. Those women who do not feel changing names corresponds to 'proper' femininity, or feel less invested in this idea, will be prepared to subvert norms and transgress ideas of 'respectability'. This is very much connected to what participants can even imagine as being possible and with the time in the twentieth or twenty-first century in which they grew up and married.

As Eli Adams says (1993: 208), transgression is a part of our *imaginative* lives – we have to be able to imagine the transgression to perform it. When the norm was so deeply ingrained, women could not have imagined even the possibility of transgressing it. In many ways then, transgression can be thought of as defining boundaries by pointing out their contours: 'transgression is a component of the rule' (Jenks, 2003: 7). Jenks argues that transgression can be looked upon as a productive force for change, but that, nevertheless, for this to be possible we must 'know the collective orders, to recognise the edges in order to transcend them' (2003: 7). Change in this area is slow, but it is true that the ability to think of and enact such a transgression has allowed for the opening up of discussion around the naming norm and the kind of family forms it indicates as being acceptable.

As Goffman (1990 [1963]: 9) indicates, stigma is attached to those who are not fully socially accepted. The stigma around families which do not share one name, though far less than in previous decades, continues to exist. As the participant quotes above show, the norm of one name in a family remains strong and the idea of not following this would be seen to question family relationships and authenticity as a couple and, for some, as a mother. In comparing the Japanese situation[1] with that of Western countries without laws on names, Ueno argues that even when no laws exist to force couples to share names, the mother's surname retains the stigma of having been born out of wedlock (Ueno, 2009: 204). The patrilineal conventions of family surname usage and the practices by which last names are passed on, ensure that men's names have a higher (moral) status than women's. More varied and complex family forms would suggest that all children born from the same mother should take her surname, rather than women and children being expected to take on the name of the appropriate (husband–father) man (Ueno, 2009: 204), but there is little call for this in a society which continues to see women's names as inferior (Ueno, 2009: 204).

The need to justify one's actions and follow rules of femininity and respectable heterosexuality can be enough to put women off transgressing rules. As P35 (name changer) stated: 'If the other options were more common I might have chosen one of them' – to put oneself outside the norm can be a burden not worth shouldering.

Bureaucracy: encouraging us not to transgress

The statement from P35 may seem unreasonable, as there is no legal obstacle to her doing something unusual with her last name. However, as this study shows, the importance of social norms, traditions, and affective relationships should not be underestimated in influencing our seemingly personal decision-making. The encouragement not to transgress our social norms has become embedded in the everyday ways in which we organise and monitor people in a highly bureaucratised state. These mundane ways in which we are encouraged not to transgress become so normalised they can easily be forgotten.

As Beck and Beck-Gernsheim argue, the institutions of the state remain important to governing our lives (2010: 2). The bureaucracy which is linked to these institutions follows us from birth to death and encourages socially acceptable ways of accounting for and categorising the self: the 'tick-box' and 'empty line to fill in' self is pre-defined by those who make the questionnaires and encourages certain ways of recording it. When bureaucracy makes it clear certain ways of recording, and therefore living, a certain selfhood are easier and more intelligible, it discourages others, and embeds (and re-embeds) our social values in mundane and everyday processes.

Forms encourage women not only to reveal their marital status with the re-inscription of their gendered titles, but to fill in a space for 'maiden name'. A gendered and sexualised name space, suggesting a place for women only. This discourages men from changing their names by invoking the gender binary of 'something for women is not for men' (see Lucal (1999) and Connell (2009: 10) for a discussion of the poverty of the idea of binaries) and vice versa, while continuing to connect adult womanhood with sexual activity and, at the most reduced level, the hymen, as well as with the ritual of marriage and its patriarchal, heterosexual connections with subordination. These forms reiterate certain ways of being, based on a gendered structuring of social relationships; a person may even have to fit themselves to them and hence cover over their own life choices and different ways of being. In so doing, and without necessarily wishing to, this confirms the form's validity and records the person formally in a way which may not reflect the full truth or their own self.

While much bureaucracy is beginning to wake up to the gendered nature of 'maiden name' and move to 'previous name' in greater numbers – which also reflects the fact there may be many reasons other than marriage why a person might have a previous name – the marriage ceremony itself continues to reinscribe gender using the name and signature. On the wedding day itself a woman may sign the marriage certificate with her new name and use this certificate as proof of her new identity when she then in turn changes her legal name on other documents. A man may not do this. To sign with a new name on his wedding day he must first change his name by deed poll, meaning he must go through an entirely separate process and payment to be able to 'prove' his legal name before signing the marriage certificate.

In making the heterosexual marriage contract so specifically geared towards women changing their name, it reinforces the name-changing act: an act only

144 *Accounting for transgression*

for women to be done as 'part and parcel' of getting married. Men are actively penalised for changing their name on marriage, by having to pay an extra amount in getting the deed poll and having to go through an extra layer of bureaucracy to do so. The name change continues to be considered something women do rather than men and all of the processes are designed to help women do exactly this, as easily and quickly as possible, while men are hindered and discouraged. Instead of a smooth easy path – making their decision look natural and 'right' – the system seems to be asking men to justify their transgression of the norm at each stage, making the process difficult and off-putting. The mundane paperwork of name changing makes it very clear that this is a gendered process, one in which women do the name changing and men do not.

As an example of this working out in a participant's life aside from the marriage contract and more everyday paperwork, P63 spoke of arriving in Britain for the first time at the start of her journey to becoming a British citizen. She came from a country and culture in which women changing their name on marriage was not expected, but was told explicitly by immigration that if she was going to try and live in Britain her life would be made easier if her family shared one name: 'I was told on coming to the UK [by immigration officials] that it would be easier for benefits etc. if I have his name.' Without doubt, this is the most explicit example of a woman in my sample being told to change her name to 'fit in' and to make her life 'easier' (and less 'troublesome' for immigration officials and the immigration process). She followed the immigration officer's advice and has remained ambivalent about it ever since, showing that though the bureaucracy surrounding her and her family, and the intelligibility of them as a family may be easier, this does not necessarily square with feeling comfortable in yourself. This is a relational move and not one associated with any sense of growing individualism.

Conclusions

Acting in an unusual, 'deviant' manner – transgressing social norms – calls for accounting in a way acting with the grain of the norm does not. Name retainers had to deal with negative, questioning reactions to their naming decision and had to be prepared with an acceptable form of justification. Transgressions may be small, but they have powerful consequences and speak to what is lauded in society, who the powerful are, what acts are meaningful, and why. Transgressing is hard work; justifications become key ways in which to give your actions some coherence and credibility, but also provide a means to defend yourself from criticism and, at the extreme ends of transgression, social ostracisation. In the end, the effort of transgression – its bureaucracy, its explanation – may be off-putting enough that the norm is followed and the status quo maintained.

Note

1 In Japan, married couples must legally share one name. This usually means the man's name is shared. There are ongoing discussions in Japan about this law.

References

Beasley, C., Brook, H., and Holmes, M. (2012). *Heterosexuality in Theory and Practice.* Abingdon: Routledge.

Beck, U. and Beck-Gernsheim, E. (2010). *Individualization.* London: Sage.

Bourdieu, P. (1991). *Language and Symbolic Power.* Cambridge: Polity Press.

Connell, R. (2009). *Gender.* Cambridge: Polity Press.

Eli Adams, J. (1993). 'The Banality of Transgression? Recent Works on Masculinity'. *Victorian Studies*. 36 (2): 207–213.

Garfinkel, H. (2002). *Ethnomethodology's Program* (this edition edited by A.W. Rawls). Lanham, MD: Rowman and Littlefield.

Goffman, E. (1990 [1959]). *The Presentation of Self in Everyday Life.* London: Penguin Books.

Goffman, E. (1990 [1963]). *Stigma.* London: Penguin Books.

Heritage, J. (2008 [1984]). *Garfinkel and Ethnomethodology.* Cambridge: Polity Press.

Jenks, C. (2003). *Transgression.* London: Routledge.

Lucal, B. (1999). 'What It Means to Be Gendered Me: Life on the Boundaries of a Dichotomous Gender System'. *Gender and Society*. 13 (6): 781–797.

Mead, G.H. (1964). *On Social Psychology.* Chicago: The University of Chicago.

Mills, C.W. (1940). 'Situated Actions and Vocabularies of Motive'. *American Sociological Review*. 5 (6): 904–913.

Pateman, C. (1988). *The Sexual Contract.* Stanford, CA: Stanford University Press.

Rawls, A.W. (2002). 'Editor's Introduction' in H. Garfinkel (this edition edited by Rawls) *Ethnomethodology's Program*. Lanham, MD: Rowman and Littlefield: 1–64.

Scott, M.B. and Lyman, S.M. (1968). 'Accounts'. *American Sociological Review*. 33 (1): 46–62.

Ueno, C. (2009). *The Modern Family in Japan.* Balwyn North: Trans Pacific Press.

10 Conclusion

The norm of name changing in Britain continues to manage societal relationships and organisation. First, names are both a part of and reflect systems, and systems reflect ideas and ideals. A particular, socially constructed system of name taking and sharing prevails. The 'one name' in families could after all be the woman's or a completely new name made up by couples on marrying. Instead the name is the man's name and this reflects the gendered hierarchy within the institution of marriage. I would argue that the fact the naming norm continues to be so powerful is a part of deep-rooted gendered inequality which continues to exist within British society. The naming norm is a symbol of this inequality and is difficult to erode due to the depth with which these convictions are held.

Second, it simplifies bureaucracy for state institutions: the name sets up clearly who is connected with whom and who can therefore be called upon to take responsibility for whom. This system is by no means perfect and is certainly culturally constructed: Spain, Iceland, and China, for example, manage to exist as nations without the same naming practices as Britain. It remains, however, that changing the system seems overly complicated for state institutions, as a proliferation of names would make family relationships harder to discern. This is surely a part of the reason why complex family formations are difficult for state institutions to deal with: proliferation equals greater complexity. Names are the symbols of this change in family formations and social organisation and it is discouraged in everyday, seemingly mundane ways.

As Leonard has argued (1980: 265), paying attention to symbols is important. A decision to change or retain one's name in the modern day is also a decision about the ideas and ideals one is willing to embody. Though changing a name is unlikely to be a conscious decision to consider oneself lesser than one's husband, it feeds into the gendered inequality that exists within this country and the idea that women's selfhoods are of less consequence than men's (Hochschild, 2003a: 57, 165). It does not necessarily compel one to live one's life in this way, but it is a public statement of acceptance of these ideas on a symbolic and powerful level.

Names and naming are suffused with power: they can quickly connect a person with a set of classed ideas and connotations; furthermore, names can connect people to an ethnic, cultural, and national background. They can 'place' a person within a society and allow others to place them – as insider or as outsider. The gendered power to give a name to a woman in marriage, or the expectation that a woman will take on a man's name, makes plain the symbolic hierarchy of significance and power in marriage. This symbolic hierarchy is a part, though, of real and effective gender inequality and has real consequences: more care and emotional labour undertaken by women, for example. Other naming ideas are discouraged within this unequal system.

What is socially and legally *discouraged* expresses what social ideals and values are looked down upon; what is legally and socially *encouraged* expresses those ideals and values which are lauded: this is contextual and constructed. Keeping one's own name now would not be the same action as that of a Scottish woman pre-nineteenth century, who would be keeping her name as part of the normalised, patriarchal system of marriage in her country; today keeping one's own name is a stand against the prevailing system and the gendered ideals that remain meaningful to this system. The UK now shares a naming norm and the social, legal, and economic position of women has changed a great deal since the nineteenth century. The paradox is that the English naming norm, historically so connected with women losing their legal personhood and becoming a part of their husband's public identity, remains so powerful across the UK at a time in which women are apparently becoming increasingly independent. Also, the Western world is meant to be a part of individualising trends which suggest that one's own public identity would be an important thing to keep and sustain, rather than being defined in relation to another.

It would appear that individualisation theorists like Bauman and Giddens overestimate the extent to which the Western world has individualised and lost its need for outward systems of reference and approval. Tradition and the influence of the past continue to be significant to the decisions we make and the roles we play. Women are certainly still invested in the relational roles of wife and mother and the name change represents the extent of this: losing a symbol of individual self to become more embedded in the familial. Name retainers may be closer to the self of individualisation theories, as they attempt to maintain their individual self within the marriage. However as Young (1997: 124) has argued, no one can be completely independent and live without considering others' wishes; we are all interdependent. I would therefore look to argue with Beck and Beck-Gernsheim (2010: 56) that the women in my study are 'in-between' the self of individualisation theories and more relational and traditional identities.

The self, as Mead (1964: 205) has argued, is made up of the dynamic relationship between self and other (be that the 'other' of family and friends, institutions, or a generalised society). This interaction is clear in the decisions of my participants as they work to reconcile the thoughts of loved ones, the comments and assumptions of those working in institutions, and the expectations and pressures of the society in which they live. Name changers are working *with* the social norm and are influenced to comply; name retainers have worked against it, influenced by other groupings and life experiences, but having to justify themselves to those around them. Whatever decision is made, the naming norm must be negotiated in some way, as a part of the organising principle of heterosexuality in Britain, which in turn limits the possibilities for selfhood.

The naming norm is therefore a 'technology of the self' (Foucault, 1988), influencing behaviour and what kind of persona the named individual wants to present to the world. Name and title changing allow one to present oneself as a wife with the connotations of adulthood, responsibility, and 'appropriate femininity' that go with this. To avoid these connotations and try to redefine heterosexual married identity, name retaining is an option – a quiet subversion (Beasley et al., 2012: 67). Women do have choices, but these choices are limited by a great number of factors including the presentation of (a socially acceptable) self to a wider world.

Appearing to have made an individual and informed choice remains highly significant to my sample. They have been influenced by the idea of choice as key to a well-lived life which pervades modern society, however restricted, in fact, choices may be. Feminists are themselves often deeply embedded in this narrative, hoping the feminist movement can open up choices for women. Though this is a positive goal it should not stop critical engagement with the kinds of choices open to women. In terms of naming decisions, encouraging support for all decisions women make is affirmative but can prevent critical interrogation of the underlying gendered significance of the norm.

The norm is gendered, and conspicuous commitment and love work are encouraged so that women display their married selves and their 'proper' femininity through name changing. The name changing norm encourages women to build their identity around the idea of a loving, family-orientated wife (and mother) who puts the feelings of others first. Attempting to thwart the naming norm is an attempt to keep marriage a private event, refuse the public identity of wife, and 'quietly subvert' (Beasley et al., 2012: 67) heterosexual tropes.

Children are highly important to naming decisions. Participants are looking ahead to possible future children in many cases and wanting to have a clear, intelligible connection to them. The understandings of others are important here: to make it easy for *others* to connect child and mother, women change their names. The self interacts with others to become intelligible and socially acceptable. Familial identity takes precedence, with the help of the bureaucracy of institutions cementing the norm into everyday life. Those who keep their own name must face the questioning of others who cannot understand relationships of care without a shared name. Names are integrated into pivotal gendered moments of heterosexual life stories and are therefore a part of making a credible, understandable account of a life. When names become problematic it suggests a controversial decision, a transgression, which must then be explained and justified. This explanation will be the only way to make a couple or family intelligible.

Participants did not have simplistic ideas of names and family, some seeing names as unnecessary or secondary to a sense of family life. However, sharing a name within a family was seen generally as a positive thing and names were used to cement biological links, create social links to smooth over the lack of biological ties, and indeed to take on the heritage of a partner, which was discussed in a

Conclusion   149

literal way by participants. Names are the social signs of biological connections – held up as a significant sign of family in this culture – and could be used to 'create' a family even if biological links were missing.

Finally, the gendered importance of the norm to a sense of self remains significant. There continues to be upset when women suggest not changing names, threats of not going ahead with the marriage, and a great deal of silence around other possibilities (aided by classed ideas of other options). A type of masculinity is bound up in the naming norm, as well as a type of femininity. The authority of the father–husband, head-of-household continues to be important to a large number of a partners within this study and therefore possibly to others like them. Their wives were also a part of this gendering, some wondering whether they could look at themselves as truly committed and loving if they did not follow the norms of marriage, significantly name changing. Their submission to the views of others was a part of their appropriately feminine behaviour. Among the name-retaining women, though many of their partners accepted their decision and a small number took their wife's name, some faced an uphill battle against pressure and disagreement from their partner and others. The upset name retaining caused to the gender and social order was perceived as threatening. These participants were called to account in a way name changers were not (except when explaining their feminist beliefs in relation to their naming decision).

'Deviant' decisions still need to be explained – and these explanations need to be socially understandable to be credible. It is useful for name retainers to use a narrative of selfhood which suggests unbroken linear growth and the desire not to disrupt this through the name change, however much this may smooth over and even hide fragmentation and disruption. Name changers, however, could discuss fluidity, disruption, and even fragmentation in their lives and use names to make sense of it; their lives could be presented as creative and adaptable, often therefore hiding the traditional nature of the naming decision they had made. Whatever the decision, the ability to tell a coherent life story was fundamental and paramount.

To end then, names are significant both to individual identity and to how British society is organised and operates. They are an important part of marriage as a rite of passage and a turning point in the life course, and they have a wider political symbolism and power, which is a part of maintaining unequal gendered social relations. They are a part of the everyday and therefore often go unquestioned, but to ignore them is to ignore the more subtle workings of society and to miss the continuing gendered hierarchy within Britain today.

References

Beasley, C., Brook, H., and Holmes, M. (2012). *Heterosexuality in Theory and Practice.* Abingdon: Routledge.

Beck, U. and Beck-Gernsheim, E. (2010). *Individualization.* London: Sage.

Foucault, M. (1988). 'Technologies of the Self' in L.H. Martin, H. Gutman, and P.H. Hutton (eds.) *Technologies of the Self.* London: Tavistock Publications: 16–49.

150   *Conclusion*

Hochschild, A.R. (2003a [1983]). *The Managed Heart*. Berkeley, CA: University of California Press.

Leonard, D. (1980). *Sex and Generation*. London: Tavistock Publications.

Mead, G.H. (1964). *On Social Psychology*. Chicago: The University of Chicago.

Young, I.M. (1997). *Intersecting Voices*. Princeton, NJ: Princeton University Press.

Index

Abbott, D. 65
active agents 10, 13, 55; *see also* agency
Adam and Eve 63
Adams, E. 14, 136, 142
adoption 7, 16, 30, 97
agency 54–5, 141; active 10, 13, 55, 58; individual 10, 13–14; in naming decisions 141; of women 80–1, 141; *see also* choice
American slavery 61–2
APracticalWedding.com 69
Askham, J. 125

Bauman, Z. 33–4
Beck, U. 34–5, 52, 89, 143, 147
Beck-Bernsheim, E. 34–5, 52, 89, 143, 147
belonging 108–11
Bible, story of Adam and Eve 63
birth families, connection to 97–9
Bourdieu, P. 9, 12–13, 139
brides, feminist 69
British naming conventions 38, 47; English law 18; gendered 64; historical 15–17; modern 22–30; Scots law 17
Butler, J. 118

capitalism, neoliberal 50–2
cartoons, anti-feminist and anti-suffrage 64–65
censorship, cultural 45
children: changing names of 110; and the decision to marry 106; and naming decisions 68, 107–8, 111–14, 148; names of 22; and naming norms 103–5
Chodorow, N. 118
choice: factors influencing 51; feminist rhetoric of 51–2; gendered aspects of 57–9; in late modernity 50; in modern society 9–10; narratives of 52, 54–8,

78, reflexive 50; and risk 53; of women 3–4, 41–2, 50, 64, 148; *see also* agency
Christian ethics 11
Christianity: inequality of love in 75–6; naming conventions in 62–3
civil partnerships, same-sex 77
class divisions 129–30
closed capital 129
commitment: conspicuous 56, 78; name changing as symbol of 56, 74, 81, 83, 138; privatisation of 89–90
communities: behaviors shaped by 35; perception of self by 126–31; social 14
confluent love 6
Cook, J. 62
core selves 119–20, 125–6
couples: gay and lesbian 7, 95; heterosexual 5–6, 9
culture, and class 129

Daly, M. 62
data, sorting and coding 26–7
Davies, H. 110
de Certeau, M. 52
deep acting 79, 81
divorce 24, 26, 30, 39, 86–7
domestic life, heterosexual 5–6
Douglass, F. 62
doxa 12
Dumm, T. 33

emotion work 4–7, 59, 73, 78, 83
emotions, participant 80–1
England, naming traditions in *see* British naming conventions
English law 18
equality, social 50
Erickson, R. 79
ethics 11

152   *Index*

family and families: and belonging
   108–11; biological vs. social 95–8, 102;
   conceptualisation of 7–8; doing and
   displaying 8, 99–103; as genetic lineage
   94–5; inequalities in 7–8; intelligibility
   of 104; and naming conventions 101,
   107–8; one name shared by 39, 68,
   94, 101–3, 107–8, 111–14, 142,
   146; varieties of 7, 99–101; *see also*
   marriage
family building 96, 97, by lesbian
   couples 95
family names 16–17; *see also* surnames
family values 94
femininity 46–7, 133, 142
feminism 3–4, 118; and the heterosexual
   life 5; and the last name 64–6; and
   naming decisions 66–9; and the rhetoric
   of choice 51–2, 70; second wave 64–6,
   68–9
first names 1
Fluke, S. 65
Foucault, M. 148; and the technologies of
   the self 9, 10–11
framing, gendered 80

Garfinkel, H. 141
gay couples 7, 95
gender, and the construction of self 1; *see
   also* hierarchy, gendered; inequality and
   inequalities, gendered; men; women
gender differences 23
gender order 46
gender relations 26, 88
genealogy 94–5
generalisability 24–5
Gergen, J.K. 14, 117–18, 124, 126
Giddens, A. 6, 33–4, 39–40, 50, 53, 55,
   57, 64, 90–1, 124, 126, 147
Goffman, E. 9, 142
Greek ethics 11

habitus 9, 12–13
Hegel, G. 84
heteronormativity 70, 73, 80
heterosexual imaginary 5
heterosexuality 4–7, 47, 90–1; feminist
   analyses of 120; hegemonic 90–1; and
   love 73–4; and naming norms 103;
   as norm 91; as organising principle of
   society 4–7, 120, 148; respectability of
   106; sub-institutions of 45
hierarchy: gendered 9, 11, 18, 77, 146, 149

Hochschild, A. 56, 78–9, 83
humanism 126
husbands: expectations of 80; as name
   changers 130, 149; name discussion
   with 43–4, 46; reaction to naming
   decisions 40, 55–8, 68, 97, 138–9;
   see also men
hyphenated names 129–30; *see also*
   surnames, double-barrelled

identity: collective 1, 4; complexity of
   117; construction of 2, 4, 12–13; ethnic
   127–8; familial 8, 96, 148; feminist 66;
   gendered 2–3, 131–3; individual 1, 4;
   loss of 62; masculine 133; and names 2,
   119; and social positioning 10
incest taboos 96
individualisation 36, 52, 53, 123, 147
inequality and inequalities 50; gendered
   23, 35, 53, 59, 75, 118, 146; in marriage
   58, 73, 77, 79, 89; in name changing 46,
   51, 82; of name change and power 40
interviews 25; as exchange of information
   29–30; life history 27–9; personal
   details 30; transcribing 28–30
Invention of Tradition, The (Hobsbawm
   and Ranger) 37
Ireland, naming practices in 16
Islamic culture 127

Japan, war orphans in 8
Jenks, C. 142

kinship affinity 96
kinship narratives 95
Kristeva, J. 118

last names 1
late modernity 3, 9, 33–5, 50, 118
lesbian couples 7, 95
life history interviews 27–9
life narratives 132; and the vocabulary of
   marriage 125–6
loneliness 33
love 4–9; and biology 74–5; confluent 6;
   gendered inequality of 53; gendering 74;
   inequality of 75; in marital relationships
   73–4, 79; and marriage 53, 73–4;
   narratives of 6–7, 82; romantic 6; rules
   of 90; as secular religion 7; and selfhood
   8–9; social construction of 6; *see also*
   true love
love narratives 87

Index   153

love power 53, 78, 81
love work 53, 59, 74, 78–81, 85
Lucy Stone League 65

maiden name 143
Malcolm X 62
marriage 6, 9; as choice 53; of convenience
76; cross-border 76–7; emotion norms
in 84; and love 79; gendered hierarchy
in 146; heterosexual 143; identity and
stability in 125; inequity in 58, 72, 77,
79, 89; and naming rituals 1; power
in 18, 39, 147; as rite of passage 120,
139; rules of 78–9; same-sex 7, 77;
and selfhood 8–9, 119–20; sine manu
17; and social groupings 12; as symbol
of commitment 86; as technology of
self 12; therapeutic model of 87–8;
vocabulary of 125–6
marriage ceremony, gender reinforcement
in 143
masculinity, and the shared name 131
Matthews, J. J. 46
May, S. 82
May, V. 36, 109–10
Mead, G. H. 45, 117, 124, 126, 127, 132,
137, 147; theory of selfhood 9, 13–14
men: gendered sense of self 57; and
the inequalities of marriage 73; and
masculine identity 133; see also
husbands
Mills, C. W. 141
modernisation, reflexive 9–10

name changers: discussions with partner
43–4; feminist 69; husbands as 130,
149; and the love narrative 81–5;
narratives of 121–2; as situated agents
39; see also name changing
name changing 22–3, 36; as emotion
work 80; as heterosexual ideal 91;
inequalities of 40, 46, 51, 82, 123;
influences on decision 41, 51, 53, 56,
66–7, 147; and the issue of choice 78;
legal ramifications of 23; and the love
narrative 82; and marriage 64; as norm
22–3, 38–9, 44–7, 132, 146; and power
70; as public symbol of marriage 120; as
sign of commitment 56, 74, 81, 83, 138;
as symbol of gendered hierarchy 77;
see also name changers
name retainers: feminist 66–8; and love
85–6; need for justification by 45,

58, 66, 89–90, 124–5, 130, 137–40,
144, 147, 149; and the significance of
one name 39, 68, 94, 101–3, 107–8,
111–14, 142, 146; ways of justifying
140–2; see also name retaining
name retaining 22–3; discussion about
43–4, 46; husbands' reactions to 40,
55–8, 68, 97, 138–9; as transgression
137–40; as unequal 85–6
names: biological vs. social 97–8, 102;
connections to class 129–30; ethnic
identity 127–8; on forms 143; maiden
143; masculine endings for 16; as means
of social organisation 1; power of 146;
previous 143; sharing 142; significance
of 1–2; as signs of self 85; as symbols
2, 88; see also first names; last names;
surnames
naming: as political act 61–4; power of
63–5, 146
naming conventions: in American slavery
61–2; British history of 15–18; for
children 22; and the choice narrative
54–5; and feminism 3–4, 66–9;
in heterosexual partnerships 58–9;
influences on 42, 51, 53, 56, 66–7;
medieval 15; and names shared by
a family 39, 68, 94, 101–3, 107–8,
111–14, 142, 146; participants' feeling
about 44–5; of royalty 15; tradition and
choice 2–3; see also naming norm(s)
naming norm(s) 148; and respectability
101–7; as normalised 47; and the sense
of self 9; as technology of self 118
narrative(s): of choice 55–8, 78;
dominant 42; kinship 95; of love 82;
of self 54–5
neoliberal capitalism 50–2
norms: gendered 23, 51, 148–9; taken-for-
granted 56; vocabulary of following
141; see also naming norm(s)

online survey 25–6
original family name (OFN) 30
other, generalised 13, 14, 40, 45, 46, 68,
111, 126, 127, 131, 141

participant emotions 80–1
philosophy, feminist 118
place names 62
Plato 76, 117
politics, transformational 126
postmodernism 117–18

154 *Index*

power: balance of 18; gendered 57–8, 91, 133, 147; hierarchies of 109; of names 146; naturalization of 42; and tradition 37–9
power relations 5
power structures 35, 65
property rights 17–18, 132
pure relationships 6, 34, 90

questions, open- and closed- 25–6

reflexive modernisation 9–10
reflexivity 9–10, 13; self- 34
relationships: as ephemeral 33–4; gendered 40, 75, 143; heterosexual 35; long-distance 91; mother-child 104, 107; parent-child 76; pure 6, 34, 90
reproductive rights 51, 64
reproductive technologies 95
research design and methodology: British women's name decisions 22–3; interviews 27–9; mixed methods 25–6; references to participants 30; sample 23–5; survey 26; survey coding 26–7; transcription and write-up 29–30
research sample: education 24; ethnicity 23–4
respectability: of heterosexuality 106; and marriage 125; and the naming norm 101–7
Roman ethics 11
Roman law 17
rootedness 82–3

sacrifice, gendered 57
Sartre, J. -P. 9
Scotland, naming traditions in 17, 38–40
Scots law 17
sedimentation 36
self: Bourdieu's view of 12–13; and community 126–31; construction of 1, 13, 147; experiential 126; Mead's theory of 13–14; narrative of 55, 125; reflexive project of 50, 64; relational 118; technology of 9–11, 118, 148
selfhood 8, 110, 117, 119, 123
self-reflexivity 34
sexuality 63, 106
silence: on love and commitment 88; about name-changing norm 45; as part of dominant discourse 46; power of 42–3
slaves, names of 61–2
social community 14

social positioning 10
social relations, gendered 40, 143
Spender, D. 63
stigma: of name retaining 142; of out-of-wedlock birth 105–6, 142
storytelling 28–9
subjectivity 9, 126
subversion, quiet 91, 137–8
surnames 142; double-barrelled 105, 113–14, 129–30; gender differences in 15; historical use of 15–16; indicating masculine/feminine relationships 16
survey: coding 26–7; online 26
symbols: importance of 9, 146; in the marriage ceremony 77
Symposium (Plato) 76

TheFeministBride.com 69
tradition(s) 3, 42; and choice 2–3; meaning-making 35–6; moving away from 53; and name changing 40–1; and the past 36–7; regulative 35; rejection of 46; temporal 37–9; unthinking 68
transformational politics 126
transgression 14–15, 140–4; defined 136–7; discouraged by bureaucracy 143–4; reactions to 137–40; talking about 140–2
true love 74, 76, 80, 81, 84, 86, 89, 90, 136

unthinkingness 12, 37, 42, 50

vocabularies, as social control 126

Wales, use of surnames in 16
women: agency of 80–1, 141; as bearers of class 129; changing place of in society 35–6; choices of 3–4, 42, 50, 64, 148; connotations of Ms. and Mrs. 122; dependency of 118; and the desire to please 80; experiences of 63; exploitation of 74; and love work 84–5; as property 67, 85, 123; property rights of 17–18; Roman 17; sacrifices of 57, 74; in Scotland 17; sexuality of 63, 106; societal expectations of 46–7; subjectivity of 9, 126; submission of 133; subordination of 10, 18

Young, I. M. 118, 123, 147